Lecture Notes in Computer Science 9542

Commenced Publication in 1973
Founding and Former Series Editors:
Gerhard Goos, Juris Hartmanis, and Jan van Leeuwen

Editorial Board

More information about this series at http://www.springer.com/series/7410

Tim Güneysu · Gregor Leander
Amir Moradi (Eds.)

Lightweight Cryptography for Security and Privacy

4th International Workshop, LightSec 2015
Bochum, Germany, September 10–11, 2015
Revised Selected Papers

 Springer

Editors
Tim Güneysu
University of Bremen and DFKI
Bremen
Germany

Amir Moradi
Ruhr-Universität Bochum
Bochum
Germany

Gregor Leander
Ruhr-Universität Bochum
Bochum
Germany

ISSN 0302-9743   ISSN 1611-3349 (electronic)
Lecture Notes in Computer Science
ISBN 978-3-319-29077-5   ISBN 978-3-319-29078-2   (eBook)
DOI 10.1007/978-3-319-29078-2

Library of Congress Control Number: 2015960227

LNCS Sublibrary: SL4 – Security and Cryptology

Printed on acid-free paper

This Springer imprint is published by SpringerNature
The registered company is Springer International Publishing AG Switzerland

Preface

The International Workshop on Lightweight Cryptography for Security and Privacy (LightSec) was established to promote novel research on the security and privacy issues for applications that can be termed as lightweight security due to the associated constraints on metrics such as available power, energy, computing ability, area, execution time, and memory requirements. While such applications are becoming ubiquitous in daily life, they are also affecting a greater portion of society, leading to a plethora of economic-, security- and privacy-related concerns. The first three editions of LightSec took place in Turkey. This fourth edition of LightSec was held in Germany and was organized by the Horst Görtz Institute for IT Security (HGI) at Ruhr University Bochum (RUB). The workshop had 53 participants from 12 different countries. LightSec 2015 received generous financial support by the Ruhr University Bochum, the graduate school Ubicrypt, and eurobits.

LightSec received 17 submissions that underwent a review process. Each paper was reviewed by three reviewers. The entire double-blinded review process took more than two months in which the merits and weaknesses of each paper were carefully taken into account. The Program Committee finally accepted 10 original articles that were presented at the workshop and published in these proceedings.

LightSec featured four invited talks. On the first day Christian Rechberger from the Technical University Denmark and Miroslav Knezevic from NXP Semiconductor gave excellent lectures on "Lightweight Crypto on a Full Circle: From Industry to Academia and Back" and "Designing Crypto for Low Energy and Low Power," respectively. The second day featured invited talks by Roberto Avanzi from QUALCOMM on "What the Industry Really Needs" in the area of lightweight crypto, and by Meltem Sömez Turan from the National Institute of Standards and Technology (NIST) about the NIST initiative on lightweight cryptography.

We thank all the Program Committee members and external reviewers for their invaluable contribution to the selection process. Their technical comments and insights ensured the quality of the selected papers in these proceedings. Of course, we would also like to thank the authors for submitting their original research papers to LightSec 2015. We are very much indebted to our four invited speakers for their extremely interesting and entertaining presentations.

Last but not least, the successful organization of the event would not have been possible without the great reliable help of Irmgard Kühn, who took care of all the big and small issues that arose. Finally, we hope that these proceedings are as interesting to read as it was to compile them. We are already looking forward to the next editions of LightSec, wherever they take place.

November 2015

Tim Güneysu
Gregor Leander
Amir Moradi

Organization

LightSec 2015 was organized by Horst Görtz Institute for IT Security at Ruhr-Universität Bochum, Germany.

Conference General Chair

Tim Güneysu	University of Bremen and DFKI, Germany
Amir Moradi	Ruhr-Universität Bochum, Germany
Christof Paar	Ruhr-Universität Bochum, Germany

Conference Program Co-chairs

Tim Güneysu	University of Bremen and DFKI, Germany
Gregor Leander	Ruhr-Universität Bochum, Germany
Amir Moradi	Ruhr-Universität Bochum, Germany

Program Committee

Mohamed Ahmed Abdelraheem	Technical University of Denmark, Denmark
Tolga Acar	Microsoft Research, USA
Onur Aciicmez	Samsung, USA
Zahra Ahmadian	University of Shahid Beheshti, Iran
Jean-Phillipe Aumasson	Kudelski Security, Switzerland
Reza Azarderakhsh	Rochester Institute of Technology, USA
Guido Bertoni	STMicroelectronics, Italy
Elif Bilge Kavun	Infineon, Germany
Andrey Bogdanov	Technical University of Denmark, Denmark
Chris Gaj	George Mason University, USA
Berndt Gammel	Infineon, Germany
Pascal Junod	HEIG-VD, Switzerland
Albert Levi	Sabanci University, Turkey
Nele Mentens	Katholieke Universiteit Leuven, Belgium
Mehran Mozaffari Kermani	Rochester Institute of Technology, USA
Ventzislav Nikov	NXP Semiconductors, Belgium
Svetla Nikova	Katholieke Universiteit Leuven, Belgium
Erdin Öztürk	Istanbul Commerce University, Turkey
Thomas Peyrin	Nanyang Technological University, Singapore
Francisco Rodríguez-Henríquez	CINVESTAV-IPN, Mexico
Mehmet Sabir Kiraz	TÜBİTAK BİLGEM, Turkey
Erkay Savas	Sabanci University, Turkey
Nitesh Saxena	University of Alabama at Birmingham, USA

Peter Schwabe	Radboud University, The Netherlands
Kerem Varici	UC Louvain, Belgium
Amr Youssef	Concordia University, Canada

Additional Reviewers

Riham Altawy
Emrah Karagöz
Patrick Longa
Reza Rezaeian Farashahi
Gokay Saldamli
Maliheh Shirvanian
Prakash Shrestha

Sponsoring Institutions

Rectorate of the Ruhr University Bochum
Cryptography in Ubiquitous Computing (UbiCrypt)
European Competence Center for IT Security (eurobits)

Contents

Cryptanalysis

Meet-in-the-Middle Attacks on Reduced Round Piccolo

Mohamed Tolba, Ahmed Abdelkhalek, and Amr M. Youssef[(✉)]

Concordia Institute for Information Systems Engineering,
Concordia University, Montréal, Québec, Canada
youssef@ciise.concordia.ca

Abstract. Piccolo is a lightweight block cipher designed by Sony Corporation and published in CHES 2011. It inherits the Generalized Feistel Network (GFN) structure and operates on a 64-bit state. It has two versions; Piccolo-80 and Piccolo-128 with 80-bit and 128-bit keys, respectively. In this paper, we propose meet-in-the-middle attacks on 14-round reduced Piccolo-80 and 16, 17-round reduced Piccolo-128. First, we build a 5-round distinguisher by using specific properties of the linear transformation of Piccolo. This 5-round distinguisher is then used to launch a 14-round attack on Piccolo-80. As Piccolo-128 uses a different key schedule than what is used in Piccolo-80, we utilize the key dependent sieving technique to construct a 7-round distinguisher which is then employed to mount an attack on 16-round reduced Piccolo-128. To extend the attack to 17 rounds, we build a different 6-round distinguisher. For Piccolo-80, the time, data, and memory complexities of the 14-round attack are $2^{75.39}$ encryptions, 2^{48} chosen plaintexts, and $2^{73.49}$ 64-bit blocks, respectively. For Piccolo-128, the data complexity of both the 16-round and 17-round attacks is 2^{48} chosen plaintexts. The time and memory complexities of the 16-round (resp. 17-round) attack are 2^{123} (resp. $2^{126.87}$) encryptions, and $2^{113.49}$ (resp. $2^{125.99}$) 64-bit blocks. To the best of our knowledge, these are currently the best published attacks on both Piccolo-80 and Piccolo-128.

Keywords: Cryptanalysis · Meet-in-the-middle attacks · Generalized type-2 Feistel structure

1 Introduction

Recently, there is a huge demand for deploying resource-constrained devices such as RFID tags and wireless sensor nodes. To provide cryptographic security to such resource-constrained devices, new block ciphers of simple round function, and modest, or even no, key schedule are developed. As such, the design and analysis of hardware-oriented lightweight block ciphers have become a hot topic. HIGHT [16], mCrypton [23], DESL/DESXL [21], PRESENT [6], KATAN/KTANTAN [8], PRINTcipher [20], and Piccolo [27] are just few examples of such lightweight block ciphers that are designed to be efficiently deployed on resource-constrained devices.

© Springer International Publishing Switzerland 2016
T. Güneysu et al. (Eds.): LightSec 2015, LNCS 9542, pp. 3–20, 2016.
DOI: 10.1007/978-3-319-29078-2_1

Piccolo [27] is a hardware-oriented lightweight block cipher designed by Sony Corporation in 2011. It operates on a 64-bit state and has two versions; Piccolo-80 and Piccolo-128 with 80-bit and 128-bit keys, respectively. The differences between the two versions are the key schedule and the number of rounds. The structure of Piccolo inherits the Generalized Feistel Network (GFN) construction and has 4 branches, each of 16-bit length. Piccolo has been analyzed extensively where most of the results are reached using the biclique cryptanalysis technique [18,19,28,30]. The biclique cryptanalysis attack uses weaknesses that exist in the block cipher to accelerate the brute force attack and so it is regarded as a bruteforce-like attack.

Meet-in-the-Middle (MitM) attack is a single-key attack and it is the attack applied to Piccolo-80 and Piccolo-128 in [17] by the authors of Piccolo. The drawback of these two MitM attacks is that they require the full codebook, i.e., 2^{64} plaintexts/ciphertexts pairs and as explicitly mentioned in [17] the number of the attacked rounds would be reduced if the full codebook is not allowed. In addition, under the single-key setting Piccolo-80 and Piccolo-128 have been analyzed using the impossible differential attack [4]. Under the related-key setting, Piccolo has been analyzed using related-key impossible differential attack [25].

The MitM attack was first proposed by Diffie and Hellman in 1977 to be used in the cryptanalysis of Data Encryption Standard (DES) [13]. This attack splits the block cipher into two sub-ciphers such that $E = G_{K_2} \circ F_{K_1}$, where K_1 and K_2 are two distinct key sets which are used in F and G, respectively. Since the MitM attack requires low data complexity, it is considered as one of the major cryptanalysis techniques on block ciphers. However, finding two distinct key sets, K_1 and K_2, that cover a large number of rounds is quite challenging, especially in the block ciphers that use nonlinear key schedule. The three-subset MitM attack proposed by Bogdanov and Rechberger [7] solves this problem by splitting the key into three-subsets K_1, K_2, and K_c such that the key sets K_1 and K_2 may have common key bits that define the set K_c. The attack is then repeated for each possible value of the key bits in K_c. This approach succeeded in attacking the full KTANTAN cipher [7]. In addition to block ciphers, the MitM attack was applied to hash functions to launch preimage or second preimage attacks on Whirlpool [26] and Streebog [3], just to name a few.

Another line of research on the MitM attacks was triggered by Demirci and Selçuk when they were able to attack 8 rounds of both AES-192 and AES-256 [10]. In this attack, the cipher is split into three sub-ciphers, not just two as before, such that $E = E_2 \circ E_{mid} \circ E_1$, where E_{mid} exhibits a distinguishing property that is evaluated offline independently of the middle rounds keys. Then the keys used in E_1 and E_2 are guessed and checked in an online phase whether they verify the distinguishing property or not. The main downside of this attack is the high memory requirement to save a precomputation table. Later on, Dunkelman, Keller and Shamir [14] suggested two techniques to tackle the issue of the high memory requirement; differential enumeration and multisets which helped reduce the memory requirement but not enough to attack AES-128, however. Afterwards, Derbez et al. [11] reduced the memory requirement further by using a rebound-like idea and succeeded in attacking AES-128.

Table 1. Summary of the cryptanalysis results on Piccolo-80 (RK: Related-Key Setting Attack, SK: Single-Key Setting Attack, Pre: Pre-whitening Key, Post: Post-whitening Key, CC: Chosen Ciphertext, CP: Chosen Plaintext, †: Requires the full codebook or more)

Attack	Setting	# Rounds	Pre/Post	Time	Data	Memory	Reference
Impossible differential	RK	14	None	$2^{68.19}$	$2^{68.19†}$	N.A.	[25]
MitM	SK	14	None	2^{73}	$2^{64†}$	2^5	[17]
Impossible differential	SK	12	Pre	$2^{55.18}$	$2^{36.34}$ CC	2^{63}	[4]
Impossible differential	SK	13	None	$2^{69.7}$	$2^{43.25}$ CP	2^{62}	[4]
MitM	SK	14	None	$2^{75.39}$	2^{48} CP	$2^{73.49}$	Sect. 3

Finally, Li, Jia and Wang proposed a key-dependent sieve [22] to further reduce the memory complexity of Derbezs attack and presented an attack on 9-round AES-192 and 8-round PRINCE. The MitM attack is not only applied to Substitution Permutation Network (SPN) block ciphers such as AES, Hierocrypt-3 [1] or Hierocrypt-L1 [2] but also on Feistel Structure as exemplified by the generic work presented by Guo *et al.* [15] and Lin *et al.* [24]. It is worth noting that despite its high memory requirement, the MitM attack based on Demirci and Selçuk technique proves to be quite successful as represented by the recent work against the SPN structure PRINCE [12] and the Feistel constructions TWINE [5] and Khudra [29].

In this paper, we present MitM attacks on 14-round reduced Piccolo-80 and 16, 17-round reduced Piccolo-128. In the attack on Piccolo-80, we first construct a 5-round distinguisher then append 4 rounds at its top and 5 rounds at its bottom. The time, data, and memory complexities of the 14-round attack on Piccolo-80 are $2^{75.39}$ encryptions, 2^{48} chosen plaintexts, and $2^{73.49}$ 64-bit blocks, respectively. To attack 16-round reduced Piccolo-128, we build a 7-round distinguisher then append 3 rounds at its top and 6 rounds at its bottom. Extending the attack by one round using that 7-round distinguisher would require the whole key to be guessed. Hence, we construct a 6-round distinguisher, append 4 rounds at its top and 7 rounds at its bottom. The data complexity of both attacks on 16 and 17-round reduced Piccolo-128 is 2^{48} chosen plaintexts. The time, and memory complexities of the 16-round attack on Piccolo-128 are 2^{123} encryptions, and $2^{113.49}$ 64-bit blocks, respectively. The time, and memory complexities of the 17-round attack on Piccolo-128 are $2^{126.87}$ encryptions, and $2^{125.99}$ 64-bit blocks, respectively. Tables 1 and 2 summarize our results and the previous results on Piccolo-80 and Piccolo-128, respectively.

The rest of the paper is organized as follows. In Sect. 2, we provide the notations used throughout the paper and a brief description of Piccolo. Our attacks on 14 rounds of Piccolo-80 and 16, 17 rounds of Piccolo-128 are presented in Sect. 3 and the paper is concluded in Sect. 4.

Table 2. Summary of the cryptanalysis results on Piccolo-128 (RK: Related-Key Setting Attack, SK: Single-Key Setting Attack, Pre: Pre-whitening Key, Post: Post-whitening Key, CP: Chosen Plaintext, †: Requires the full codebook or more)

Attack	Setting	# Rounds	Pre/Post	Time	Data	Memory	Reference
Impossible differential	RK	21	None	$2^{117.77}$	$2^{117.77†}$	N.A	[25]
MitM	SK	21	None	2^{121}	$2^{64†}$	2^6	[17]
Impossible differential	SK	15	Post	$2^{125.4}$	$2^{58.7}$ CP	2^{61}	[4]
MitM	SK	16	Post	2^{123}	2^{48} CP	$2^{113.49}$	Sect. 3
MitM	SK	17	Post	$2^{126.87}$	2^{48} CP	$2^{125.99}$	Sect. 3

2 Specifications of Piccolo

2.1 Notations

The following notations are used throughout the rest of the paper:

- $a_{(b)}$: A word a of length b bits.
- $a||b$: Concatenation of the two words a and b.
- a^t: Transposition of the vector or the matrix a.
- a_b: Representation of the word a in base b.
- K: The master key.
- k_i: The ith 16-bit of K from left, where $0 \leq i < 5$ in Piccolo-80 and $0 \leq i < 8$ in Piccolo-128.
- rk_i: The 16-bit key used in round $\lfloor i/2 \rfloor$.
- wk_i: The 16-bit whitening key, where $0 \leq i < 4$.
- X_i: The 64-bit input to round i, where $0 \leq i \leq 26$ in Piccolo-80 and $0 \leq i \leq 32$ in Piccolo-128, X_0 is the plaintext P and X_{26} or X_{32} is the ciphertext C in Piccolo-80 and Piccolo-128, respectively.
- $X_i[j]$: The jth nibble of X_i, where $0 \leq j < 16$.
- $X_i[j : l]$: The nibbles from j to l of X_i, where $j < l$.
- $X_i[j, l]$: The nibbles j and l of X_i.
- $\Delta X_i, \Delta X_i[j]$: The difference at state X_i and nibble $X_i[j]$, respectively.
- X_i^j: The jth state of the 64-bit input to round i.

2.2 Specifications

There are two versions of Piccolo, depending on the key size, Piccolo-80 for 80-bit keys and Piccolo-128 for 128-bit keys. There are two differences between Piccolo-80 and Piccolo-128, the first is the number of rounds. Piccolo-80 iterates over 25 rounds, while Piccolo-128 runs 31 rounds. Piccolo's design employs a Generalized Feistel Network (GFN) structure and its internal state is divided into 4 words each of 16-bit length, i.e., we have 4 branches as shown in Fig. 1. Therefore, each round has two Feistel Networks (FN). Each FN has two operations: an F-function (F) and an Add key (AK). The F-function is an unkeyed 16×16-bit function and is applied to the first branch of the FN and, as depicted in the right part of Fig. 1, consists of three transformations [27]:

1. First S-box layer: A nonlinear layer that applies the same 4×4-bit bijective S-box S to the 16-bit $X_{(16)} = x_{0(4)}||x_{1(4)}||x_{2(4)}||x_{3(4)}$ data of the first branch of the FN as follows:

$$(x_{0(4)}, x_{1(4)}, x_{2(4)}, x_{3(4)}) \leftarrow (S(x_{0(4)}), S(x_{1(4)}), S(x_{2(4)}), S(x_{3(4)}))$$

2. Diffusion layer: The internal state is multiplied by a matrix M, where the multiplication is performed over $GF(2^4)$ defined by the irreducible polynomial $x^4 + x + 1$. Hence, the output of the first S-box layer is updated as follows:

$$(x_{0(4)}, x_{1(4)}, x_{2(4)}, x_{3(4)})^t \leftarrow M.(x_{0(4)}, x_{1(4)}, x_{2(4)}, x_{3(4)})^t,$$

3. Second S-box layer: It resembles the first S-box layer but applied to the output of the diffusion layer.

Each round of Piccolo contains two round keys used in the two FNs. Moreover, there are two pre-whitening keys wk_0, wk_1 that are xored with the internal state before the first round and two post-whitening keys wk_2, wk_3 that are xored with the internal state after the last round. After applying the two FN operations in each round, a permutation is performed on the byte level, as shown in Fig. 1.

The key schedule takes an 80-bit master key K in Piccolo-80 such that $K = k_0||k_1||k_2||k_3||k_4$ or an 128-bit master key K in Piccolo-128 such that $K = k_0||k_1||k_2||k_3||k_4||k_5||k_6||k_7$ and generates the 4 16-bit whitening keys wk_i, $0 \leq i < 4$ and 50 16-bit round keys in Piccolo-80, as per Algorithm 1 or 62 16-bit round keys in Piccolo-128, as per Algorithm 2.

Data: Key Scheduling(k_0, k_1, k_2, k_3, k_4)
Result: $wk_i, 0 \leqslant i < 4$ and $rk_i, 0 \leqslant i < 50$
$wk_0 \leftarrow k_0^L||k_1^R, wk_1 \leftarrow k_1^L||k_0^R, wk_2 \leftarrow k_4^L||k_3^R, wk_3 \leftarrow k_3^L||k_4^R;$
for $i \leftarrow 0$ *to* 24 **do**

$$(rk_{2i}, rk_{2i+1}) \leftarrow (con_{2i}^{80}, con_{2i+1}^{80}) \oplus \begin{cases} (k_2, k_3) & \text{if } i \bmod 5 = 0 \text{ or } 2 \\ (k_0, k_1) & \text{if } i \bmod 5 = 1 \text{ or } 4 \\ (k_4, k_4) & \text{if } i \bmod 5 = 3, \end{cases}$$

end

Algorithm 1. The Key Schedule employed in Piccolo-80 [27]

In both algorithms, k_i^L and k_i^R are the left and right half byte of k_i. In Algorithm 1, $(con_{2i}^{80}||con_{2i+1}^{80})$ is calcualted as $(con_{2i}^{80}||con_{2i+1}^{80}) \leftarrow (c_{i+1}||c_0||c_{i+1}||00_2 ||c_{i+1}||c_0||c_{i+1}) \oplus 0f1e2d3c_{16}$, where c_i is a 5-bit representation of i. In Algorithm 2, we have $(con_{2i}^{128}||con_{2i+1}^{128}) \leftarrow (c_{i+1}||c_0||c_{i+1}||00_2||c_{i+1}||c_0||c_{i+1}) \oplus 6547a98b_{16}$.

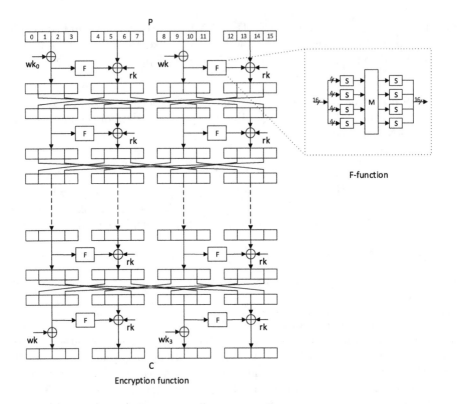

P

Fig. 1. Structure of Piccolo

Data: Key Scheduling$(k_0, k_1, k_2, k_3, k_4, k_5, k_6, k_7)$
Result: $wk_i, 0 \leqslant i < 4$ and $rk_i, 0 \leqslant i < 62$
$wk_0 \leftarrow k_0^L || k_1^R, wk_1 \leftarrow k_1^L || k_0^R, wk_2 \leftarrow k_4^L || k_7^R, wk_3 \leftarrow k_7^L || k_4^R;$
for $i \leftarrow 0$ *to* 61 **do**
  if $(i + 2) \bmod 8 = 0$ **then**
    | $(k_0, k_1, k_2, k_3, k_4, k_5, k_6, k_7) \leftarrow (k_2, k_1, k_6, k_7, k_0, k_3, k_4, k_5);$
  end
  $rk_i \leftarrow k_{(i+2) \bmod 8} \oplus con_i^{128},;$
end
Algorithm 2. The Key Schedule employed in Piccolo-128 [27]

We measure the memory complexity of our attacks as 64-bit Piccolo blocks and the time complexity in terms of the equivalent number of reduced-round Piccolo encryptions.

3   MitM Attacks on Reduced Round Piccolo

Generally in the MitM attacks, a reduced round block cipher is split into three sub-ciphers such that $E = E_2 \circ E_{mid} \circ E_1$, where E_{mid} exhibits a distinguishing property. This distinguishing property is evaluated in the offline phase. Then, in the online phase, the keys used in the analysis rounds E_1 and E_2 are guessed and checked whether they verify the distinguishing property or not. If they verify it, they are considered as key candidates, otherwise they are discarded. In our attacks, the distinguishing property is a truncated differential where its input takes a set of possible values and its output is a parameterized function of the input. The values of the output corresponding to the input form an ordered sequence that is used as our property to identify the right key guess. All the ordered sequences resulting from all the possible combinations of the parameters are stored in a precomputation table. As the size of this precomputation table is usually huge, we use two techniques inspired by the MitM attacks on SPN [12,22] to reduce its size and hence we are able to attack more rounds than what we can attack without these techniques.

The δ-set concept [9], as captured by Definition 1, is used to build our distinguishers.

Definition 1 (δ-set, [9]). *A δ-set for nibble-oriented cipher is a set of 16 state values that are all different in one nibble (the active nibble) and are all equal in the remaining nibbles (the inactive nibbles).*

The following subsections contain a detailed description of our attacks on 14-round Piccolo-80 and 16, 17-round Piccolo-128, respectively.

3.1 A MitM Attack on 14-Round Piccolo-80

In Piccolo, by noting that when the δ-set is chosen at the second input branch of the FN and the corresponding ordered sequence is evaluated at its first output branch, a distinguisher that minimizes the number of parameters can be constructed. However, such distinguisher does not lead to the best attack on Piccolo-80 since it can be extended upwards in the plaintext direction by two rounds only. If a third round is appended, the full codebook is needed due to the diffusion transformation utilized in Piccolo. Hence, to increase the number of rounds appended on top of the distinguisher, the δ-set is chosen at the first (instead of the second) input branch of the FN which, unfortunately, increases the number of parameters by two additional parameters. Then, in order to reduce the number of parameters, we exploit the properties of the diffusion operation M. In particular, we choose the δ-set to be after the first S-box layer of the first F-function such that after the diffusion transformation, only two nibbles are active, as shown in Fig. 2. By enumerating all the possible values of three active input nibbles of the linear diffusion, it was found that such δ-set that has three active nibbles at the input of the linear transformation, and two active nibbles at its output contains 15 differences. Such δ-set enables us to build a 5-round distinguisher and overcome the problem of the two additional parameters when the δ-set is chosen at the first branch of the FN, as depicted in Fig. 2, and captured by the following proposition:

Proposition 1. *Consider the encryption of a δ-set $\{Y^0 = P'^0[0 : 3]||P^0[4 : 15], Y^1 = P'^1[0 : 3]||P^1[4 : 15], \cdots, Y^{15} = P'^{15}[0 : 3]||P^{15}[4 : 15]\}$ through 5 rounds of Piccolo. The ordered sequence $[X_5^0[14 : 15] \oplus X_5^1[14 : 15], X_5^0[14 : 15] \oplus X_5^2[14 : 15], \cdots, X_5^0[14 : 15] \oplus X_5^{15}[14 : 15]$ is fully determined by the following 5 16-bit parameters, $X_0^0[0 : 3]$, $X_1^0[8 : 11]$, $X_2^0[0 : 3]$, $X_2^0[8 : 11]$ and $X_3^0[0 : 3]$.*

The above proposition means that we have $2^{5 \times 16} = 2^{80}$ ordered sequences out of the $2^{15 \times 8} = 2^{120}$ theoretically possible ones.

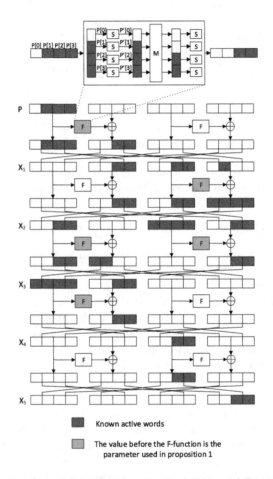

Fig. 2. 5-Round Distinguisher to attack 14-round Piccolo-80

Proof. The knowledge of the δ-set $= \{Y^0, Y^1, \cdots, Y^{15}\}$ allows us to determine $[Y^0 \oplus Y^1, Y^0 \oplus Y^2, \cdots, Y^0 \oplus Y^{15}]$. In the sequel, we show that the ordered sequence at $X_5[14 : 15]$ can be determined uniquely by the knowledge of the 5

16-bit parameters mentioned in proposition 1. As the δ-set is chosen at the input of the linear transformation M, it has to be propagated forward through M and backward through the first S-box layer to be able to determine the difference $\Delta X_1[6:7, 10:11, 13]$. To do this, we need to know three nibbles after the first S-box layer and two nibbles before the second S-box layer of the first F-function in the first round. However, the knowledge of only 4 nibbles $X_0^0[0:3]$ suffices to bypass the F-function and to compute $\Delta X_1[6:7, 10:11, 13]$. It is to be noted that only two nibbles are active after the F-function due to the restriction we place on the choice of our δ-set. Then, we bypass the second round by the knowledge of $X_1^0[8:11]$ which allows us to compute $\Delta X_2[2:3, 8:11, 14:15]$. By repeating the previous steps and propagating the differences further, $\Delta X_5[14:15]$ is computed. It is worth noting that there are nibbles which should have difference but appear in Fig. 2 as if they do not have any difference, because their knowledge do not impact the computation of the ordered sequence at $X_5[14:15]$. For instance, after the third (resp. fourth) round, the difference at $X_3[8:11]$ (resp. $X_4[0:1]$) should be non-zero because the difference at $X_2[2:3, 8:11]$ (resp. $X_3[0:3]$) is non-zero.

In what follows we show how to utilize the above described distinguisher to attack 14-round Piccolo-80 starting from the 5th round (round 4) till the 18th round (round 17) without the pre-whitening or the post-whitening keys. The attack relies on the previous proposition and exploits the linearity of the key schedule to build a 5-round distinguisher and then append 4 rounds above it and 5 rounds below it, as seen in Fig. 3. The attack has two phases as follows:

Offline Phase. As demonstrated in Proposition 1, we determine all the 2^{80} ordered sequences and store them in a hash table H.

Online Phase. The online phase, as seen in Fig. 3, proceeds as follows:

1. A plaintext P^0 is chosen as a reference to all the differences in the δ-set.
2. The δ-set P^0, P^1, $\cdots$, P^{15} is determined by guessing the state variables $X_6^0[8:11]$, $X_6^0[6:7, 12:13]$, $X_8^0[4:5, 14:15]$, and $X_8^0[1:3]$ to decrypt the δ-set differences.
3. The corresponding ciphertexts C^0, C^1, $\cdots$, C^{15} are requested.
4. The ordered sequence differences $[X_{13}^0[14:15] \oplus X_{13}^1[14:15], X_{13}^0[14:15] \oplus X_{13}^2[14:15], \cdots, X_{13}^0[14:15] \oplus X_{13}^{15}[14:15]]$ are determined by guessing the state variables $X_{13}^0[8:11]$, $X_{14}^0[0:3]$, $X_{14}^0[8:11]$, $X_{15}^0[0:3]$, $X_{15}^0[8:11]$, $X_{16}^0[0:3]$, $X_{16}^0[8:11]$ that are required to decrypt the ciphertext differences $[C^0 \oplus C^1, C^0 \oplus C^2, \cdots, C^0 \oplus C^{15}]$.
5. The guessed state variables are filtered by checking if the computed ordered sequence exists in H or not.

The evaluation of the δ-set and the corresponding ordered sequence as demonstrated in steps 2 and 4 require the guessing of 43 internal state nibbles. Guessing these 43 internal state nibbles makes the attack complexity exceeds the exhaustive search. Therefore, we analyze the key schedule searching for relations

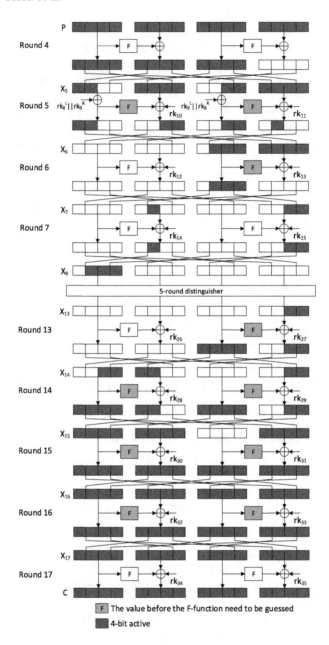

Fig. 3. 14-Round attack on Piccolo-80

between the round keys to reduce the number of guessed parameters. As a result, we find that starting the attack from the 5th round, i.e., round 4 is the best choice to reduce the number of the guessed parameters. Indeed, by only guessing k_0, k_1, k_2, k_3 and with the knowledge of P^0, we are able to compute $X_6^0[8:11]$,

$X_6^0[6:7, 12:13]$, $X_6^0[4:5, 14:15]$, and $X_8^0[1:3]$. The knowledge of $[C^0, C^1, \cdots, C^{15}]$, $[C^0 \oplus C^1, C^0 \oplus C^2, \cdots, C^0 \oplus C^{15}]$ and the same keys guessed above enables us to evaluate the state variables $X_{13}^0[8:11]$, $X_{14}^0[0:3]$, $X_{14}^0[8:11]$, $X_{15}^0[0:3]$, $X_{15}^0[8:11]$, $X_{16}^0[0:3]$, $X_{16}^0[8:11]$. Consequently, we have to guess 4 round keys (16 nibbles) instead of guessing 43 internal state nibbles. Moreover and in order to reduce the memory complexity of the attack even further, we choose to compute the ordered sequence at only 6-bit instead of 8-bit, where any arbitrary 6-bit from the 8-bit can be chosen. Therefore, the probability of a wrong key to be a key candidate is $2^{80-(15\times 6)} = 2^{-10}$. As we have 2^{64} keys to be guessed, we expect that only $2^{64-10} = 2^{54}$ keys to remain after step 5. Hence, to recover the master key we guess k_4 and test the 2^{54} key candidates along with k_4 with just two plaintext/ciphertext pairs.

Attack Complexity. The memory complexity is determined by the size of the hash table H created in the offline phase. This table contains 2^{80} ordered sequences, where each ordered sequence has 15 6-bit differences. Therefore, the memory complexity is $2^{80} \times 90/64 = 2^{80.49}$ 64-bit blocks. To reduce the memory complexity below 2^{80}, we use a simple tradeoff and store a fraction $1/\alpha$ of H and repeat the attack α times as now we have decreased the chance to hit one element in H. We choose $\alpha = 2^7$ to reduce the memory complexity while still having a non-marginal time complexity. Hence, the memory complexity of the attack is $2^{73.49}$. As depicted in Fig. 3, we shift the round keys rk_8, rk_9 from the 5th round to the 6th round. This round keys shift enable us to append 4 rounds, and not just 3 rounds, on top of our 5-round distinguisher with the same data complexity and without requiring the full codebook. To illustrate how this is possible, we choose our plaintexts such that after the 5th round the words $X_5[2:3, 8:9]$ take a fixed value while the remaining words of X_5 take all the possible values. Hence, the data required can be formed using one structure that contains 2^{48} states of X_5. In order to obtain its corresponding plaintexts, we simply decrypt this structure as no keys are involved in this round any more. Accordingly, the data complexity is upper bounded by 2^{48} chosen plaintexts. Repeating the attack 2^7 times does not increase the data complexity as we just choose a different reference plaintext P^0. The time complexity of the offline phase is determined by the time needed to build the hash table H that now contains 2^{73}, instead of 2^{80}, ordered sequences. Therefore, the time complexity of the offline phase is $2^{73} \times 16 \times 5/(2 \times 14) = 2^{74.51}$. The time complexity of the online phase consists of two parts: the time required to filter the key space which is estimated to be $2^7 \times 2^{64} \times 16 \times (6+9)/(2 \times 14) = 2^{74.1}$ and the time to recover the master key which is estimated to be $2 \times 2^{(64-10)} \times 2^{16} = 2^{71}$. Hence, the total time complexity of the attack is $2^{74.51} + 2^{74.1} + 2^{71} \approx 2^{75.39}$ 14-round Piccolo-80 encryptions.

3.2   A MitM Attack on 16-Round Piccolo-128

Reusing the ideas of the attack on Piccolo-80 does not lead to the best attack on Piccolo-128 because the key schedule of the latter is different. Therefore, we use the key dependent sieving technique in order to build a longer distinguisher with the least number of parameters. As depicted in Fig. 4, we construct a 7-round distinguisher, that we employ to attack 16-round Piccolo-128 from the 2nd round (round 1) to the 17th round (round 16) with the post-whitening keys. The δ-set of our 7-round distinguisher is chosen to be active at $P[7]$ and our distinguisher is built using Proposition 2.

Proposition 2. *Consider the encryption of a δ-set $\{P^0, P^1, \cdots, P^{15}\}$ through 7 rounds of Piccolo. The ordered sequence $[X_7^0[13:15] \oplus X_7^1[13:15], X_7^0[13:15] \oplus X_7^2[13:15], \cdots, X_7^0[13:15] \oplus X_7^{15}[13:15]]$ is fully determined by the following 8 16-bit parameters $X_1^0[8:11]$, $X_2^0[0:3]$, $X_2^0[8:11]$, $X_3^0[0:3]$, $X_3^0[8:11]$, $X_4^0[0:3]$, $X_4^0[8:11]$ and $X_5^0[0:3]$.*

The previous 5-round distinguisher of our attack on 14-round Piccolo-80 is independent of the round keys while our 7-round distinguisher that we utilize to attack 16-round Piccolo-128 uses the round keys to reduce the number of parameters. Assuming that we know the internal state X_3^0, i.e., 4 parameters, and the round keys rk_6, rk_7, we can evaluate X_4^0. Therefore, the 6 F-functions from the third round to the fifth round of the distinguisher can be bypassed. To bypass the other two F-functions, we need to know rk_4^L, rk_5^R, rk_8^L, and rk_9^R only. If rk_4, rk_8 depend on the same k_i and rk_5, rk_9 rely on the same k_j then we can bypass the other two F-functions by guessing only k_i^L, and k_j^R. In such case, we can bypass the 8 F-functions of our 7-round distinguisher by guessing 7 parameters only. By placing our distinguisher to cover from the 5th round (round 4) to the 11th round (round 10), the number of parameters in proposition 2 is reduced to 7 parameters only. In that case, k_i is k_4 and k_j is k_5 and the 7 16-bit parameters of our distinguisher are the state X_7^0, k_1, k_6, k_4^L, and k_5^R. Our 16-round attack is then built by appending 3 and 6 rounds at the top and the bottom of our 7-round distinguisher, respectively. As shown in Fig. 5, the attack follows the same steps as the previous attack on Piccolo-80 while considering the new position of the δ-set at $X_4[7]$ and the different position of the corresponding ordered sequence at $X_{11}[13:15]$. In the online phase, the knowledge of P^0 and the guessing of k_4, k_5, k_6^L, and k_7^R enable us to partially decrypt $X_4[7]$ and determine the δ-set. From the other direction, by the knowledge of $[C^0, C^1, \cdots, C^{15}]$, $[C^0 \oplus C^1, C^0 \oplus C^2, \cdots, C^0 \oplus C^{15}]$ and the guessing of k_0, k_1, k_2, k_3^R, k_5, k_6, and k_7, we can compute the ordered sequence at $X_{11}[13:15]$. Hence, in total we need to guess seven and half keys, i.e., k_0, k_1, k_2, k_3^R, k_4, k_5, k_6, and k_7, in order to mount our attack on 16-round Piccolo-128.

Attack Complexity. The memory complexity is estimated to be $2^{7*16} \times (15 \times 12)/64 \approx 2^{113.49}$ 64-bit blocks and the data complexity is 2^{48} chosen plaintexts. The time complexity is $2^{112} \times 16 \times 8/(2 \times 16) + 2^{120} \times 16 \times (5 + 11)/(2 \times 16) + 2 \times 2^{(120-68)} \times 2^8 = 2^{114} + 2^{123} + 2^{61} \approx 2^{123}$ 16-round Piccolo-128 encryptions.

3.3   A MitM Attack on 17-Round Piccolo-128

To extend the attack on Piccolo-128 by one more round, we have to build another distinguisher, as illustrated in Fig. 6 because using the previous 7-round

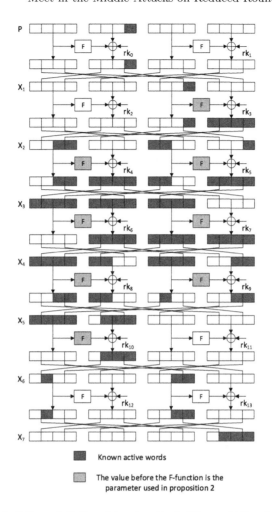

Fig. 4. 7-Round distinguisher to attack 16-round Piccolo-128

distinguisher requires the guessing of the whole key space. Using this new 6-round distinguisher, which needs 8 parameters, we attack 17-round Piccolo-128 from the 5th round (round 4) to the 21st round (round 20) with the post-whitening keys. We append 4 and 7 rounds at the top and the bottom of our 6-round distinguisher, respectively. To launch the attack on 17-round Piccolo-128, we need to guess seven and half keys, as shown in Fig. 7. These keys are $k_0^R, k_1, k_2, k_3, k_4, k_5, k_6, k_7$. The attack procedure follows the same steps of the previous attacks.

Attack Complexity. The memory complexity is estimated to be $2^{8 \times 16} \times (15 \times 12)/64 \approx 2^{129.49}$ 64-bit blocks. Since the memory complexity exceeds 2^{128}, we store a fraction $1/\alpha$ of the hash table H. $\alpha = 2^{3.5}$ is chosen so that the memory complexity does not exceed 2^{128} while having a non-marginal time complexity.

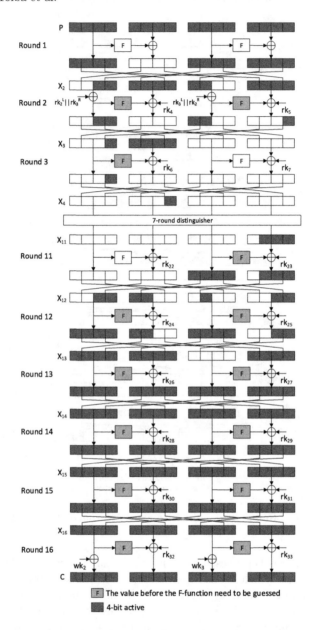

Fig. 5. 16-Round attack on Piccolo-128

Therefore, the memory complexity is $2^{125.99}$ 64-bit blocks. The data complexity is 2^{48} chosen plaintexts. Regarding the time complexity, since we do not store a fraction of the hash table, we have to repeat the online attack $2^{3.5}$ times. The time complexity of the offline phase is estimated to be $2^{128-3.5} \times 16 \times 8/(2 \times 17) \approx 2^{126.41}$. We use the partial computation technique in order to reduce

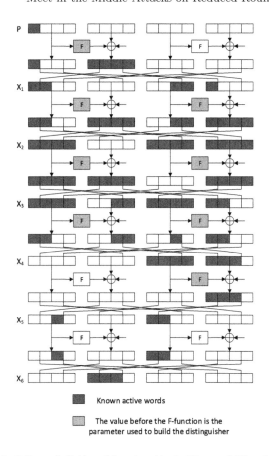

Known active words

The value before the F-function is the
parameter used to build the distinguisher

Fig. 6. 6-Round distinguisher to attack 17-round Piccolo-128

the time complexity of the online phase. First, guessing the keys k_0^R, k_3^L, k_6, k_7
enables us to identify the δ-set and the time of this step is evaluated to be
$2^{48} \times 16 \times 5/(2 \times 17) \approx 2^{49.23}$. By guessing k_4, k_5 we can partially decrypt through
round 20 and this step is estimated to be $2^{80} \times 16 \times 2/(2 \times 17) \approx 2^{79.91}$. Then,
guessing k_2 enables us to compute the output of the first F-function in round
19 and is estimated to be $2^{96} \times 16 \times 1/(2 \times 17) \approx 2^{94.91}$. Afterwards, guessing
k_1 enables us to partially decrypt through round 19 and 18 as well as the first
F-function of round 17 and needs $2^{112} \times 16 \times 4/(2 \times 17) \approx 2^{112.91}$ encryptions.
Finally, guessing k_3^R enables us to compute the ordered sequence and this step
needs $2^{120} \times 16 \times 6/(2 \times 17) \approx 2^{121.5}$ encryptions. Accordingly, the time complexity
of the online phase is $2^{49.23} + 2^{79.91} + 2^{94.91} + 2^{112.91} + 2^{121.5} \approx 2^{121.5}$ and it will
be repeated $2^{3.5}$ times so, all in all, it is estimated to be 2^{125}. Recovering the
master key using two plaintext/ciphertext pairs requires $2 \times 2^{120} \times 2^{128-180} \times 2^8 =
2^{77}$. The total time complexity of the attack is $2^{126.41} + 2^{125} + 2^{77} \approx 2^{126.87}$
encryptions.

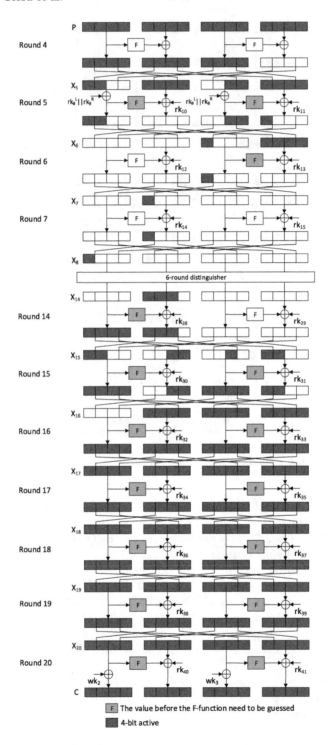

Fig. 7. 17-Round attack on Piccolo-128

4   Conclusion

In this work, we presented MitM attacks on 14-round reduced Piccolo-80 and 16, 17-round reduced piccolo-128. All these attacks on Piccolo-80 and Piccolo-128 require the same data complexity of 2^{48} chosen plaintexts. The time complexities of the MitM attacks on 14-round Piccolo-80 and 16, 17-round Piccolo-128 are $2^{75.39}$, 2^{123}, and $2^{126.87}$, respectively. Their memory complexities are $2^{73.49}$, $2^{113.49}$, and $2^{125.99}$ for the 14-round Piccolo-80 and 16, 17-round Piccolo-128, respectively.

References

1. Abdelkhalek, A., AlTawy, R., Tolba, M., Youssef, A.M.: Meet-in-the-middle attacks on reduced-round Hierocrypt-3. In: Lauter, K., Rodríguez-Henríquez, F. (eds.) LatinCrypt 2015. LNCS, vol. 9230, pp. 187–203. Springer, Heidelberg (2015)
2. Abdelkhalek, A., Tolba, M., Youssef, A.: Improved key recovery attack on round-reduced hierocrypt-L1 in the single-key setting. In: Chakraborty, R., Schwabe, P., Solworth, J. (eds.) Security, Privacy, and Applied Cryptography Engineering. Lecture Notes in Computer Science, vol. 9354, pp. 139–150. Springer International Publishing, Switzerland (2015)
3. AlTawy, R., Youssef, A.M.: Preimage attacks on reduced-round stribog. In: Pointcheval, D., Vergnaud, D. (eds.) AFRICACRYPT. LNCS, vol. 8469, pp. 109–125. Springer, Heidelberg (2014)
4. Azimi, S., Ahmadian, Z., Mohajeri, J., Aref, M.: Impossible differential cryptanalysis of Piccolo lightweight block cipher. In: 11th International ISC Conference on Information Security and Cryptology (ISCISC), pp. 89–94, September 2014
5. Biryukov, A., Derbez, P., Perrin, L.: Differential analysis and meet-in-the-middle attack against round-reduced TWINE. In: Leander, G. (ed.) FSE 2015. LNCS, vol. 9054, pp. 3–27. Springer, Heidelberg (2015)
6. Bogdanov, A., et al.: PRESENT: an ultra-lightweight block cipher. In: Paillier, P., Verbauwhede, I. (eds.) CHES 2007. LNCS, vol. 4727, pp. 450–466. Springer, Heidelberg (2007)
7. Bogdanov, A., Rechberger, C.: A 3-subset meet-in-the-middle attack: cryptanalysis of the lightweight block cipher KTANTAN. In: Biryukov, A., Gong, G., Stinson, D.R. (eds.) SAC 2010. LNCS, vol. 6544, pp. 229–240. Springer, Heidelberg (2011)
8. Cannière, C., Dunkelman, O., Knežević, M.: KATAN and KTANTAN — a family of small and efficient hardware-oriented block ciphers. In: Clavier, C., Gaj, K. (eds.) CHES 2009. LNCS, vol. 5747, pp. 272–288. Springer, Heidelberg (2009)
9. Daemen, J., Knudsen, L., Rijmen, V.: The block cipher SQUARE. In: Biham, E. (ed.) FSE 1997. LNCS, vol. 1267, pp. 149–165. Springer, Heidelberg (1997)
10. Demirci, H., Selçuk, A.A.: A meet-in-the-middle attack on 8-Round AES. In: Nyberg, K. (ed.) FSE 2008. LNCS, vol. 5086, pp. 116–126. Springer, Heidelberg (2008)
11. Derbez, P., Fouque, P.-A., Jean, J.: Improved key recovery attacks on reduced-round AES in the single-key setting. In: Johansson, T., Nguyen, P.Q. (eds.) EUROCRYPT 2013. LNCS, vol. 7881, pp. 371–387. Springer, Heidelberg (2013)
12. Derbez, P., Perrin, L.: Meet-in-the-middle attacks and structural analysis of round-reduced PRINCE. In: Leander, G. (ed.) FSE 2015. LNCS, vol. 9054, pp. 190–216. Springer, Heidelberg (2015)

13. Diffie, W., Hellman, M.E.: Special feature exhaustive cryptanalysis of the NBS data encryption standard. Computer **10**(6), 74–84 (1977)
14. Dunkelman, O., Keller, N., Shamir, A.: Improved single-key attacks on 8-Round AES-192 and AES-256. In: Abe, M. (ed.) ASIACRYPT 2010. LNCS, vol. 6477, pp. 158–176. Springer, Heidelberg (2010)
15. Guo, J., Jean, J., Nikolić, I., Sasaki, Y.: Meet-in-the-middle attacks on generic Feistel constructions. In: Sarkar, P., Iwata, T. (eds.) ASIACRYPT 2014. LNCS, vol. 8873, pp. 458–477. Springer, Heidelberg (2014)
16. Hong, D., et al.: HIGHT: a new block cipher suitable for low-resource device. In: Goubin, L., Matsui, M. (eds.) CHES 2006. LNCS, vol. 4249, pp. 46–59. Springer, Heidelberg (2006)
17. Isobe, T., Shibutani, K.: Security analysis of the lightweight block ciphers XTEA, LED and Piccolo. In: Susilo, W., Mu, Y., Seberry, J. (eds.) ACISP 2012. LNCS, vol. 7372, pp. 71–86. Springer, Heidelberg (2012)
18. Jeong, K.: Cryptanalysis of block cipher Piccolo suitable for cloud computing. J. Supercomputing **66**(2), 829–840 (2013)
19. Jeong, K., Kang, H., Lee, C., Sung, J., Hong, S.: Biclique cryptanalysis of lightweight block ciphers PRESENT, Piccolo and LED. IACR Cryptology ePrint Archive 2012/621 (2012). https://eprint.iacr.org/2012/621.pdf
20. Knudsen, L., Leander, G., Poschmann, A., Robshaw, M.: PRINTCIPHER: a block cipher for IC-Printing. In: Mangard, S., Standaert, F.-X. (eds.) CHES 2010. LNCS, vol. 6225, pp. 16–32. Springer, Heidelberg (2010)
21. Leander, G., Paar, C., Poschmann, A., Schramm, K.: New lightweight DES variants. In: Biryukov, A. (ed.) FSE 2007. LNCS, vol. 4593, pp. 196–210. Springer, Heidelberg (2007)
22. Li, L., Jia, K., Wang, X.: Improved meet-in-the-middle attacks on AES-192 and PRINCE. IACR Cryptology ePrint Archive 2013/573 (2013). https://eprint.iacr.org/2013/573.pdf
23. Lim, C.H., Korkishko, T.: mCrypton – a lightweight block cipher for security of low-cost RFID tags and sensors. In: Song, J.-S., Kwon, T., Yung, M. (eds.) WISA 2005. LNCS, vol. 3786, pp. 243–258. Springer, Heidelberg (2006)
24. Lin, L., Wu, W.: Improved meet-in-the-middle distinguisher on Feistel schemes. IACR Cryptology ePrint Archive 2015/051 (2015). https://eprint.iacr.org/2015/051.pdf
25. Minier, M.: On the security of Piccolo lightweight block cipher against related-key impossible differentials. In: Paul, G., Vaudenay, S. (eds.) INDOCRYPT 2013. LNCS, vol. 8250, pp. 308–318. Springer, Heidelberg (2013)
26. Sasaki, Y., Wang, L., Wu, S., Wu, W.: Investigating fundamental security requirements on whirlpool: improved preimage and collision attacks. In: Wang, X., Sako, K. (eds.) ASIACRYPT 2012. LNCS, vol. 7658, pp. 562–579. Springer, Heidelberg (2012)
27. Shibutani, K., Isobe, T., Hiwatari, H., Mitsuda, A., Akishita, T., Shirai, T.: Piccolo: an ultra-lightweight blockcipher. In: Preneel, B., Takagi, T. (eds.) CHES 2011. LNCS, vol. 6917, pp. 342–357. Springer, Heidelberg (2011)
28. Song, J., Lee, K., Lee, H.: Biclique cryptanalysis on lightweight block cipher: HIGHT and Piccolo. Int. J. Comput. Math. **90**(12), 2564–2580 (2013)
29. Tolba, M., Abdelkhalek, A., Youssef, A.: Meet-in-the-middle attacks on round-reduced khudra. In: Chakraborty, R., Schwabe, P., Solworth, J. (eds.) Security, Privacy, and Applied Cryptography Engineering, pp. 127–138. Springer International Publishing, Switzerland (2015)
30. Wang, Y., Wu, W., Yu, X.: Biclique cryptanalysis of reduced-round piccolo block cipher. In: Ryan, M., Smyth, B., Wang, G. (eds.) ISPEC 2012. LNCS, vol. 7232, pp. 337–352. Springer, Heidelberg (2012)

Differential Factors Revisited: Corrected Attacks on PRESENT and SERPENT

Cihangir Tezcan[1,2,3](✉)

[1] Department of Mathematics, Middle East Technical University, Ankara, Turkey
cihangir@metu.edu.tr
[2] CYDES Laboratory, Department of Cyber Security, Institute of Informatics,
Middle East Technical University, Ankara, Turkey
[3] Department of Cryptography, Institute of Applied Mathematics,
Middle East Technical University, Ankara, Turkey

Abstract. Differential factors, which prevent the attacker to distinguish some of the guessed keys corresponding to an active S-box during a differential attack on a block cipher, are recently introduced at Lightsec 2014 and used to reduce the time complexities of the previous differential-linear attacks on SERPENT. Key recovery attacks generally consists of two parts: Key guess using the distinguisher and exhaustive search on the remaining key bits. Thus, we show that differential factors can reduce the time complexity of the former and increase the latter since the attacker does not need to guess the keys which cannot be distinguished. As an example for the latter, we show that the best known differential attack on PRESENT overlooked its six differential factors and the corrected attack actually requires a time complexity increased by a factor of 64. Moreover, we show that differential factors also reduce data complexity of the differential attacks since less number of pairs are required to distinguish the correct key when the key space is reduced. This reduction in data complexity also reduces the time complexity. By using SERPENT's differential factors, we further reduce the data and time complexity of the differential-linear attacks on this cipher to obtain the best attacks.

Keywords: S-box · Differential factor · SERPENT · PRESENT

1 Introduction

Confusion layer of symmetric cryptography algorithms mostly consists of substitution boxes (S-boxes) and in order to provide better security against known attacks, S-boxes are selected depending on their cryptographic properties. Low non-linear and differential uniformity [24] provide resistance against linear [21]

C. Tezcan—This work was supported by The Scientific and Technological Research Council of Turkey (TÜBİTAK) under the grant 115E447 titled "Quasi-Differential Factors and Time Complexity of Block Cipher Attacks". Part of this work was done when the author was visiting Department of Electrical Engineering, ESAT/COSIC, Katholieke Universiteit Leuven, Belgium.

© Springer International Publishing Switzerland 2016
T. Güneysu et al. (Eds.): LightSec 2015, LNCS 9542, pp. 21–33, 2016.
DOI: 10.1007/978-3-319-29078-2_2

and differential cryptanalysis [6], respectively and most of the time these are the only properties designers focus on. However, it is shown that resistance against algebraic [11] and cube [12] attacks can be obtained by high algebraic degree and branch number. Moreover, lack of undisturbed bits [28] provides resistance against truncated [17], impossible [2], and improbable [27] differential cryptanalysis. It was shown in [20] that undisturbed bits are actually linear structures in coordinate functions. Thus, it is better to avoid linear structures to get better security against these kind of attacks. Resistance against side-channel attacks like differential power analysis [18] can be obtained depending on the number of shares [7] in threshold implementations. Implementation invariant resistance against these attacks can be obtained by S-boxes with a low transparency order [25] but low transparency order is not sufficient alone to directly achieve a satisfying level of security [10].

Recently it was shown in [29] that S-boxes may have parameters called differential factors which does not change the output difference of an S-box when they are XORed with the input pair. Thus, some counters of the guessed keys in a differential variant attack become the same, which prevents the attacker from fully capturing the attacked round keys. This may benefit the attacker because reduction in the attacked key space reduces the time complexity of many attacks. For instance, the 10, 11, and 12-round differential-linear attacks of [13] on SERPENT [1] tries to capture 40, 48, and 160 bits of the key, respectively. However, it was shown in [29] that these attacks can only obtain advantages of 38, 46, and 157 bits on the key due to differential factors and these attacks can actually be performed with time complexities reduced by a factor of 4, 4, and 8, respectively.

Most of the statistical attacks on blocks ciphers consists of two steps: Capturing partial information about the key via distinguishers and obtaining the remaining key bits via exhaustive search. We note that although differential factors reduce the time complexity of the former, they increase the time complexity of the latter. In this work we use this observation to correct the differential attack of [31] on PRESENT [9] which due to six differential factors requires a time complexity of 2^{70} memory accesses instead of 2^{64} memory accesses as it is claimed in [31].

Moreover, we show that differential factors also reduces the data complexity of differential attacks since the reduction in the key space allows us to use less number of pairs to distinguish the correct key. This observation also reduces the memory required to store the key counters and time complexity since the attack procedure is repeated for every data. We use our findings to obtain best differential-linear attacks on SERPENT by reducing the data and time complexity of the previous attacks.

2   Differential Factors

Definition 1 ([29]). *Let S be a function from $\mathbb{F}_2^n$ to $\mathbb{F}_2^m$. For all $x, y \in \mathbb{F}_2^n$ that satisfy $S(x) \oplus S(y) = \mu$, if we also have $S(x \oplus \lambda) \oplus S(y \oplus \lambda) = \mu$, then we say that the S-box has a* differential factor λ *for the output difference μ. (i.e. μ remains invariant for λ).*

PRESENT's S-box is given as an example in Table 1 which has $\lambda = 1$ as a differential factor for $\mu = 5$.

Table 1. PRESENT's S-box ordered in pairs where the output difference is $\mu = 5$. Note that XOR of any pair with $\lambda = 1$ gives another pair that has output difference $\mu = 5$.

x	5	1	E	C	F	D	8	2	B	7	4	0	6	A	3	9
S(x)	0	5	1	4	2	7	3	6	8	D	9	C	A	F	B	E

The following theorem shows that the number of differential factors of an S-box is the same with the number of differential factors of its inverse. Moreover, it also provides the differential factors of the inverse S-box when we know the differential factors of the S-box. Hence, there is no need to check the differential factors of the inverse of S-boxes. This theorem is useful in practice since inverse of an S-box is used for decryption in substitution permutation networks.

Theorem 1 ([29]). *If a bijective S-box S has a differential factor λ for an output difference μ, then S^{-1} has a differential factor μ for the output difference λ.*

Moreover, differential factors for the same μ form a vector space.

Theorem 2 ([29]). *If λ_1 and λ_2 are differential factors for an output difference μ, then $\lambda_1 \oplus \lambda_2$ is also a differential factor for the output difference μ. i.e. All differential factors λ_i for μ form a vector space.*

Differential factors are observed mostly in small S-boxes. For instance, 73.3 % of all 3×3 bijective S-boxes contain differential factors. Moreover, a list of ciphers and hash functions whose 4×4 S-boxes contain differential factors are provided in [29].

2.1 Differential Factors and Time Complexity

We start by recalling the definition of advantage.

Definition 2 ([26]). *If an attack on an m-bit key gets the correct value ranked among the top r out of 2^m possible candidates, we say the attack obtained an $(m - log(r))$-bit advantage over exhaustive search.*

Differential attacks on block ciphers use a differential as a distinguisher and the attack is performed by adding a few more rounds on the top or bottom of this differential. Pairs that may satisfy this differential are partially encrypted or decrypted under the possible subkeys and counters of these keys are incremented when the differential is satisfied. In a one round attack, one can obtain these counters just by looking at a precomputed table. However, more complicated attacks may require to repeat partial encryptions under every possible subkey. In these cases, differential factors reduce the time complexity of this step as follows.

Theorem 3 ([29]). *In a block cipher let an S-box S contain a differential factor λ for an output difference μ and the partial round key k is XORed with the input of S. If an input pair provides the output difference μ under a partial subkey k', then the same output difference is observed under the partial subkey $k' \oplus \lambda$. Therefore, during a differential attack involving the guess of a partial subkey corresponding to the output difference μ, the advantage of the cryptanalyst is reduced by 1 bit and the time complexity of this key guess step is halved.*

Proof. In a differential attack for any key k', k' and $k' \oplus \lambda$ would get the same number of hits since λ is a differential factor. Hence the attacker cannot distinguish half of the guessed keys with the other half. Therefore during the key guessing step, the attacker does not need to guess half of the keys. Thus, the time complexity of this step is halved.   □

From Theorems 2 and 3 we obtain the following Corollary.

Corollary 1 ([29]). *During a differential attack involving the guess of a partial subkey corresponding to the output difference μ of an S-box that has a vector space of differential factors of dimension r for μ, the advantage of the cryptanalyst is reduced by r bits and the time complexity of the key guess step is reduced by a factor of 2^r.*

Most of the statistical attacks on blocks ciphers first tries to capture partial information about the secret key and then the full key is obtained by exhaustive search. Thus, if possible, the attacker tries to balance these two steps to obtain the optimal time complexity for the attack. Although differential factors reduce the time complexity of the former, they increase the time complexity of the latter. We provide our first observation in Corollary 2.

Corollary 2. *Differential factors reduce the time complexity of capturing partial information about the key which uses differentials but they increase the time complexity of the exhaustive search for obtaining the remaining key bits.*

Thus, the attacker should take into account differential factors when trying to balance the time complexities of these two parts. We show the importance of Corollary 2 in Sect. 4 by proving that Wang's differential attack on PRESENT is actually wrong and the corrected attack requires 2^{70} memory accesses instead of 2^{64} as it is claimed in [31].

2.2   Differential Factors and Data Complexity

Statistical attacks use a distinguisher which is observed with different probabilities p_0 and p for the correct key and the wrong keys, respectively. For instance, the attacker uses N plaintext pairs in differential attack and counts the times each subkey satisfies this distinguisher. The correct key is expected to be above some threshold T since we have $p_0 > p$. Thus, the number of hits a wrong (right) subkey gets can be seen as a random variable of a binomial distribution with parameters N and p (p_0). We denote the non-detection error probability, which is the probability of the counter for the right subkey to be less than T, by p_{nd}; and the false alarm error probability, which is the probability of the counter for a wrong subkey to be higher than or equal to T, by p_{fa}.

Theorem 4. *Differential factors reduce the key space for the key guess process and therefore reduce the data complexity of the attack. Thus, memory required to keep the counters for the guessed keys also reduces. Reduction in the data complexity may also reduce the time complexity depending on the attack.*

Proof. The amount of required plaintext pairs N to perform the attack with the desired success probability depends also on the number of wrong keys. Because they determine the number of binomial distributions from which we try to distinguish the correct key. Since the existence of the differential factors reduces the wrong subkey space, the number of pairs required to perform the attack also reduces. Thus, memory required to keep the counters for the guessed keys also reduces. Moreover, the attack procedure is repeated for every pair in most of the attacks. Therefore, this reduction in the data complexity further reduces the time complexity. □

When differential factors were introduced in [29], their effect on the data and memory complexity were overlooked. By using differential factors that appear in the differential-linear attacks on SERPENT, we reduce the data complexity of these attacks in Sect. 5. Since the data and time complexities of these attacks are directly proportional, we further reduce the time complexities of these attacks. Moreover, we reduce the data and memory complexity of the differential attack on PRESENT in Sect. 4 using Theorem 4.

Success probability of differential attacks are generally calculated easily using Selçuk's formula [26] and it is used in the original PRESENT attack. However, in this work we use BLONDEAU-GÉRARD-TILLICH algorithm [8] since it is valid for both differential and differential-linear attacks. This algorithm takes p, p_0, p_{nd}, and p_{fa} as input and provides N and T as output.

3   PRESENT and SERPENT

PRESENT [9] is a 31-round SPN (Substitution Permutation Network) type block cipher with block size of 64 bits that supports 80 and 128-bit secret key. It has been internationally standardized by ISO/IEC 29192-2:2012 [16] as a lightweight block cipher. Round function of PRESENT, which is depicted in Fig. 1, is same for both versions of PRESENT and consists of standard operations such as subkey XOR, substitution and permutation: At the beginning of each round, 64-bit input of the round function is XORed with the subkey. Just after the subkey XOR, 16 identical 4×4-bit S-boxes are used in parallel as a non-linear substitution layer and finally a permutation is performed so as to provide diffusion.

SERPENT [1] was designed by Anderson, Biham and Knudsen in 1998. It was submitted to the AES contest and became one of the five finalists. It has a block

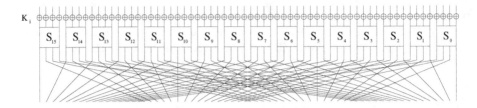

Fig. 1. Round function of PRESENT

size of 128 bits and accepts any key size of length 0 to 256 bits. It is a 32-round SPN, where each round consists of key mixing, a layer of S-boxes and a linear transformation.

The 128-bit input value before round i is denoted by $\hat{B}_i$, $i \in \{0, \ldots, 31\}$. Each $\hat{B}_i$ is composed of four 32-bit words X_0, X_1, X_2, X_3 where X_0 is the leftmost word.

Three round operations are specified as follows:

1. Key Mixing: At each round R_i, a 128-bit subkey K_i is XORed with the current intermediate data $\hat{B}_i$.
2. S-boxes: At each round, R_i uses a single S-box S_j, where $i \equiv j \pmod 8$ and $i \in \{0, \ldots, 31\}$, 32 times in parallel. In this paper, we use the bitsliced version of SERPENT. For example, in the first round the first copy of S_0 takes the least significant bits from X_0, X_1, X_2, X_3 and returns the output to the same bits. Thus, we obtain 32 4-bit slices referred as b_i's, where $i \in \{0, \ldots, 31\}$ and b_0 is the right most slice.
3. Linear Transformation: The four 32-bit words X_0, X_1, X_2, X_3 are linearly mixed by the following linear operations:

$$X_0 := X_0 \lll 13$$
$$X_2 := X_2 \lll 3$$
$$X_1 := X_1 \oplus X_0 \oplus X_2$$
$$X_3 := X_3 \oplus X_2 \oplus (X_0 \ll 3)$$
$$X_1 := X_1 \lll 1$$
$$X_3 := X_3 \lll 7$$
$$X_0 := X_0 \oplus X_1 \oplus X_3$$
$$X_2 := X_2 \oplus X_3 \oplus (X_1 \ll 7)$$
$$X_0 := X_0 \lll 5$$
$$X_2 := X_2 \lll 22$$
$$\hat{B}_{i+1} := X_0, X_1, X_2, X_3$$

where $\lll$ denotes the left rotation operation and $\ll$ denotes the left shift operation.

32-round SERPENT cipher may be described by the following equations:

$$\hat{B}_0 := P \qquad \hat{B}_{i+1} := R_i(\hat{B}_i), \ i \in \{0, \ldots, 31\} \qquad C := \hat{B}_{32}$$

where

$$R_i(X) = LT(\hat{S}_i(X \oplus K_i)), \ i \in \{0, \ldots, 30\}$$
$$R_{31}(X) = \hat{S}_{31}(X \oplus K_{31}) \oplus K_{32}$$

and $\hat{S}_i$ is the application of the S-box $S_{(i \ (mod \ 8))}$ 32 times in parallel, and LT is the linear transformation.

In this paper, we use P, S, I to the denote output of the permutation layer, output of the substitution layer, and input of a round, respectively.

Differential factors of PRESENT and SERPENT's S-boxes are provided in Table 2.

Table 2. Differential factors of PRESENT and SERPENT's S-boxes

S-box	0123456789ABCDEF	λ	μ
PRESENT	C56B90AD3EF84712	1_x	5_x
PRESENT	C56B90AD3EF84712	F_x	F_x
SERPENT S_0	38F1A65BED42709C	4_x	4_x
SERPENT S_0	38F1A65BED42709C	D_x	F_x
SERPENT S_1	FC27905A1BE86D34	4_x	4_x
SERPENT S_1	FC27905A1BE86D34	F_x	E_x
SERPENT S_2	86793CAFD1E40B52	2_x	1_x
SERPENT S_2	86793CAFD1E40B52	4_x	D_x
SERPENT S_6	72C5846BE91FD3A0	6_x	2_x
SERPENT S_6	72C5846BE91FD3A0	F_x	F_x

4 Differential Attacks on PRESENT

The best known differential attack on PRESENT is obtained in [31] by adding two rounds to the bottom of the 24 different 14-round differentials which has different input and same output difference. These differentials hold with probability $p = 2^{-62}$ and Δ_1 is an example for these differentials

$$\Delta_1 : 070000000000700 \rightarrow_{14r} 0000000900000009$$

This differential attack captures 32 bits of the key with a time complexity of $2^{33.18}$ 2-round PRESENT encryptions, a data complexity of 2^{64} chosen plaintexts, and a memory complexity of 2^{32} 6-bit counters. This part of the attack works with a success probability of 99.9999939 % and then the remaining 48 bits are obtained via exhaustive search which requires 2^{48} 16-round PRESENT encryptions or equivalently 2^{64} memory accesses.

It is claimed that these 14-round characteristics activates two S-boxes at the round 15 and due to the undisturbed bits of the S-box, it activates at most six S-boxes instead of eight in round 16. If activated, the input difference of these S-boxes must be 1. PRESENT's S-box has a differential factor $\lambda = 1$ for $\mu = 5$. Thus, the inverse of the S-box has a differential factor $\lambda = 5$ for $\mu = 1$ by Theorem 1. Since $\mu = 1$ coincides with the input difference of these six S-boxes, the advantage of this attack is actually 26 bits instead of 32 bits. This theoretical result can easily be observed experimentally by performing this attack by removing the first few rounds of the 14-round differential so that it remains within our computational power. This attack is summarized in Table 3.

Table 3. 16-round differential-linear attack of [31]. Output differences μ that contain differential factors, which is $\lambda = 1$ for the inverse S-box, are shown in bold.

Rounds	Differences in bits															
	x_{15}	x_{14}	x_{13}	x_{12}	x_{11}	x_{10}	x_9	x_8	x_7	x_6	x_5	x_4	x_3	x_2	x_1	x_0
$X_{1,I}$	0000	0111	0000	0000	0000	0000	0000	0000	0000	0000	0000	0000	0000	0111	0000	0000
14-Round Differential Δ_1																
$X_{14,P}$	0000	0000	0000	0000	0000	0000	0000	1001	0000	0000	0000	0000	0000	0000	0000	1001
$X_{15,S}$	0000	0000	0000	0000	0000	0000	0000	???0	0000	0000	0000	0000	0000	0000	0000	???0
$X_{15,P}$	0000	000?	0000	**000?**	0000	000?	0000	**000?**	0000	**000?**	0000	**000?**	0000	0000	0000	0000
$X_{16,S}$	0000	????	0000	????	0000	????	0000	????	0000	????	0000	????	0000	0000	0000	0000

This observation reduces the time complexity of the first part of the attack to $2^{27.18}$ 2-round PRESENT encryptions and the memory complexity to 2^{26} 6-bit counters. However, the time complexity of exhaustive search for the remaining bits of the key is 2^{54} 16-round PRESENT encryptions or equivalently 2^{70} memory accesses. Therefore, the correct time complexity of Wang's differential attack on PRESENT [31] is 2^{70} memory accesses, instead of 2^{64}.

Another correction we make for this attack is due to Theorem 4. The original attack uses the whole codebook and achieves a success probability of 0.999999939. However, the original attack tries to capture 32 bits of the key. Thus, we need $p_{fa} \leq 2^{-33}$ to have only the correct key counter above the threshold T. Since the six differential factors used in the attack reduces the key space for the key guess process, we can choose $p_{fa} = 2^{-27}$ to prevent any wrong key to get a counter higher than T. Using the BLONDEAU-GÉRARD-TILLICH algorithm with parameters $p = 2^{-64}$, $p_0 = 24 \cdot 2^{-62}$, $p_{nd} = 1 - 0.999999939$, and $p_{fa} = 2^{-27}$ shows that

Table 4. Comparison of Wang's original differential attack on PRESENT and our corrected one. *MA - Memory Accesses, b - bits, CP - Chosen Plaintexts.*

	Rounds	Data	Time	Memory	Success	Reference
Original	16	2^{64} CP	2^{64} MA	$6 \cdot 2^{32}$ b	99.9999939 %	[31]
Corrected	16	$2^{63.58}$ CP	2^{70} MA	$6 \cdot 2^{26}$ b	99.9999939 %	Sect. 4

this attack can be performed with $2^{63.58}$ data complexity to achieve the success probability of the original attack. This change reduces the memory required for the guessed key counters to $6 \cdot 2^{26}$ bits from $6 \cdot 2^{32}$ bits. These corrections are summarized in Table 4.

5   Differential-Linear Attacks on SERPENT

The most successful differential-linear attacks on SERPENT were provided by Dunkelman *et al.* in [13] for 10, 11, and 12 rounds for the key sizes 128, 192, and 256, respectively. These attacks combine the 3-round differential

$$\Delta : 00000000000000000000000040050000 \rightarrow 0??00?000?000000000?00?0??0??0?0$$

Table 5. 12-round differential-linear attack of [13]. Output differences μ that contain differential factors, which are $\mu = 4$ and $\mu = E$ for S_1 and $\mu = 4$ for S_0, are shown in bold. Undisturbed bits are shown in italic.

Input	X_0:	????	????	0???	0???	????	????	????	00??
	X_1:	????	????	0???	0???	????	????	????	00??
	X_2:	????	????	0???	0???	????	???*1*	????	00??
	X_3:	????	????	0???	0???	????	????	????	00??
S_0	X_0:	??0?	00?0	**0000**	0?00	00?0	**0000**	00??	00??
	X_1:	??0?	????	00?0	0???	0???	??**?0**	0?00	**0000**
	X_2:	000?	00??	0**?**?0	0?00	??00	?00**1**	0?00	**0000**
	X_3:	?0??	?0??	00??	0???	??0?	0?**?0**	?00**1**	**0000**
LT	X_0:	?000	0000	0000	0??0	0?00	?000	0000	0000
	X_1:	?000	0000	0000	0??0	0?00	?000	0000	0000
	X_2:	?000	0000	0000	0??0	0?00	?000	0000	0000
	X_3:	?000	0000	0000	0*1*?0	0?00	*1*000	0000	0000
S_1	X_0:	0000	0000	0000	0100	0000	**0000**	0000	0000
	X_1:	1000	0000	0000	0010	0100	**0000**	0000	0000
	X_2:	0000	0000	0000	0000	0100	**1000**	0000	0000
	X_3:	0000	0000	0000	0010	0100	**0000**	0000	0000
LT	X_0:	0000	0000	0000	0000	0000	0000	0001	0000
	X_1:	0000	0000	0000	0000	0000	0000	0000	0000
	X_2:	0000	0000	0000	0000	0000	0000	1001	0000
	X_3:	0000	0000	0000	0000	0000	0000	0000	0000

9-Round Differential-Linear Characteristic $\Delta \circ \Lambda$

Last Round

Table 6. Summary of attacks on SERPENT. Our observations on differential factors in Theorem 4 convert the attacks of [29] to the best attacks for this cipher. *En - Encryptions, MA - Memory Accesses, B - bytes, AC - Adaptive Chosen Plaintexts, CP - Chosen Plaintexts, KP - Known Plaintexts.*

# Rounds	Attack Type	Key Size	Data	Time	Memory	Advantage	Success	Reference
6	Meet-in-the-middle	256	512 KP	2^{247} En	2^{246} B	-	-	[19]
6	Differential	All	2^{83} CP	2^{90} En	2^{40} B	-	-	[19]
6	Differential	All	2^{71} CP	2^{103} En	2^{75} B	-	-	[19]
6	Differential	192, 256	2^{41} CP	2^{163} En	2^{45} B	124	-	[19]
7	Differential	256	2^{122} CP	2^{248} En	2^{126} B	128	-	[19]
7	Improbable	All	$2^{116.85}$ CP	$2^{117.57}$ En	2^{113} B	112	99.9 %	[30]
7	Differential	All	2^{84} CP	2^{85} MA	2^{56} B	-	-	[4]
10	Rectangle	192, 256	$2^{126.3}$ CP	$2^{173.8}$ MA	$2^{131.8}$ B	80	-	[5]
10	Boomerang	192, 256	$2^{126.3}$ AC	$2^{173.8}$ MA	2^{89} B	80	-	[5]
10	Differential-Linear	All	$2^{101.2}$ CP	$2^{115.2}$ En	2^{40} B	40	84 %	[13]
10	Differential-Linear	All	$2^{101.2}$ CP	$2^{113.2}$ En	2^{40} B	38	84 %	[29]
10	**Differential-Linear**	**All**	$2^{100.55}$ **CP**	$2^{112.55}$ **En**	2^{40} **B**	**38**	**84 %**	**Sect. 5**
11	Linear	256	2^{118} KP	2^{214} MA	2^{85} B	140	78.5 %	[3]
11	Multidimensional Linear[a]	All	2^{116} KP	$2^{107.5}$ En	2^{108} B	48	78.5 %	[23]
11	Multidimensional Linear[b]	All	2^{118} KP	$2^{109.5}$ En	2^{104} B	44	78.5 %	[23]
11	Nonlinear	192, 256	$2^{120.36}$ KP	$2^{139.63}$ MA	$2^{133.17}$ B	118	78.5 %	[22]
11	Filtered Nonlinear	192, 256	$2^{114.55}$ KP	$2^{155.76}$ MA	$2^{146.59}$ B	132	78.5 %	[22]
11	Differential-Linear	192, 256	$2^{121.8}$ CP	$2^{135.7}$ En	2^{76} B	48	84 %	[13]
11	Differential-Linear	192, 256	$2^{121.8}$ CP	$2^{133.7}$ En	2^{76} B	46	84 %	[29]
11	**Differential-Linear**	**192, 256**	$2^{120.8}$ **CP**	$2^{132.7}$ **En**	2^{76} **B**	**46**	**84 %**	**Sect. 5**
12	Multidimensional Linear[c]	256	2^{116} KP	$2^{237.5}$ En	2^{125} B	174	78.5 %	[23]
12	Differential-Linear	256	$2^{123.5}$ CP	$2^{249.4}$ En	$2^{128.5}$ B	160	84 %	[13]
12	Differential-Linear	256	$2^{123.5}$ CP	$2^{246.4}$ En	$2^{128.5}$ B	157	84 %	[29]
12	**Differential-Linear**	**256**	$2^{122.45}$ **CP**	$2^{244.35}$ **En**	$2^{128.5}$ **B**	**156**	**84 %**	**Sect. 5**

[a] [22] shows that this attack requires $2^{125.81}$ KP and $2^{101.44}$ En $+2^{114.13}$ MA.
[b] [22] shows that this attack requires $2^{127.78}$ KP and $2^{97.41}$ En $+2^{110.10}$ MA.
[c] [22] shows that this attack requires $\geq 2^{125.81}$ KP $2^{229.44}$ En $+2^{242.13}$ MA.

that has an experimental probability of 2^{-7} with the 6-round linear approximation

$$\Lambda : 20060040000001001000000000000000 \rightarrow 00001000000000005000010000100001$$

of [3] that has bias $q = 2^{-27}$. By performing experiments on the first four rounds of this 9-round differential-linear distinguisher, it was shown in [13] that for the full distinguisher, the probability of pairs to have the same parity in the masked outputs is $1/2 + 2^{-57.75}$. The 11-round attack adds one round to the top of this distinguisher and one round to the bottom. The 12-round attack adds an extra round to the top, which is provided in Table 5. Since the time complexity of the 11-round attack exceeds the exhaustive search of 128 bits, the 10-round attack removes the last round of the distinguisher so that it becomes applicable to SERPENT with 128-bit keys. These attacks partially encrypt the top rounds under every possible subkey to obtain the input difference of Δ. Then the last round is decrypted to check the parity of the correct pairs which is actually performed by using precomputed lookup tables.

It was claimed that these attacks can capture 40, 48, and 160 bits of the subkey. Later it was shown in [29] that these attacks overlooked the differential factors of SERPENT's S-boxes S_0 and S_1 and the actual advantages are 38, 46, and 157 bits, respectively. Since the attack procedure is repeated for every guess of the subkey bits, existence of differential factors also reduced the time complexities of these attacks by a factor of 4, 4, and 8, respectively.

However, we can further improve these attacks using Theorem 4. We also not that a differential factor was overlooked in the 12-round attack of [29] and therefore the advantage of the attack is actually 156 bits, not 157. Since the differential factors used in the attacks reduce the key space to 38, 46, and 156 bits, we choose the false alarm probability for these attacks in BLONDEAU-GÉRARD-TILLICH algorithm as $p_{fa} = 2^{-39}$, $p_{fa} = 2^{-47}$, and $p_{fa} = 2^{-157}$, respectively. This analysis shows that these attacks can actually be performed with data complexities $2^{100.55}$, $2^{120.8}$, and $2^{122.45}$ instead of $2^{101.2}$, $2^{121.8}$, and $2^{123.5}$ respectively. Since the data and time complexities of these attacks are directly proportional, we further reduce the time complexities of these attacks to $2^{112.55}$, $2^{132.7}$, and $2^{244.35}$ from $2^{113.2}$, $2^{133.7}$, and $2^{246.4}$, respectively. The attacks on SERPENT are summarized in Table 6.

6   Conclusion

Many attacks on ciphers require data, time, and memory complexities that are beyond our computational powers. Thus, experiments on the reduced versions of these theoretical attacks are vital to check the validity in practice. For instance, it was believed that the key bits corresponding to active S-boxes in a differential attack could be fully captured in a differential attack. However, differential factors which are introduced in Lightsec 2014 show that this is not always the case. Differential factors were used to correct the differential-linear attacks on SERPENT and the resulting attacks have reduced time complexities. Key recovery attacks generally consists of two parts and in this work we show that differential factors reduce the time complexity of the key guess using a distinguisher step but increase the time complexity of exhaustive search on the remaining key bits step. As an example, we show that the best differential attack on PRESENT in the literature overlooked the differential factors and the attack actually requires 2^{70} memory accesses instead of 2^{64}. Hence, differential factors affect the attacker adversely if the exhaustive search step of the attack requires time complexity more than the key guess step.

Moreover, we further investigate the effects of differential factors and observe that existence of differential factors in an attack reduces the memory complexity required for the key counters and the data complexity. This is because differential factors reduce the size of the key space for the key guess part of the attack which allows the attacker to distinguish the correct key from the wrong ones with a reduced number of data. The reduction in the data complexity may result in a similar reduction in the time complexity since data and time complexities are directly proportional in most of the attacks. Using these observations, we further reduce the data and time complexities of the best differential-linear attacks on SERPENT to obtain the best attacks for this cipher. Moreover, we show that the differential attack on PRESENT actually requires less data and memory complexity.

References

1. Biham, E., Anderson, R., Knudsen, L.R.: Serpent: a new block cipher proposal. In: Vaudenay, S. (ed.) FSE 1998. LNCS, vol. 1372, pp. 222–238. Springer, Heidelberg (1998)
2. Biham, E., Biryukov, A., Shamir, A.: Cryptanalysis of skipjack reduced to 31 rounds using impossible differentials. J. Cryptology **18**(4), 291–311 (2005)
3. Biham, E., Dunkelman, O., Keller, N.: Linear cryptanalysis of reduced round serpent. In: Matsui, M. (ed.) FSE 2001. LNCS, vol. 2355, pp. 16–27. Springer, Heidelberg (2002)
4. Biham, E., Dunkelman, O., Keller, N.: The rectangle attack - rectangling the serpent. In: Pfitzmann, B. (ed.) EUROCRYPT 2001. LNCS, vol. 2045, pp. 340–357. Springer, Heidelberg (2001)
5. Biham, E., Dunkelman, O., Keller, N.: New results on boomerang and rectangle attacks. In: Daemen, J., Rijmen, V. (eds.) FSE 2002. LNCS, vol. 2365, pp. 1–16. Springer, Heidelberg (2002)
6. Biham, E., Shamir, A.: Differential cryptanalysis of DES-like cryptosystems. J. Cryptology **4**(1), 3–72 (1991)
7. Bilgin, B., Nikova, S., Nikov, V., Rijmen, V., Stütz, G.: Threshold implementations of all 3×3 and 4×4 S-boxes. In: Prouff, E., Schaumont, P. (eds.) CHES 2012. LNCS, vol. 7428, pp. 76–91. Springer, Heidelberg (2012)
8. Blondeau, C., Gérard, B., Tillich, J.P.: Accurate estimates of the data complexity and success probability for various cryptanalyses. Des. Codes Crypt. **59**(1–3), 3–34 (2011)
9. Bogdanov, A., Knudsen, L.R., Leander, G., Paar, C., Poschmann, A., Robshaw, M.J.B., Seurin, Y., Vikkelsoe, C.: PRESENT: an ultra-lightweight block cipher. In: Paillier, P., Verbauwhede, I. (eds.) CHES 2007. LNCS, vol. 4727, pp. 450–466. Springer, Heidelberg (2007)
10. Chakraborty, K., Sarkar, S., Maitra, S., Mazumdar, B., Mukhopadhyay, D., Prouff, E.: Redefining the transparency order. Cryptology ePrint Archive, Report 2014/367 (2014)
11. Courtois, N.T., Pieprzyk, J.: Cryptanalysis of block ciphers with overdefined systems of equations. In: Zheng, Y. (ed.) ASIACRYPT 2002. LNCS, vol. 2501, pp. 267–287. Springer, Heidelberg (2002)
12. Dinur, I., Shamir, A.: Cube attacks on tweakable black box polynomials. In: Joux, A. (ed.) EUROCRYPT 2009. LNCS, vol. 5479, pp. 278–299. Springer, Heidelberg (2009)

13. Dunkelman, O., Indesteege, S., Keller, N.: A differential-linear attack on 12-round serpent. In: Chowdhury, D.R., Rijmen, V., Das, A. (eds.) INDOCRYPT 2008. LNCS, vol. 5365, pp. 308–321. Springer, Heidelberg (2008)
14. Eisenbarth, T., Öztürk, E. (eds.): LightSec 2014. LNCS, vol. 8898. Springer, Heidelberg (2015)
15. Helleseth, T. (ed.): EUROCRYPT 1993. LNCS, vol. 765. Springer, Heidelberg (1994)
16. ISO/IEC 29192–2:2012: Information technology - security techniques - lightweight cryptography - part 2: Block ciphers (2011)
17. Knudsen, L.R.: Truncated and higher order differentials. In: Preneel, B. (ed.) FSE 1994. LNCS, vol. 1008, pp. 196–211. Springer, Heidelberg (1995)
18. Kocher, P.C., Jaffe, J., Jun, B.: Differential power analysis. In: Wiener, M. (ed.) CRYPTO 1999. LNCS, vol. 1666, pp. 388–397. Springer, Heidelberg (1999)
19. Kohno, T., Kelsey, J., Schneier, B.: Preliminary cryptanalysis of reduced-round Serpent. In: AES Candidate Conference, pp. 195–211 (2000)
20. Makarim, R.H., Tezcan, C.: Relating undisturbed bits to other properties of substitution boxes. In: Eisenbarth and Öztürk [14], pp. 109–125
21. Matsui, M.: Linear cryptoanalysis method for DES cipher. In: Helleseth [15], pp. 386–397
22. McLaughlin, J., Clark, J.A.: Filtered nonlinear cryptanalysis of reduced-round serpent, and the wrong-key randomization hypothesis. In: Stam, M. (ed.) IMACC 2013. LNCS, vol. 8308, pp. 120–140. Springer, Heidelberg (2013)
23. Nguyen, P.H., Wu, H., Wang, H.: Improving the algorithm 2 in multidimensional linear cryptanalysis. In: Parampalli, U., Hawkes, P. (eds.) ACISP 2011. LNCS, vol. 6812, pp. 61–74. Springer, Heidelberg (2011)
24. Nyberg, K.: Differentially uniform mappings for cryptography. In: Helleseth [15], pp. 55–64
25. Prouff, E.: DPA attacks and S-boxes. In: Gilbert, H., Handschuh, H. (eds.) FSE 2005. LNCS, vol. 3557, pp. 424–441. Springer, Heidelberg (2005)
26. Selçuk, A.A.: On probability of success in linear and differential cryptanalysis. J. Cryptology 21(1), 131–147 (2008)
27. Tezcan, C.: The improbable differential attack: cryptanalysis of reduced round CLEFIA. In: Gong, G., Gupta, K.C. (eds.) INDOCRYPT 2010. LNCS, vol. 6498, pp. 197–209. Springer, Heidelberg (2010)
28. Tezcan, C.: Improbable differential attacks on PRESENT using undisturbed bits. J. Comput. Appl. Math. 259, Part B(0), 503–511 (2014)
29. Tezcan, C., Özbudak, F.: Differential factors: improved attacks on SERPENT. In: Eisenbarth and Öztürk [14], pp. 69–84
30. Tezcan, C., Taskin, H.K., Demircioglu, M.: Improbable differential attacks on serpent using undisturbed bits. In: Poet, R., Rajarajan, M. (eds.) Proceedings of the 7th International Conference on Security of Information and Networks, p. 145. ACM, New York (2014)
31. Wang, M.: Differential cryptanalysis of reduced-round PRESENT. In: Vaudenay, S. (ed.) AFRICACRYPT 2008. LNCS, vol. 5023, pp. 40–49. Springer, Heidelberg (2008)

Lightweight Constructions

A Light-Weight Group Signature Scheme with Time-Token Dependent Linking

Keita Emura[✉] and Takuya Hayashi

Security Fundamentals Laboratory, Network Security Research Institute,
National Institute of Information and Communications Technology (NICT),
Tokyo, Japan
k-emura@nict.go.jp

Abstract. Group signature is a central topic of cryptography with anonymity, and its several applications have been considered so far, e.g., privacy-preserving vehicle communications. Since anonymity (a.k.a. unlinkability) is quite strong in certain situations and it requires heavy cryptographic costs, group signatures with relaxed anonymity also have been proposed. For example, group signatures with controllable linkability was proposed by Hwang et al., (LightSec 2011) where an authority called Linker can anonymously check whether two group signatures are made by the same signer or not by using a linking key. However, the linking algorithm requires a heavy computation, i.e., bilinear pairings. In this paper, we propose the notion group signatures with time-token dependent Linking (GS-TDL), where a signer is unlinkable unless it generates multiple signatures at the same time period. It is particularly worth noting that our linking algorithm does not require cryptographic computations (i.e., comparisons to determine two elements are the same). Moreover, the signature size is 25 % shorter than that of the Hwang et al. scheme, and is 34 % shorter than that of the Boneh-Boeyn-Shacham short group signature scheme. Our GS-TDL scheme supports verifier-local revocation (VLR), which maintains constant signing and verification costs by using the linkable part of signatures. These appear to be related to independent interests. Finally, we provide our experimental results (using the TEPLA library on a cheap and constrained computational power device, Raspberry Pi).

1 Introduction

Group Signature: Digital signature is widely recognized as an important tool for current information-oriented society, where a verifier can check whether a signature is made by a specific signer or not. That is, the verifier identifies the signer. However, in a certain situation, this identification infringes privacy of signer, and group signature, which was proposed by Chaum and van Heyst [17], considers such a privacy infringement, where a verifier can anonymously check the signer whether a signer is a member of the group or not. Bellare, Micciancio, and Warinschi (BMW) [10] formalized group signature, and showed that full-anonymity and full-traceability are enough to construct a secure group signature

© Springer International Publishing Switzerland 2016
T. Güneysu et al. (Eds.): LightSec 2015, LNCS 9542, pp. 37–57, 2016.
DOI: 10.1007/978-3-319-29078-2_3

scheme, and the BMW model is widely recognized as a de-facto standard for group signature. Briefly, full-anonymity requires that no one, except the group manager, can link whether two group signatures are made by the same signer or not. Bellare, Shi, and Zhang (BSZ) [11] and Kiayias and Yung (KY) [33] showed an extension of the BMW model for dynamic group setting, and Sakai et al. [45] further extended the BSZ model to prevent signature hijacking attack.

Our Motivation: When defining a security-level of a system, it should be decided whether full anonymity (or more precisely, unlinkability) must be guaranteed or not. For example, in a vehicle ad-hoc network (VANET) system with anonymity, e.g., [48], linkable information (such as travel routes) is also important when local information is collected. That is, no such linkable information can be collected when a full-anonymous group signature scheme is employed as its building tool. Moreover, system efficiency may be drastically improved if unlinkability is not required, because the theoretical gap between a group signature scheme with unlinkability and one without unlinkability is significantly large [44]. More concretely, group signature without unlinkability can be constructed from one-way functions, whereas group signature with unlinkability implies chosen-ciphertext secure public key encryption. Especially, group signature with opening soundness [45] implies pubic key encryption with non-interactive opening [19]. As another example, Baldimtsi and Lysyanskaya proposed a light-weight version of anonymous credentials [6], where no pairing computation is required under a relaxed anonymity definition. Conversely, continuous linkability (via pseudonyms, for example) is problematic from the viewpoint of privacy. For example, a vehicle with continuous linkability is tracked from the time the vehicle is acquired up until the time it is sold, and parking spaces, which may include the driver's home and work place, are revealed. Therefore, suitably defining "moderate" anonymity with practical efficiency is an important issue that must be resolved.

Our Contribution: In this paper, we propose group signatures with time-token dependent linking (GS-TDL), where a signer is unlinkable unless it generates multiple signatures at the same time period, and give a *light-weight* instantiation. We assume that a Token Generation Unit (TGU) generates a time-dependent token t_T at a time T and broadcasts it, and each signer, who uses a unique identity ID, generates a group signature σ by using t_T and its signing key $\mathsf{sigk_{ID}}$. In GS-TDL, nobody can distinguish whether two signatures were generated by the same signer or not if $(\mathsf{ID}, T) \neq (\mathsf{ID}', T')$ for identities of signers ID and ID' and time periods T and T'.

Our GS-TDL is secure in the random oracle model, because we pursue a light-weight implementation of the system, under the q-strong Diffie-Hellman (q-SDH) assumption [13] and the strong decisional Diffie-Hellman inversion (SDDHI) assumption [16,23]. The group signature size in our scheme is shorter than that of previous schemes owing to time-dependent linkability. Specifically, a signature contains only 6 group elements, whereas that of the short group signature scheme [14] contains 9 group elements, that of the short controllable linkable group signature scheme [29] contains 8 group elements, and that of the controllable linkable group signature scheme (for dynamic group setting) [30] contains 12 group elements. Recently, though a short dynamic controllable linkable group signature scheme is proposed [28], a signature contains 8 group elements.[1] In addition to the signature size, our linking algorithm does not require cryptographic computations (i.e., comparisons to determine two elements are the same).

Our GS-TDL supports verifier-local revocation (VLR) [15,34,38,42,43], where no signer is involved in the revocation procedure. In particular, our GS-TDL achieves backward unlinkability [38,42,43], which prevents adversaries from breaking anonymity, even after signers are revoked. Our time-dependent linking properties enable us to achieve *constant verification costs* by using the linkable part of signatures, whereas those of previous schemes are $O(r)$, where r is the number of revoked users. This appear to be related to independent interest.

Finally, we provide the experimental results of our GS-TDL scheme, and show that it is feasible in practice. To implement GS-TDL, we use the TEPLA library [1]. We note that we employ asymmetric pairing settings ((type III) Barreto-Naehrig (BN) curves [8]) with 254-bit order due to the recent novel works for solving the discrete logarithm problem over certain elliptic curves with symmetric pairing settings, e.g., [7,25].

Application: As an application of GS-TDL, we can construct an anonymous time-dependent authentication system in the VANET setting, in which two group signatures become linkable if a signer (vehicle) generates a group signature twice in the same time period. Time-dependent linking appears to be more suitable for a VANET system than a system based on message-linkable group signature (MLGS) [48], where two group signatures become linkable if a signer (vehicle) generates a group signature for the same message twice. For example, a vehicle is always linkable if it generates group signatures on the same message, and this situation might occur when a vehicle is used for work trips and uses the same road each day. This may infringe privacy of drivers.[2] We note that no formal security definition for MLGS is provided in [48], and therefore the security proofs are informal. As a result, we can show an attack against the MLGS scheme of Wu et al., where anyone can generate a valid-but-untraceable group signature without using a secret key. We give the attack and the detailed system construction based on GS-TDL in the full version of this paper.

Related Work: Nakanishi et al. proposed linkable group signature [41], where anyone can determine whether two signatures were made by the same signer or not. As a difference from GS-TDL, no time-dependent token is required

---

[1] We remark that these schemes [14,28–30] also achieve only CPA-anonymity (i.e., no opening oracle access is allowed in anonymity game) as in ours.

[2] Even if a random nonce is included as a part of signed message, no linking algorithm works and this leads to a wag-the-dog situation. Even if a time T is included, e.g., sign $M||T$ by using a message-dependent linking group signature scheme, anyone can manipulate T and such a signer-driven anonymous system must be avoided because vehicles have incentive to hide identity. On the contrary, in GS-TDL, time T is authorized by TGU and no vehicle can manipulate T.

for linking. That is, two group signatures made by the same signer are always linkable. A group signature with a relaxed anonymity (for VANET) has been considered in [40]. But the link algorithm is not publicly executable, and an authority called Link Manager is introduced. That is, two group signatures made by the same signer are always linkable from the viewpoint of Link Manager. Moreover, pairing computations are required for linking. Abe et al. [2] proposed double-trapdoor anonymous tags which can generally construct traceable signatures [32]. Since a signer is always linkable after the corresponding token is broadcasted, we cannot use traceable signatures instead of GS-TDL. As a special case of traceable signatures, group signatures with controllable linkability has been proposed [28–30,47], where a link key is defined for the linking procedure. However, pairing computations are required for linking, which lead to inefficiency. Yang et al. [49] considered special unlinkability which has a similar functionality of time-dependent linking. However, the group manager needs to publish a token for each group member per a period whereas the group manager just publishes a small-size token (which can be commonly used by group members) in our scheme.

2 Preliminaries

Complexity Assumptions: Let $\mathcal{G}$ be a probabilistic polynomial-time algorithm that takes a security parameter λ as input and generates a parameter $(p, \mathbb{G}_1, \mathbb{G}_2, \mathbb{G}_T, e, g_1, g_2)$ of bilinear groups, where p is a λ-bit prime, $\mathbb{G}_1, \mathbb{G}_2$ and $\mathbb{G}_T$ are groups of order p, e is a bilinear map from $\mathbb{G}_1 \times \mathbb{G}_2$ to $\mathbb{G}_T$, and g_1 and g_2 are generators of $\mathbb{G}_1$ and $\mathbb{G}_2$, respectively. Here we use the asymmetric setting, i.e., $\mathbb{G}_1 \neq \mathbb{G}_2$.

Definition 1 (SDDHI Assumption [16]). *We say that the SDDHI (Strong Decisional Diffie-Hellman Inversion) assumption holds if for all PPT adversaries $\mathcal{A}$, $|\Pr[(p, \mathbb{G}_1, \mathbb{G}_2, \mathbb{G}_T, e, g_1, g_2) \xleftarrow{\$} \mathcal{G}(1^\lambda); x \xleftarrow{\$} \mathbb{Z}_p; (T, st) \leftarrow \mathcal{A}^{\mathcal{O}_x}(p, \mathbb{G}_1, \mathbb{G}_2, \mathbb{G}_T, e, g_1, g_2, g_1^x); \tau_0 = g_1^{\frac{1}{x+T}}; \tau_1 \xleftarrow{\$} \mathbb{G}_1; b \xleftarrow{\$} \{0,1\}; b' \leftarrow \mathcal{A}^{\mathcal{O}_x}(\tau_b, st) : b = b'] - \frac{1}{2}|$ is negligible, where $\mathcal{O}_x$ is an oracle which takes as input $z \in \mathbb{Z}_p^* \setminus \{T\}$, outputs $g_1^{\frac{1}{x+z}}$.*

We remark that the underlying bilinear group must not be symmetric.

Definition 2 (q-SDH Assumption [13]). *We say that the q-SDH (q-Strong Diffie-Hellman) assumption holds if for all PPT adversaries $\mathcal{A}$, $\Pr[(p, \mathbb{G}_1, \mathbb{G}_2, \mathbb{G}_T, e, g_1, g_2) \xleftarrow{\$} \mathcal{G}(1^\lambda); \gamma \xleftarrow{\$} \mathbb{Z}_p; (x, g_1^{\frac{1}{x+\gamma}}) \leftarrow \mathcal{A}(p, \mathbb{G}_1, \mathbb{G}_2, \mathbb{G}_T, e, g_1, g_1^\gamma, \ldots, g_1^{\gamma^q}, g_2, g_2^\gamma); x \in \mathbb{Z}_p^* \setminus \{-\gamma\}]$ is negligible.*

Digital Signature: Let (Gen, Sign, Verify) be a digital signature scheme. The key generation algorithm Gen takes as input a security parameter λ, and outputs a pair of verification/signing key (vk, sigk). The signing algorithm Sign takes as input sigk and a message to be signed M, and outputs a signature Σ.

The verification algorithm Verify takes as input vk, Σ and M, and outputs 0/1. We require the following correctness property: for all $(\mathsf{vk}, \mathsf{sigk}) \leftarrow \mathsf{Gen}(1^\lambda)$ and M, $\Pr[\mathsf{Verify}(\mathsf{vk}, \mathsf{Sign}(\mathsf{sigk}, M), M) = 1] = 1$ holds. Next, we define existential unforgeability against chosen message attack (EUF-CMA) as follows. Let $\mathcal{C}$ be the challenger, and $\mathcal{A}$ be an adversary. $\mathcal{C}$ runs $(\mathsf{vk}, \mathsf{sigk}) \leftarrow \mathsf{Gen}(1^\lambda)$ and gives vk to $\mathcal{A}$. $\mathcal{A}$ is allowed to issue signing queries M. $\mathcal{C}$ runs $\Sigma \leftarrow \mathsf{Sign}(\mathsf{sigk}, M)$ and returns Σ to $\mathcal{A}$. Finally, $\mathcal{A}$ outputs (Σ^*, M^*). We say that a digital signature scheme $(\mathsf{Gen}, \mathsf{Sign}, \mathsf{Verify})$ is EUF-CMA if the probability, that $\mathsf{Verify}(\mathsf{vk}, \Sigma^*, M^*) = 1$ and $\mathcal{A}$ did not send M^* as a signing query, is negligible.

3   Definitions of GS-TDL

In this section, we give the syntax and security definitions of GS-TDL by adding the time-dependent linkability to the BMW model [10] which is recognized as a de-facto standard for group signatures. In order to implement the time-dependent linkability, we introduce Token Generation Unit who generates time tokens and broadcasts the tokens. As in the conventional group signatures, an authority called Group Manager issues signing keys for users. A user generates a group signature by using own secret signing key and the corresponding time token. If a user generates two group signatures by using the same time token, then these signatures are linkable whereas two signatures are unlinkable if two signatures are generated by different time tokens respectively.

Design Principle: Because we pursued a light-weight implementation of the system, there is a room for discussion about whether the open functionality should be utilized or not. In the open functionality, an authority (called an opener) can determine the identity of the actual signer by using a secret opening key. For example, the open functionality is implemented by using public key encryption (PKE) or non-interactive zero-knowledge proof of knowledge, and could be an efficiency bottleneck. It has been reported that the signature size of the Furukawa-Imai group signature scheme [24] can be reduced by 50 % if the open functionality is removed [20]. It also has been reported that implementing the open functionality without using PKE leads to a short group signature scheme at the expense of the signature opening costs [12]. Given the above facts, we do not consider the open functionality (we only consider the linking functionality). Moreover, we assume that the signing key of a signer is embedded in a device during the setup phase, and therefore we remove an interactive join algorithm from our syntax. Finally, we consider the revocation functionality, especially verifier-local revocation (VLR) where no signer is involved in revocation procedures.

Definition 3 (Syntax of GS-TDL). *A group signature scheme with time-token dependent linking* $\mathcal{GS\text{-}TDL}$ *consists of the algorithms* (Setup, GKeyGen, TKeyGen, Join, TokenGen, GSign, Revoke, GVerify, Link) *as follows:*

- Setup: *The setup algorithm takes as input a security parameter λ, and outputs a public parameter params.*
- GKeyGen: *The group key generation algorithm takes as input params, and outputs a group public key gpk, a group master key gsk, an initial revocation storage grs := $\emptyset$ and an initial revocation list RL_0 := $\emptyset$.*
- TKeyGen: *The token key generation algorithm takes as input params, and outputs a public key tpk and a secret key tsk.*
- Join: *The join algorithm takes as input gsk, grs and a unique identity ID, and outputs a signing key $sigk_{ID}$ and updated revocation storage. We remark that this algorithm is not required to be interactive.*
- TokenGen: *The token generation algorithm takes as inputs tsk and a time T, and outputs a token t_T.*
- GSign: *The signing algorithm takes as inputs gpk, tpk, t_T, $sigk_{ID}$, and a message M to be signed, and outputs a group signature σ.*
- Revoke: *The revocation algorithm takes as inputs gpk, grs, and a set of revoked users at a time T $\{ID_{T,1}, \dots, ID_{T,n_T}\}$, and outputs RL_T. Here, n_T is the number of users that are additionally revoked on T.*
- GVerify: *The verification algorithm takes as inputs gpk, tpk, RL_T, σ, and M, and outputs 0 (invalid) or 1 (valid).*
- Link: *The linking algorithm takes as inputs gpk, tpk, and RL_T, and two signatures and messages (σ_0, M_0, T_0) and (σ_1, M_1, T_1), and outputs 1 if two signatures are made by the same signer, and 0 otherwise. We remark that the* Link *algorithm outputs 0 does not guarantee two signatures are made by the different signers. For example, if a signature is invalid, then the algorithm outputs 0.*

We require the following correctness, where any honestly generated signature is valid, and the Link algorithm correctly links two signatures if these are generated by the same signing key with the same token, unless the corresponding signer is not revoked. Moreover, we require that a signature is invalid if the corresponding signer is revoked.[3]

Definition 4 (Correctness). *For any probabilistic polynomial time (PPT) adversary $\mathcal{A}$ and the security parameter $\lambda \in \mathbb{N}$, we define the experiment* $\mathrm{Exp}_{GS\text{-}TDL,\mathcal{A}}^{corr}(\lambda)$ *as follows.*

---

[3] As a remark, the case that an adversary generates a valid signature using a revoked user's signing key cannot be captured by unforgeability since the open algorithm is not defined. Instead, we consider the case that a signature is invalid when the corresponding signer is revoked in correctness, though it might be additionally defined such as revocation soundness.

$\mathrm{Exp}_{\mathsf{GS\text{-}TDL},\mathcal{A}}^{corr}(\lambda):$

    $ms \leftarrow \mathsf{Setup}(1^\lambda)$

    $(\mathsf{gpk}, \mathsf{gsk}, \mathsf{grs}, \mathsf{RL}_0) \leftarrow \mathsf{GKeyGen}(params)$

    $(\mathsf{tpk}, \mathsf{tsk}) \leftarrow \mathsf{TKeyGen}(params); \ \mathsf{GU} := \emptyset$

    $(\mathsf{ID}^*, T^*, M_0, M_1) \leftarrow \mathcal{A}^{\mathsf{AddU}(\cdot), \mathsf{Revoke}(\mathsf{grs}, \cdot)}(\mathsf{gpk}, \mathsf{tpk})$

    $\mathsf{ID}^* \in \mathsf{GU}; \ t_{T^*} \leftarrow \mathsf{TokenGen}(\mathsf{tsk}, T^*)$

    $\sigma_0 \leftarrow \mathsf{GSign}(\mathsf{gpk}, \mathsf{tpk}, t_{T^*}, \mathsf{sigk}_{\mathsf{ID}^*}, M_0)$

    $\sigma_1 \leftarrow \mathsf{GSign}(\mathsf{gpk}, \mathsf{tpk}, t_{T^*}, \mathsf{sigk}_{\mathsf{ID}^*}, M_1)$

    Return 1 *if the following holds* :

    $\big[\mathsf{ID}^* \notin \mathsf{RL}_{T^*} \wedge \big((\mathsf{GVerify}(\mathsf{gpk}, \mathsf{tpk}, \mathsf{RL}_{T^*}, M_0, \sigma_0) = 0$

    $\vee \ \mathsf{GVerify}(\mathsf{gpk}, \mathsf{tpk}, \mathsf{RL}_{T^*}, M_1, \sigma_1) = 0)$

    $\vee \ \mathsf{Link}(\mathsf{gpk}, \mathsf{tpk}, \mathsf{RL}_{T^*}, (M_0, \sigma_0, T^*), (M_1, \sigma_1, T^*)) = 0)\big]$

    $\vee \big[\mathsf{ID}^* \in \mathsf{RL}_{T^*} \wedge \big((\mathsf{GVerify}(\mathsf{gpk}, \mathsf{tpk}, \mathsf{RL}_{T^*}, M_0, \sigma_0) = 1$

    $\vee \ \mathsf{GVerify}(\mathsf{gpk}, \mathsf{tpk}, \mathsf{RL}_{T^*}, M_1, \sigma_1) = 1)\big]$

    Otherwise return 0

- AddU: *The add user oracle allows an adversary $\mathcal{A}$ to add honest users to the group. On input an identity* ID, *this oracle runs* $\mathsf{sigk}_{\mathsf{ID}} \leftarrow \mathsf{Join}(\mathsf{gsk}, \mathsf{grs}, \mathsf{ID})$. ID *is added to* GU.
- Revoke: *Let* $T - 1$ *be the time that the oracle is called. The revocation oracle allows an adversary $\mathcal{A}$ to revoke honest users. On input identities* $\{\mathsf{ID}_{T,1}, \ldots, \mathsf{ID}_{T,n_T}\}$, *this oracle runs* $\mathsf{RL}_T \leftarrow \mathsf{Revoke}(\mathsf{gpk}, \mathsf{grs}, \{\mathsf{ID}_{T,1}, \ldots, \mathsf{ID}_{T,n_T}\})$. *We remark that* T^* *is the challenge time that $\mathcal{A}$ outputs* $(\mathsf{ID}^*, M_0, M_1)$.

$\mathcal{GS}\text{-}\mathcal{TDL}$ *is said to be satisfying correctness if the advantage* $\mathrm{Adv}_{\mathsf{GS},\mathcal{A}}^{corr}(\lambda) := \Pr[\mathrm{Exp}_{\mathsf{GS\text{-}TDL},\mathcal{A}}^{corr}(\lambda) = 1]$ *is negligible for any PPT adversary $\mathcal{A}$.*

Next, we give our anonymity definition which guarantees that no adversary who has tsk can distinguish whether two signatures are generated by the same signer or not, if the corresponding linkable signatures are not generated. In contrast to the BMW model, $\mathcal{A}$ is not allowed to obtain signing keys of challenge users (selfless anonymity). This is a reasonable setting since $\mathcal{A}$ can trivially break anonymity if $\mathcal{A}$ obtains such signing keys. For example, let $\mathcal{A}$ have $\mathsf{sigk}_{\mathsf{ID}_{i_0}}$. Then, $\mathcal{A}$ can make a signature σ on T_0 using $\mathsf{sigk}_{\mathsf{ID}_{i_0}}$ (with arbitrary message M), and can check whether $\mathsf{Link}(\mathsf{gpk}, \mathsf{tpk}, \mathsf{RL}_{T_0}, (M_0, \sigma^*, T_0), (M, \sigma, T_0)) = 1$ or not, where σ^* is the challenge signature. Instead, $\mathcal{A}$ is allowed to access the GSign oracle in our definition. Moreover, we consider backward unlinkability, where no adversary can break anonymity even after the challenge signers are revoked.

Definition 5 (Anonymity). *For any PPT adversary $\mathcal{A}$ and a security parameter $\lambda \in \mathbb{N}$, we define the experiment $\mathrm{Exp}_{GS\text{-}TDL,\mathcal{A}}^{anon\text{-}tg\text{-}b}(\lambda)$ as follows.*

$$\mathrm{Exp}_{GS\text{-}TDL,\mathcal{A}}^{anon\text{-}tg\text{-}b}(\lambda):$$

$$params \leftarrow \mathsf{Setup}(1^\lambda)$$
$$(\mathsf{gpk}, \mathsf{gsk}, \mathsf{grs}, \mathsf{RL}_0) \leftarrow \mathsf{GKeyGen}(params);$$
$$(\mathsf{tpk}, \mathsf{tsk}) \leftarrow \mathsf{TKeyGen}(params); \ \mathsf{GU} := \emptyset; \ \mathsf{STSet} := \emptyset$$
$$d \leftarrow \mathcal{A}^{\mathsf{AddU}(\cdot),\mathsf{Revoke}(\mathsf{grs},\cdot),\mathsf{GSign}(\cdot,\cdot,\cdot),\mathsf{Ch}(b,\cdot,\cdot,\cdot,\cdot,\cdot,\cdot)}(\mathsf{gpk}, \mathsf{tpk}, \mathsf{tsk})$$
$$Return \ d$$

- AddU: *The same as before.*
- Revoke: *The same as before. We remark that if $T_0 \neq T_1$ and assume that $T_0 < T_1$, then ID_{i_0} and/or ID_{i_1} can be revoked after T_1. If $T_0 = T_1$, then ID_{i_0} and/or ID_{i_1} can be revoked after T_0.*
- GSign: *The signing oracle takes as input ID, t_T, and a message M. We assume that t_T is a valid token which means that the $\mathsf{GVerify}$ algorithm outputs 1 for all honestly generated signatures with t_T, even though this is made by $\mathcal{A}$. If $\mathsf{ID} \notin \mathsf{GU}$, then the oracle runs $\mathsf{AddU}(\mathsf{ID})$. The oracle returns $\sigma \leftarrow \mathsf{GSign}(\mathsf{gpk}, \mathsf{tpk}, t_T, \mathsf{sigk}_{\mathsf{ID}}, M)$ and stores (ID, T) in STSet.*
- Ch: *The challenge oracle takes as input ID_{i_0}, ID_{i_1}, t_{T_0}, t_{T_1}, M_0^*, and M_1^* where $\mathsf{ID}_{i_0} \neq \mathsf{ID}_{i_1}$ and $\mathsf{ID}_{i_0}, \mathsf{ID}_{i_1} \in \mathsf{GU}$. Return signature(s) according to the following cases:*
  - *$T_0 = T_1$: If $(\mathsf{ID}_{i_0}, T_0), (\mathsf{ID}_{i_1}, T_1) \notin \mathsf{STSet}$, then compute $\sigma^* \leftarrow \mathsf{GSign}(\mathsf{gpk}, \mathsf{tpk}, t_{T_b}, \mathsf{sigk}_{\mathsf{ID}_{i_b}}, M^*)$, and return σ^*. Without loss of generality, we set $M^* = M_0^* = M_1^*$.*
  - *$T_0 \neq T_1$: If $(\mathsf{ID}_{i_0}, T_0), (\mathsf{ID}_{i_1}, T_1), (\mathsf{ID}_{i_0}, T_1) \notin \mathsf{STSet}$, then compute $\sigma_0^* \leftarrow \mathsf{GSign}(\mathsf{gpk}, \mathsf{tpk}, t_{T_0}, \mathsf{sigk}_{\mathsf{ID}_{i_0}}, M_0^*)$ and $\sigma_1^* \leftarrow \mathsf{GSign}(\mathsf{gpk}, \mathsf{tpk}, t_{T_1}, \mathsf{sigk}_{\mathsf{ID}_{i_b}}, M_1^*)$, and return σ_0^* and σ_1^*.*

  Moreover, we assume that t_{T_0} and t_{T_1} are valid tokens even though these are made by $\mathcal{A}$, which means that the $\mathsf{GVerify}$ algorithm outputs 1 for all honestly generated signatures with t_{T_0} or t_{T_1}.[4]

$\mathcal{GS}\text{-}\mathcal{TDL}$ *is said to be satisfying anonymity if the advantage $\mathrm{Adv}_{GS\text{-}TDL,\mathcal{A}}^{anon\text{-}tg}(\lambda) := |\Pr[\mathrm{Exp}_{GS\text{-}TDL,\mathcal{A}}^{anon\text{-}tg\text{-}1}(\lambda) = 1] - \Pr[\mathrm{Exp}_{GS,\mathcal{A}}^{anon\text{-}tg\text{-}0}(\lambda) = 1]|$ is negligible for any PPT adversary $\mathcal{A}$.*

When $T_0 = T_1$, our definition guarantees that two different signers are unlinkable even if they generate signatures at the same time period. We note that if $\mathcal{A}$ obtains two signatures even though $T_0 = T_1$, then $\mathcal{A}$ can break anonymity

---

[4] This condition must be required to exclude the trivially-broken case, e.g., $\mathcal{A}$ honestly generates t_{T_0} and sets t_{T_1} as arbitrary value. Then, $\mathcal{A}$ can check whether σ^* is valid or not. If yes, then $b = 0$ and $b = 1$ otherwise.

by using the Link algorithm. Therefore, $\mathcal{A}$ is allowed to obtain one challenge signature σ^* only. When $T_0 \neq T_1$, our definition guarantees that a signer is still unlinkable if the signer respectively generates two signatures on different time periods. That is, when $\mathcal{A}$ obtains σ_0^*, which is generated by ID_{i_0} at a time T_0, and σ_1^*, which is generated by ID_{i_b} at a time $T_1 \neq T_0$, no $\mathcal{A}$ can distinguish whether two signatures are respectively made by the same user ID_{i_0} or different users ID_{i_0} and ID_{i_1}. In order to prevent a trivial linking attack, $\mathcal{A}$ is not allowed to obtain a signature for (ID_{i_0}, T_1) in this case.

We note that we do not have to consider the case $\mathsf{ID}_{i_0} = \mathsf{ID}_{i_1}$ and $T_0 \neq T_1$, since time T is an input of the verification algorithm. That is, $\mathcal{A}$ can easily break anonymity in this case: $\mathcal{A}$ just obtains $\sigma^* \leftarrow \mathsf{GSign}(\mathsf{gpk}, \mathsf{tpk}, t_{T_b}, \mathsf{sigk}_{\mathsf{ID}_{i_0}}, M^*)$ and checks whether $\mathsf{GVerify}(\mathsf{gpk}, \mathsf{tpk}, \mathsf{RL}_{T_0}, M^*, \sigma^*) = 1$ or not.

Next, we define unforgeability which guarantees that nobody who does not have a signing key or does not have a token can generate a valid signature.

Definition 6 (Unforgeability). *For any PPT adversary $\mathcal{A}$ and security parameter $\lambda \in \mathbb{N}$, we define the experiment $\mathrm{Exp}_{\mathsf{GS\text{-}TDL},\mathcal{A}}^{unf}(\lambda)$ as follows, where $\mathcal{O} := (\mathsf{AddU}(\cdot), \mathsf{Revoke}(\mathsf{grs}, \cdot), \mathsf{TokenGen}(\mathsf{tsk}, \cdot), \mathsf{SetToken}(\cdot), \mathsf{GSign}(\cdot, \cdot, \cdot), \mathsf{USK}(\cdot), \mathsf{TSK}(\cdot))$.*

$$\mathrm{Exp}_{\mathsf{GS\text{-}TDL},\mathcal{A}}^{unf}(\lambda):$$

$params \leftarrow \mathsf{Setup}(1^\lambda)$

$(\mathsf{gpk}, \mathsf{gsk}, \mathsf{grs}, \mathsf{RL}_0) \leftarrow \mathsf{GKeyGen}(params)$

$(\mathsf{tpk}, \mathsf{tsk}) \leftarrow \mathsf{TKeyGen}(params)$

$\mathsf{GU} := \emptyset; \ \mathsf{TSet} := \emptyset; \ \mathsf{SSet} := \emptyset$

$(M, \sigma) \leftarrow \mathcal{A}^{\mathcal{O}}(\mathsf{gpk}, \mathsf{tpk})$

Return 1 *if* $(1) \wedge (2) \wedge ((3) \vee (4))$ *hold*:

(1) $\mathsf{GVerify}(\mathsf{gpk}, \mathsf{tpk}, \mathsf{RL}_{T^*}, M, \sigma) = 1$

(2) $(T^*, M, \sigma) \notin \mathsf{SSet}$

(3) $T \notin \mathsf{TSet} \wedge \mathsf{TSK}(\cdot)$ *has not been called*

(4) $\mathsf{TSK}(\cdot)$ *has been called with non-$\perp$ output*

Otherwise return 0

- AddU: *The same as before.*
- Revoke: *The same as before. We note that T^* is the challenge time that $\mathcal{A}$ outputs (M, σ).*
- TokenGen: *The token generation oracle takes as input a time T. This oracle runs $t_T \leftarrow \mathsf{TokenGen}(\mathsf{tsk}, T)$, stores T in TSet, and returns t_T.*
- SetToken: *The token setting oracle takes as input t_T, and sets t_T as the token at a time T. Without loss of generality, we assume that if the TokenGen oracle is called, the SetToken oracle is also called right after calling the TokenGen oracle. We remark that $\mathcal{A}$ can set arbitrary value as t_T via this oracle.*

- GSign: *The signing oracle takes as input* ID, T, *and a message* M. *If* ID $\notin$ GU, *then the oracle runs* AddU(ID). *If* t_T *is not generated via the* TokenGen *oracle, then call the oracle* TokenGen(tsk, T) *and the* SetToken *oracle. The oracle returns* $\sigma \leftarrow$ GSign(gpk, tpk, t_T, sigk$_{\mathsf{ID}}$, M) *and stores* (T, M, σ) *in* SSet.
- USK: *The user key reveal oracle takes as input* ID. *If the* TSK *oracle was called before, then return* $\perp$. *If* ID $\notin$ GU, *then the oracle runs* AddU(ID). *Return* sigk$_{\mathsf{ID}}$.
- TSK: *The token key reveal oracle returns* $\perp$ *if the* USK *oracle was called before and at least one identity is not revoked.*[5] *Otherwise, return* tsk.

$\mathcal{GS}$-$\mathcal{TDL}$ *is said to be unforgeable if the advantage* $\mathrm{Adv}^{unf}_{\mathsf{GS\text{-}TDL},\mathcal{A}}(\lambda) :=$ $\Pr[\mathrm{Exp}^{unf}_{\mathsf{GS\text{-}TDL},\mathcal{A}}(\lambda) = 1]$ *is negligible for any PPT adversary* $\mathcal{A}$.

Finally, we define linking soundness which guarantees that the Link algorithm does not return 1 when two valid signatures are made by either different signers or different time tokens.

Definition 7 (Linking Soundness). *For any PPT adversary* $\mathcal{A}$ *and security parameter* $\lambda \in \mathbb{N}$, *we define the experiment* $\mathrm{Exp}^{snd}_{\mathsf{GS\text{-}TDL},\mathcal{A}}(\lambda)$ *as follows.*

$$\mathrm{Exp}^{snd}_{\mathsf{GS\text{-}TDL},\mathcal{A}}(\lambda):$$
$$params \leftarrow \mathsf{Setup}(1^\lambda)$$
$$(\mathsf{gpk}, \mathsf{gsk}, \mathsf{grs}, \mathsf{RL}_0) \leftarrow \mathsf{GKeyGen}(params)$$
$$(\mathsf{tpk}, \mathsf{tsk}) \leftarrow \mathsf{TKeyGen}(params)$$
$$(\mathsf{ID}_0, \mathsf{ID}_1, T_0, T_1, M, st) \leftarrow \mathcal{A}(\mathsf{gpk}, \mathsf{tpk})$$
$$(\mathsf{ID}_0, T_0) \neq (\mathsf{ID}_1, T_1)$$
$$\mathsf{sigk}_{\mathsf{ID}_0} \leftarrow \mathsf{Join}(\mathsf{gsk}, \mathsf{grs}, \mathsf{ID}_0);\ \mathsf{sigk}_{\mathsf{ID}_1} \leftarrow \mathsf{Join}(\mathsf{gsk}, \mathsf{grs}, \mathsf{ID}_1)$$
$$t_{T_0} \leftarrow \mathsf{TokenGen}(\mathsf{tsk}, T_0);\ t_{T_1} \leftarrow \mathsf{TokenGen}(\mathsf{tsk}, T_1)$$
$$\sigma_0 \leftarrow \mathsf{GSign}(\mathsf{gpk}, \mathsf{tpk}, t_{T_0}, \mathsf{sigk}_{\mathsf{ID}_0}, M)$$
$$(M^*, \sigma^*) \leftarrow \mathcal{A}^{\mathsf{Revoke}(\mathsf{grs}, \cdot)}(st, \mathsf{sigk}_{\mathsf{ID}_1}, t_{T_1}, \sigma_0)$$
$$Return\ 1\ if$$
$$\mathsf{Link}(\mathsf{gpk}, \mathsf{tpk}, \mathsf{RL}_{T_1}, (M, \sigma_0, T_0), (M^*, \sigma^*, T_1)) = 1$$
$$Otherwise\ return\ 0$$

- Revoke: *The same as before.*

A GS-TDL scheme is said to be satisfying linking soundness if the advantage $\mathrm{Adv}^{snd}_{\mathsf{GS\text{-}TDL},\mathcal{A}}(\lambda) := \Pr[\mathrm{Exp}^{snd}_{\mathsf{GS\text{-}TDL},\mathcal{A}}(\lambda) = 1]$ *is negligible for any PPT adversary* $\mathcal{A}$.

---

[5] That is, the TSK oracle returns tsk if all identities input in the USK oracle were revoked.

4 Proposed GS-TDL Scheme

In this section, we give our GS-TDL scheme. Since we mainly pursue a *light-weight realization* of the system, here we do not employ structure preserving signatures (e.g., [3]) and Groth-Sahai proofs [27] which are typically used for constructing group signature schemes secure in the standard model, e.g., [4, 5,26,35–37]. We employ the Fiat-Shamir transformation [22] which converts a three-move Σ protocol to non-interactive zero-knowledge (NIZK) proof as in group signature schemes secure in the random oracle model, e.g., [12,14,18,24].

The Basic Idea: Our GS-TDL scheme is based on the Furukawa-Imai group signature scheme [24] which is recognized as one of the most efficient group signature schemes. First, we exclude the open functionality from the Furukawa-Imai group signature scheme as in [20]. Next, for the linking property, we apply the Franklin-Zhang technique [23], where a group signature contains Belenkiy et al.'s verifiable random function (VRF) [9]. Concretely, the value $\tau = g^{\frac{1}{x+T}}$ is contained in a signature at a time T, where x is a (part of) signing key. Then, if a signer computes two or more group signatures at a time T, then the value τ is the same, and can be linked without any cryptographic operation. Whereas, τ itself can be seen as a random value (under the SDDHI assumption), and therefore a signer is still anonymous unless the signer computes two or more group signatures at the same time. For (verifier-local) revocation, we also apply τ such that τ is added in a revocation list. Note that the verification cost of VLR-type group signatures schemes [15,38,42,43] is $O(|\mathsf{RL}_T|)$, especially, $|\mathsf{RL}_T|$-times pairing computations are required. In order to avoid such an inefficiency, we use the linkable part τ for revocation and this setting requires no cryptographic operation.

Construction 1 (Proposed GS-TDL Scheme).

– Setup(1^λ): *Let* $(\mathbb{G}_1, \mathbb{G}_2, \mathbb{G}_T)$ *be a bilinear group with prime order* p, *where* $\langle g_1 \rangle = \mathbb{G}_1$, $\langle g_2 \rangle = \mathbb{G}_2$, *and* $e : \mathbb{G}_1 \times \mathbb{G}_2 \to \mathbb{G}_T$ *be a bilinear map. Output* $params = (\mathbb{G}_1, \mathbb{G}_2, \mathbb{G}_T, e, g_1, g_2)$.

– GKeyGen($params$): *Choose* $\gamma \xleftarrow{\$} \mathbb{Z}_p$, *and* $h \xleftarrow{\$} \mathbb{G}_1$, *and compute* $W = g_2^\gamma$. *Output* gpk $= (params, h, W, e(g_1, g_2), e(h, W), e(h, g_2), H)$, gsk $= \gamma$, *where* $H : \{0,1\}^* \to \mathbb{Z}_p$ *is a hash function modeled as a random oracle,* grs $:= \emptyset$ *and* $\mathsf{RL}_0 := \emptyset$.

– TKeyGen($params$): *Let* (Gen, Sign, Verify) *be a digital signature scheme. Run* (vk, sigk) $\leftarrow$ Gen(1^λ), *and output* tpk $:=$ vk *and* tsk $:=$ sigk.

– Join(gsk, grs, ID): *Choose* $x, y \xleftarrow{\$} \mathbb{Z}_p$, *compute* $A = (g_1 h^{-y})^{\frac{1}{\gamma+x}}$, *output* sigk$_{\mathsf{ID}} = (x, y, A)$, *and update* grs $:=$ grs $\cup \{(\mathsf{ID}, x)\}$.

– TokenGen(tsk, T): *Assume that* $T \in \mathbb{Z}_p$. *Compute* $W_T = g_2^T$ *and* $\Sigma \leftarrow$ Sign(sigk, W_T), *and output* $t_T = (T, W_T, \Sigma)$.

– GSign(gpk, tpk, t_T, sigk$_{\mathsf{ID}}$, M): *Let* sigk$_{\mathsf{ID}} = (x, y, A)$ *and* $t_T = (T, W_T, \Sigma)$. *If* Verify(vk, W_T, Σ) $= 0$, *then output* $\bot$. *Otherwise, choose* $\beta \xleftarrow{\$} \mathbb{Z}_p$, *set* $\delta =$

$\beta x - y$, and compute $C = Ah^\beta$ and $\tau = g_1^{\frac{1}{x+T}}$. Choose $r_x, r_\delta, r_\beta \xleftarrow{\$} \mathbb{Z}_p$, and compute

$$R_1 = \frac{e(h, g_2)^{r_\delta} e(h, W)^{r_\beta}}{e(C, g_2)^{r_x}}, \quad R_2 = e(\tau, g_2)^{r_x}$$

$$c = H(\mathsf{gpk}, \mathsf{tpk}, C, \tau, R_1, R_2, M)$$

$$s_x = r_x + cx, s_\delta = r_\delta + c\delta, \text{ and } s_\beta = r_\beta + c\beta,$$

and output $\sigma = (C, \tau, c, s_x, s_\delta, s_\beta)$. This proves that (1) (x, y, A) is a valid Boneh-Boyen signature under gpk (i.e., $\mathsf{sigk_{ID}}$ is issued by Group Manager) and (2) τ is computed by the same x.

Pairing-free Variant: We remark that $e(h, g_2)$ and $e(h, W)$ are pre-computable and can be contained in gpk. Moreover $e(C, g_2)^{r_x}$ and $e(\tau, g_2)^{r_x}$ can be represented as $e(A, g_2)^{r_x} e(h, g_2)^{\beta r_x}$ and $e(g_1, g_2)^{\frac{r_x}{x+T}}$, respectively. Then,

$$R_1 = \frac{e(h, g_2)^{r_\delta - \beta r_x} e(h, W)^{r_\beta}}{e(A, g_2)^{r_x}} \text{ and } R_2 = e(g_1, g_2)^{\frac{r_x}{x+T}}$$

hold. So, by assuming that $e(A, g_2)$ is pre-computable (we can simply assume that $e(A, g_2)$ is contained in $\mathsf{sigk_{ID}}$), we can remove any pairing computation from the signing algorithm, instead of adding two exponentiations over $\mathbb{G}_T$.

- Revoke($\mathsf{gpk}, \mathsf{grs}, \{\mathsf{ID}_{T,1}, \ldots, \mathsf{ID}_{T,n_T}\}$): If there exists $\mathsf{ID} \in \{\mathsf{ID}_{T,1}, \ldots, \mathsf{ID}_{T,n_T}\}$ that is not joined to the system via the Join algorithm, then output $\bot$. Otherwise, extract $(\mathsf{ID}_{T,1}, x_{T,1}), \ldots, (\mathsf{ID}_{T,n_T}, x_{n_T})$ from grs. Output $\mathsf{RL}_T :=$ $\{(\mathsf{ID}_{T,1}, g_1^{\frac{1}{x_{T,1}+T}}), \ldots (\mathsf{ID}_{T,n_T}, g_1^{\frac{1}{x_{T,n_T}+T}})\}$.

- GVerify($\mathsf{gpk}, \mathsf{tpk}, \mathsf{RL}_T, M, \sigma$): Assume that $\mathsf{Verify}(\mathsf{vk}, W_T, \Sigma) = 1$ (if not, output $\bot$). Parse $\sigma = (C, \tau, c, s_x, s_\delta, s_\beta)$. If τ is contained in RL_T such that $(\mathsf{ID}, \tau) \in \mathsf{RL}_T$ for some ID, then output 0. Otherwise, compute

$$R_1' = \frac{e(h, g_2)^{s_\delta} e(h, W)^{s_\beta}}{e(C, g_2)^{s_x}} \left(\frac{e(C, W)}{e(g_1, g_2)}\right)^{-c} \text{ and } R_2' = e(\tau, g_2)^{s_x} \left(\frac{e(g_1, g_2)}{e(\tau, W_T)}\right)^{-c},$$

and output 1 if $c = H(\mathsf{gpk}, \mathsf{tpk}, C, \tau, R_1', R_2', M)$ holds, and 0 otherwise. We remark that $e(h, g_2)$, $e(h, W)$ and $e(g_1, g_2)$ are pre-computable and contained in gpk.

- Link($\mathsf{gpk}, \mathsf{tpk}, \mathsf{RL}_T, (M_0, \sigma_0, T_0), (M_1, \sigma_1, T_1)$): Parse $\sigma_0 = (C_0, \tau_0, c_0, s_{x,0}, s_{\delta,0}, s_{\beta,0})$ and $\sigma_1 = (C_1, \tau_1, c_1, s_{x,1}, s_{\delta,1}, s_{\beta,1})$. If either $T \neq T_0$ or $T \neq T_1$, then output 0. Else if either GVerify($\mathsf{gpk}, \mathsf{tpk}, \mathsf{RL}_{T_0}, M_0, \sigma_0$) = 0 or GVerify($\mathsf{gpk}, \mathsf{tpk}, \mathsf{RL}_{T_0}, M_1, \sigma_1$) = 0, then output 0. Otherwise, output 1 if $\tau_0 = \tau_1$, and 0 otherwise.[6]

---

[6] We can assume that two group signatures input are valid. That is, the signature verification has been done before running the link algorithm. Then our linking algorithm does not require cryptographic computations (i.e., comparisons to determine two elements are the same).

Since τ just depends on T and x, and does not contain any randomness, we can directly use τ for revocation. Since we do not have to run any cryptographic operation, we can achieve the (almost) constant verification cost by using hash tables which are made in the Revoke algorithm.

As a remark, the open algorithm, where an authority can identify the actual signer, also can be implemented (though we do not use it) as follows: let (ID, g_2^x) be preserved in the join phase, and the open algorithm checks whether $e(\tau, g_2^x g_2^T) = e(g_1, g_2)$ or not. If the equation holds, then ID is the identity of the corresponding signer. This open algorithm is essentially the same as that of the Bichsel et al. scheme [12].

5   Security Analysis

Theorem 1. *The proposed GS-TDL scheme has anonymity in the random oracle model under the SDDHI assumption, where H is modeled as a random oracle.*

Proof. We define the following two games: Game 0 is the same as $\mathsf{Exp}_{\mathsf{GS\text{-}TDL},\mathcal{A}}^{anon\text{-}tg\text{-}b}(\lambda)$. Game 1 is the same as Game 0, except τ^* contained in σ^* is randomly chosen, and σ^* is generated by the simulation of NIZK. Here, we show that there exist an algorithm $\mathcal{B}$ that breaks the SDDHI problem by using $\mathcal{A}$ as follows.

Let $(p, \mathbb{G}_1, \mathbb{G}_2, \mathbb{G}_T, e, g_1, g_2)$ be a bilinear group, and (g_1, g_2, g_1^x) is an instance of the SDDHI problem. Let q be the number of AddU queries. $\mathcal{B}$ chooses $i^* \in [1, q]$ and set x is a part of signing key of the user. $\mathcal{B}$ chooses $\gamma \xleftarrow{\$} \mathbb{Z}_p$, and $h \xleftarrow{\$} \mathbb{G}_1$, computes $W = g_2^\gamma$, and sets $\mathsf{gpk} = (params, h, W, e(g_1, g_2), e(h, W), e(h, g_2), H)$, where $H : \{0, 1\}^* \to \mathbb{Z}_p$ is a hash function modeled as a random oracle. $\mathcal{B}$ also runs $(\mathsf{vk}, \mathsf{sigk}) \leftarrow \mathsf{Gen}(1^\lambda)$, and sets $\mathsf{tpk} := \mathsf{vk}$ and $\mathsf{tsk} := \mathsf{sigk}$. $\mathcal{B}$ sends gpk, tpk, and tsk to $\mathcal{A}$.

In the i-th AddU query (with input ID), where $i \neq i^*$, $\mathcal{B}$ chooses $x, y \xleftarrow{\$} \mathbb{Z}_p$, computes $A = (g_1 h^{-y})^{\frac{1}{\gamma+x}}$, sets $\mathsf{sigk}_{\mathsf{ID}} = (x, y, A)$, and adds ID to GU. In the i^*-th AddU query (with input ID^*), $\mathcal{B}$ adds ID^* to GU.

For a GSign query with input (ID, t_T, M), if $\mathsf{ID} \notin \mathsf{GU}$, then $\mathcal{B}$ runs the simulation of the AddU oracle. If $\mathsf{ID} \neq \mathsf{ID}^*$, then $\mathcal{B}$ computes a group signature σ as in the actual GSign algorithm, returns σ to $\mathcal{A}$, and adds (ID, T) to STSet. Let $\mathsf{ID} = \mathsf{ID}^*$. $\mathcal{B}$ sends T to $\mathcal{O}_x$, and obtains $\tau = g_1^{\frac{1}{x+T}}$. $\mathcal{B}$ chooses $s_x, s_\delta, s_\beta, c \xleftarrow{\$} \mathbb{Z}_p$ and $C \xleftarrow{\$} \mathbb{G}_1$, computes $R_1 = \frac{e(h, g_2)^{s_\delta} e(h, W)^{s_\beta}}{e(C, g_2)^{s_x}} \left(\frac{e(C, W)}{e(g_1, g_2)} \right)^{-c}$ and $R_2 = e(\tau, g_2)^{s_x} \left(\frac{e(g_1, g_2)}{e(\tau, W_T)} \right)^{-c}$, and patches H such that $c := H(\mathsf{gpk}, \mathsf{tpk}, C, \tau, R_1, R_2, M)$. $\mathcal{B}$ returns $\sigma = (C, \tau, c, s_x, s_\delta, s_\beta)$ to $\mathcal{A}$.

In the challenge phase, $\mathcal{A}$ sends $(\mathsf{ID}_{i_0}, \mathsf{ID}_{i_1}, t_{T_0}, t_{T_1}, M_0^*, M_1^*)$ to $\mathcal{B}$. $\mathcal{B}$ chooses $b \xleftarrow{\$} \{0, 1\}$. If $\mathsf{ID}_{i_b} \neq \mathsf{ID}^*$, then $\mathcal{B}$ aborts. Let $\mathsf{ID}_{i_b} = \mathsf{ID}^*$ (this holds with the probability at least $1/q$). Next, we consider the following two cases:

$T_0 = T_1$: Let (T, W_T) be contained in both t_{T_0} and t_{T_1}. $\mathcal{B}$ sends $T := T_0 = T_1$ to the challenger of the SDDHI problem, and obtains τ^*. We remark that

T was not sent to $\mathcal{O}_x$. $\mathcal{B}$ chooses $s_x^*, s_\delta^*, s_\beta^*, c^* \xleftarrow{\$} \mathbb{Z}_p$ and $C^* \xleftarrow{\$} \mathbb{G}_1$, computes $R_1^* = \frac{e(h,g_2)^{s_\delta^*} e(h,W)^{s_\beta^*}}{e(C,g_2)^{s_x^*}} \left(\frac{e(C,W)}{e(g_1,g_2)}\right)^{-c^*}$ and $R_2 = e(\tau^*, g_2)^{s_x^*} \left(\frac{e(g_1,g_2)}{e(\tau^*, W_T)}\right)^{-c^*}$, and patches H such that $c^* := H(\mathsf{gpk}, \mathsf{tpk}, C^*, \tau^*, R_1^*, R_2^*, M^*)$. $\mathcal{B}$ returns $\sigma^* = (C^*, \tau^*, c^*, s_x^*, s_\delta^*, s_\beta^*)$ to $\mathcal{A}$.

$T_0 \neq T_1$: Let (T_0, W_{T_0}) and (T_1, W_{T_1}) be contained in t_{T_0} and t_{T_1}, respectively. $\mathcal{B}$ sends T_0 to $\mathcal{O}_x$, and obtains $\tau_0^* = g_1^{\frac{1}{x+T_0}}$. $\mathcal{B}$ chooses $s_{x,0}^*, s_{\delta,0}^*, s_{\beta,0}^*, c_0^* \xleftarrow{\$} \mathbb{Z}_p$ and $C_0^* \xleftarrow{\$} \mathbb{G}_1$, computes $R_{1,0}^* = \frac{e(h,g_2)^{s_{\delta,0}^*} e(h,W)^{s_{\beta,0}^*}}{e(C_0^*,g_2)^{s_{x,0}^*}} \left(\frac{e(C_0^*,W)}{e(g_1,g_2)}\right)^{-c_0^*}$ and $R_{2,0}^* = e(\tau_0^*, g_2)^{s_{x,0}^*} \left(\frac{e(g_1,g_2)}{e(\tau_0^*, W_{T_0})}\right)^{-c_0^*}$, and patches H such that $c_0^* := H(\mathsf{gpk}, \mathsf{tpk}, C_0^*, \tau_0^*, R_{1,0}^*, R_{2,0}^*, M_0^*)$. Moreover, $\mathcal{B}$ sends T_1 to the challenger of the SDDHI problem, and obtains τ_1^*. We remark that T_1 was not sent to $\mathcal{O}_x$. $\mathcal{B}$ chooses $s_{x,1}^*, s_{\delta,1}^*, s_{\beta,1}^*, c_1^* \xleftarrow{\$} \mathbb{Z}_p$ and $C_1^* \xleftarrow{\$} \mathbb{G}_1$, computes $R_{1,1}^* = \frac{e(h,g_2)^{s_{\delta,1}^*} e(h,W)^{s_{\beta,1}^*}}{e(C_1^*,g_2)^{s_{x,1}^*}} \left(\frac{e(C_1^*,W)}{e(g_1,g_2)}\right)^{-c_1^*}$ and $R_{2,1}^* = e(\tau_1^*, g_2)^{s_{x,1}^*} \left(\frac{e(g_1,g_2)}{e(\tau_1^*, W_{T_1})}\right)^{-c_1^*}$, and patches H such that $c_1^* := H(\mathsf{gpk}, \mathsf{tpk}, C_1^*, \tau_1^*, R_{1,1}^*, R_{2,1}^*, M_1^*)$. $\mathcal{B}$ returns $\sigma_0^* = (C_0^*, \tau_0^*, c_0^*, s_{x,0}^*, s_{\delta,0}^*, s_{\beta,0}^*)$ and $\sigma_1^* = (C_1^*, \tau_1^*, c_1^*, s_{x,1}^*, s_{\delta,1}^*, s_{\beta,1}^*)$ to $\mathcal{A}$.

Finally, $\mathcal{A}$ outputs b'. If $\tau^* = g^{\frac{1}{x+T}}$ (or $\tau_1^* = g^{\frac{1}{x+T_1}}$), then $\mathcal{B}$ simulates Game 0, and if τ^* (or τ_1^*) is a random value, then $\mathcal{B}$ simulates Game 1. In Game 1, no information of the challenge bit b is revealed from σ^*, σ_0^*, and σ_1^*. So, $\mathcal{B}$ desides the challenge is a random value if $b' \neq b$, and it is not a random value, otherwise, and solves the SDDHI problem. We remark that $\mathcal{B}$ can revoke ID^* at a time $T' > T$ (or $T' > T_1$) using the $\mathcal{O}_x$ oracle. This concludes the proof.   □

Theorem 2. *The proposed GS-TDL scheme has unforgeability in the random oracle model if the q-SDH assumption holds and* (Gen, Sign, Verify) *is EUF-CMA, where q is the number of signers and H is modeled as a random oracle.*

Proof. We consider the following two cases. The first one is $\mathcal{A}$ produces a valid signature although $\mathcal{A}$ does not have t_T $((1) \wedge (2) \wedge (3)$ in the definition), and the second one is $\mathcal{A}$ produces a valid signature although $\mathcal{A}$ does not have a signing key $((1) \wedge (2) \wedge (4)$ in the definition).

First Case: We construct an algorithm $\mathcal{B}$ that breaks EUF-CMA security of the underlying signature scheme (Gen, Sign, Verify). The challenger of the signature scheme runs $(\mathsf{vk}, \mathsf{sigk}) \leftarrow \mathsf{Gen}(1^\lambda)$, and sends vk to $\mathcal{B}$. $\mathcal{B}$ sets $\mathsf{tpk} := \mathsf{vk}$, runs $params \leftarrow \mathsf{Setup}(1^\lambda)$ and $(\mathsf{gpk}, \mathsf{gsk}) \leftarrow \mathsf{GKeyGen}(params)$, and sends $(\mathsf{gpk}, \mathsf{tpk})$ to $\mathcal{A}$. For a TokenGen query T, $\mathcal{B}$ computes $W_T = g_2^T$, sends W_T to the challenger as a signing query, and obtains Σ. $\mathcal{B}$ sets $t_T = (T, W_T, \Sigma)$, and sends t_T to $\mathcal{A}$. Since $\mathcal{B}$ has gsk, $\mathcal{B}$ can respond all AddU, GSign, and USK queries. We remark that $\mathcal{A}$ does not access the TSK oracle. Finally, $\mathcal{A}$ outputs (T, M, σ). Since σ is a valid group signature, there exist (Σ, W_T)

such that W_T is used in the verification algorithm, and Σ is a valid signature under vk. That is, $\mathcal{A}$ produces $t_T = (T, W_T, \Sigma)$, and sets it via the SetToken oracle. Since W_T is not sent to $\mathcal{B}$ as a TokenGen query, $\mathcal{B}$ outputs (Σ, W_T) as a forgery of the signature scheme.

Second Case: We construct an algorithm $\mathcal{B}$ that breaks the q-SDH problem as follows. Let $(g_1, g_1^\gamma, \ldots, g_1^{\gamma^q}, g_2, g_2^\gamma)$ be an SDH instance. Here, q be the number of AddU queries. $\mathcal{B}$ runs $(\mathsf{vk}, \mathsf{sigk}) \leftarrow \mathsf{Gen}(1^\lambda)$, and sets $\mathsf{tpk} := \mathsf{vk}$. $\mathcal{B}$ chooses $x_1, \ldots, x_q, y_1, \ldots, y_q \xleftarrow{\$} \mathbb{Z}_p$ and $\alpha, \theta \xleftarrow{\$} \mathbb{Z}_p^*$. Let define

$$f(X) = \prod_{i=1}^{q}(X + x_q) := \sum_{i=0}^{q} \alpha_i X^i$$

and

$$f_i(X) := f(X)/(X - x_i) = \prod_{j=1, j \neq i}^{q}(X + x_i) := \sum_{i=1}^{q-1} \beta_i X^i,$$

and set $g_1' = (\prod_{i=0}^{q}(g_1^{\gamma^i})^{\alpha}_i)^\theta = g_1^{\theta f(\gamma)}$. Then, for each $i \in [1, q]$ $(\prod_{j=0}^{q-1}(g_1^{\gamma^i})^{\beta_i})^\theta = g_1^{\theta f_i(\gamma)} = g_1'^{\frac{1}{\gamma + x_i}}$ hold. Set $h := g_1'^\alpha$. For each $i \in [1, q]$, $\mathcal{B}$ computes $A_i := (g_1'^{\frac{1}{\gamma + x_i}})^{1 - y_i \alpha} = (g_1' h^{-y})^{\frac{1}{\gamma + x_i}}$. $\mathcal{B}$ sets $W := g_2^\gamma$, $params = (\mathbb{G}_1, \mathbb{G}_2, \mathbb{G}_T, e, g_1', g_2)$, and $\mathsf{gpk} = (params, h, W, e(g_1', g_2), e(h, W), e(h, g_2), H)$, and gives $(\mathsf{gpk}, \mathsf{tpk})$ to $\mathcal{A}$.

For an AddU query, $\mathcal{B}$ chooses unselected $x \in \{x_1, \ldots, x_q\}$ and sets the corresponding (x, y, A) as the signing key. Since $\mathcal{B}$ has tsk, $\mathcal{B}$ can respond TokenGen and TSK queries. Moreover, $\mathcal{B}$ can respond GSign and Revoke queries since $\mathcal{B}$ has all signing keys (x_i, y_i, A_i) for each $i \in [1, q]$.

Finally, $\mathcal{A}$ outputs a forge group signature $\sigma = (C, \tau, c, s_x, s_\delta, s_\beta)$. $\mathcal{B}$ rewinds $\mathcal{A}$ and obtains $\sigma' = (C, \tau, c', s_x', s_\delta', s_\beta')$ where $c \neq c'$ with non-negligible probability (due to the forking lemma). Set

$$\tilde{x} := \frac{s_x - s_x'}{c - c'}, \quad \tilde{y} := \frac{(s_x - s_x')(s_\beta - s_\beta') - (s_\delta - s_\delta')(c - c')}{(c - c')^2}, \quad \text{and } \tilde{\beta} := \frac{s_\beta - s_\beta'}{c - c'}.$$

Then, $\frac{e(C, W)}{e(g_1', g_2)} = \frac{e(h, g_2)^{\tilde{\beta}\tilde{x} - \tilde{y}} e(h, W)^{\tilde{\beta}}}{e(C, g_2)^{\tilde{x}}}$ and $e(\tau, g_2)^{\tilde{x}} = \frac{e(g_1', g_2)}{e(\tau, W_T)}$ hold. That is, $(\tilde{x}, \tilde{y}, \tilde{A})$ can be extracted. If $1 - \tilde{y}\alpha = 0$, then $\mathcal{B}$ aborts. Moreover, if $\tilde{x} \in \{x_1, \ldots, x_q\}$, then $\mathcal{B}$ aborts. Since α and all x are randomly chosen, the aborting probability is at most q/p, and is negligible. From now on, we assume that $1 - \tilde{y}\alpha \neq 0$ and $\tilde{x} \notin \{x_1, \ldots, x_q\}$. Since $\tilde{A}$ can be represented as $\tilde{A} = (g_1' h^{-\tilde{y}})^{\frac{1}{\gamma + \tilde{x}}}$, $\mathcal{B}$ can compute $\tilde{A}^{\frac{1}{1 - \tilde{y}\alpha}} = g_1'^{\frac{1}{\gamma + \tilde{x}}} = (g_1^{\theta f(\gamma)})^{\frac{1}{\gamma + \tilde{x}}}$. Next, $\mathcal{B}$ computes $F(X)$ and $\gamma_* \in \mathbb{Z}_p^*$ which satisfy $f(X) = (X + \tilde{x})F(X) + \gamma_*$. Finally, $\mathcal{B}$ computes $\left(((g_1^{\theta f(\gamma)})^{\frac{1}{\gamma + \tilde{x}}})^{\frac{1}{\theta}} \prod_{i=0}^{q-1}(g_1^{\gamma^i})^{-F_i}\right)^{\frac{1}{\gamma_*}} = g_1^{\frac{1}{\gamma + \tilde{x}}}$, where $F(X) := \sum_{i=0}^{q-1} F_i X^i$, and outputs $(\tilde{x}, g_1^{\frac{1}{\gamma + \tilde{x}}})$ as a solution of the SDH problem. □

Theorem 3. *The proposed GS-TDL scheme has linking soundness.*

Proof. Let $(\mathsf{ID}_0, \mathsf{ID}_1, T_0, T_1, M)$ and (M^*, σ^*) be the output of $\mathcal{A}$, where $(\mathsf{ID}_0, T_0) \neq (\mathsf{ID}_1, T_1)$. Let x_0 be contained in $\mathsf{sigk}_{\mathsf{ID}_0}$ and x_1 be contained in $\mathsf{sigk}_{\mathsf{ID}_1}$, respectively. If $\mathsf{Link}(\mathsf{gpk}, \mathsf{tpk}, \mathsf{RL}_T, (M, \sigma_0, T_0), (M^*, \sigma^*, T_1)) = 1$, then $g_1^{\frac{1}{x_0+T_0}} = g_1^{\frac{1}{x_1+T_1}}$ and $T = T_0 = T_1$ holds. Then, $x_0 = x_1$ holds. Since x_0 and x_1 are randomly chosen, this equation holds with probability at most $1/p$. This concludes the proof. □

6   Experimental Results

Here, we show experimental results of our prototype implementations and the practicality of our GS-TDL scheme. Our implementation uses TEPLA library (ver. 1.0) [1] for elliptic curve operations and the pairing operation, OpenSSL (ver. 1.0.1e)[7] for standard signing and verifying, and GLib (ver. 2.28.8)[8] for the hash table for (almost) constant-time searching.

Table 1. The number of operations for each algorithms.

Algorithm	Operations
GSign	2 Mul $(\mathbb{G}_1)$ + 1 Mul $(\mathbb{G}_2)$ + 2 Exp $(\mathbb{G}_T)$ + 2 Pairing + Verify
GSign (Pairing free)	2 Mul $(\mathbb{G}_1)$ + 4 Exp $(\mathbb{G}_T)$ + Verify
TokenGen	1 Mul $(\mathbb{G}_2)$ + Sign
GVerify	6 Exp $(\mathbb{G}_T)$ + 4 Pairing + Verify
Revoke	$|\mathsf{RL}_T|$ Mul $(\mathbb{G}_1)$

We give the number of operations for each algorithms in Table 1. In the table, Mul $(\mathbb{G}_1)$, Mul $(\mathbb{G}_2)$ and Exp $(\mathbb{G}_T)$ denote a scalar multiplication on $\mathbb{G}_1$, a scalar multiplication on $\mathbb{G}_2$ and an exponentiation on $\mathbb{G}_T$, respectively. Verify and Sign denote standard verifying and signing. We use RSA signing algorithm for them because of its efficiency in the verification. We also remark that the Revoke algorithm depends on the number of revoked signers $|\mathsf{RL}_T|$. However, since the Revoke algorithm is computed by the group manager periodically, like per day, the dependence does not reduce the practicality of our scheme.

Next, we give running time of basic operations of TEPLA library in Table 2. Even on Raspberry Pi, a cheap and constrained computational power device, the operations can be performed in practical running time.

Finally, we give our experimental results of our GS-TDL scheme in Table 3. We evaluate these results as follows:

---

[7] https://www.openssl.org.
[8] https://wiki.gnome.org/Projects/GLib.

Table 2. Basic Operations on BN curves [8] of 254-bit order. Operations are run over PC (Core i7-4770 with TurboBoost) and Raspberry Pi (ARM1176JZF-S) respectively.

Operation	PC (msec)	Raspberry Pi (msec)
Mul ($\mathbb{G}_1$)	0.330	9.030
Mul ($\mathbb{G}_2$)	0.540	16.620
Exp ($\mathbb{G}_T$)	2.840	78.580
Pairing	2.690	77.330

Table 3. Benchmarks: The signing algorithms (3072-bit RSA sign, 3072-bit DSA sign, 256-bit ECDSA (prime256v1 curve) sign, and GSign) are run over Raspberry Pi (CPU: ARM1176JZF-S), and other algorithms are run over PC (Core i7-4770 CPU with TurboBoost) respectively. We use OpenSSL for RSA, DSA, and ECDSA, and TEPLA library for pairing-related operations. The total number of signers is 10,000,000, and the number of revoked signers is specified in parentheses () in the GVerify algorithm and the Revoke algorithm. We employ BN curves [8] with 254-bit order for efficient pairings, and the hash table for (almost) constant-time searching. We also employ 3072-bit RSA as (TokenGen, Sign, Verify) used in our GS-TDL scheme since the verification cost (which is run by signers in the GSign algorithm) is faster than that of DSA and ECDSA. We remark that the Link algorithm does not require any cryptographic operation, and RSA, DSA, and ECDSA do not support anonymity.

Algorithm	PC (msec)	Raspberry Pi (msec)	Entity
GSign	(12.573)	408.943	Signer
GSign (Pairing free)	(12.105)	400.302	Signer
RSA sign	3.427	233.511	-
DSA sign	1.082	75.135	-
ECDSA sign	0.335	11.702	-
TokenGen	3.763	-	Token generation unit
GVerify(1,000)	17.990	-	Verifier
GVerify(10,000)	17.997	-	Verifier
GVerify(100,000)	17.953	-	Verifier
GVerify(1,000,000)	18.049	-	Verifier
RSA verify	0.072	5.043	-
DSA verify	1.283	87.913	-
ECDSA verify	0.382	13.719	-
Revoke(1,000)	299.829	-	Group manager
Revoke(10,000)	3023.363	-	Group manager
Revoke(100,000)	30270.951	-	Group manager
Revoke(1,000,000)	301716.554	-	Group manager

(Almost) Constant-Time Verification: First of all, we should highlight that cryptographic operations in the GVerify algorithm do not depend on the number of revoked signers (i.e., scalable) due to our time-dependent linkability, i.e., τ is deterministic, though we employ VLR-type revocation. In our implementation, a table preserves (ID, x) in the Join algorithm is regarded as grs, and ID is set as a searching key (i.e., the table as takes as input ID, and outputs the corresponding x). In the Revoke algorithm, an array (ID, x, τ) is made, and τ contained in all arrays are updated on T such that $\mathsf{RL}_T :=$ $\{(\mathsf{ID}_{T,1}, g_1^{\frac{1}{x_{T,1}+T}}), \ldots (\mathsf{ID}_{T,n_T}, g_1^{\frac{1}{x_{T,n_T}+T}})\}$, and the corresponding hash table is generated for (almost) constant-time searching. Therefore, the cost of the Revoke algorithm depends on the number of revoked signers (but we emphasize that this procedure is run by the group manager and is not related to signers). In the GVerify algorithm, the verifier can easily check whether τ is contained in RL_T or not by using the hash tables without any cryptographic operation.

Practically Efficient Signing: In a certain situation, a signer has a constrained computational power compared to the verifier, and moreover the signer needs to generate signatures in several times. In our implementation result, the signing cost is still handled millisecond order and just twice as that of the 3072-bit RSA signing algorithm, though our system additionally supports anonymity. If a signer has a standard computational power (as in the PC), then the GSign algorithm can be run at 12.573 msec (and 12.105 msec for its pairing free version). This result shows that our scheme is feasible in practice.

As a remark, there is a room for improvement of our implementations since we directly employed cryptographic libraries, TEPLA and OpenSSL, without any adequate customization. In other word, our GS-TDL scheme is feasible in practice even under such a naive implementation way. That is, we might apply some implementation techniques, e.g., [31,46,50], for improvement of the efficiency. Moreover, batch verification techniques [21,39] might be employed.

Acknowledgement. We would like to thank anonymous reviewers of LightSec 2015 and Dr. Ryo Nojima for their helpful comments and suggestions.

References

1. TEPLA: University of Tsukuba Elliptic Curve and Pairing Library. http://www. cipher.risk.tsukuba.ac.jp/tepla/index_e.html
2. Abe, M., Chow, S.S.M., Haralambiev, K., Ohkubo, M.: Double-trapdoor anonymous tags for traceable signatures. Int. J. Inf. Sec. **12**(1), 19–31 (2013)
3. Abe, M., Fuchsbauer, G., Groth, J., Haralambiev, K., Ohkubo, M.: Structure-preserving signatures and commitments to group elements. In: Rabin, T. (ed.) CRYPTO 2010. LNCS, vol. 6223, pp. 209–236. Springer, Heidelberg (2010)
4. Attrapadung, N., Emura, K., Hanaoka, G., Sakai, Y.: A revocable group signature scheme from identity-based revocation techniques: achieving constant-size revocation list. In: Boureanu, I., Owesarski, P., Vaudenay, S. (eds.) ACNS 2014. LNCS, vol. 8479, pp. 419–437. Springer, Heidelberg (2014)

5. Attrapadung, N., Emura, K., Hanaoka, G., Sakai, Y.: Revocable group signature with constant-size revocation list. Comput. J. **58**(10), 2698–2715 (2015). This is the full version of [4]

6. Baldimtsi, F., Lysyanskaya, A.: Anonymous credentials light. In: ACM CCS, pp. 1087–1098 (2013)

7. Barbulescu, R., Gaudry, P., Joux, A., Thomé, E.: A heuristic quasi-polynomial algorithm for discrete logarithm in finite fields of small characteristic. In: Nguyen, P.Q., Oswald, E. (eds.) EUROCRYPT 2014. LNCS, vol. 8441. Springer, Heidelberg (2014)

8. Barreto, P.S.L.M., Naehrig, M.: Pairing-friendly elliptic curves of prime order. In: Selected Areas in Cryptography, pp. 319–331 (2005)

9. Belenkiy, M., Chase, M., Kohlweiss, M., Lysyanskaya, A.: Compact E-cash and simulatable VRFs revisited. In: Shacham, H., Waters, B. (eds.) Pairing 2009. LNCS, vol. 5671, pp. 114–131. Springer, Heidelberg (2009)

10. Bellare, M., Micciancio, D., Warinschi, B.: Foundations of group signatures: formal definitions, simplified requirements, and a construction based on general assumptions. In: EUROCRYPT, pp. 614–629 (2003)

11. Bellare, M., Shi, H., Zhang, C.: Foundations of group signatures: the case of dynamic groups. In: Menezes, A. (ed.) CT-RSA 2005. LNCS, vol. 3376, pp. 136–153. Springer, Heidelberg (2005)

12. Bichsel, P., Camenisch, J., Neven, G., Smart, N.P., Warinschi, B.: Get shorty via group signatures without encryption. In: Garay, J.A., De Prisco, R. (eds.) SCN 2010. LNCS, vol. 6280, pp. 381–398. Springer, Heidelberg (2010)

13. Boneh, D., Boyen, X.: Short signatures without random oracles and the SDH assumption in bilinear groups. J. Cryptology **21**(2), 149–177 (2008)

14. Boneh, D., Boyen, X., Shacham, H.: Short group signatures. In: Franklin, M. (ed.) CRYPTO 2004. LNCS, vol. 3152, pp. 41–55. Springer, Heidelberg (2004)

15. Boneh, D., Shacham, H.: Group signatures with verifier-local revocation. In: ACM CCS, pp. 168–177 (2004)

16. Camenisch, J., Hohenberger, S., Kohlweiss, M., Lysyanskaya, A., Meyerovich, M.: How to win the clone wars: efficient periodic n-times anonymous authentication. In: ACM CCS, pp. 201–210 (2006)

17. Chaum, D., van Heyst, E.: Group signatures. In: Davies, D.W. (ed.) EUROCRYPT 1991. LNCS, vol. 547, pp. 257–265. Springer, Heidelberg (1991)

18. Delerablée, C., Pointcheval, D.: Dynamic fully anonymous short group signatures. In: Nguyên, P.Q. (ed.) VIETCRYPT 2006. LNCS, vol. 4341, pp. 193–210. Springer, Heidelberg (2006)

19. Emura, K., Hanaoka, G., Sakai, Y., Schuldt, J.C.N.: Group signature implies public-key encryption with non-interactive opening. Int. J. Inf. Sec. **13**(1), 51–62 (2014)

20. Emura, K., Kanaoka, A., Ohta, S., Takahashi, T.: Building secure and anonymous communication channel: formal model and its prototype implementation. In: ACM Symposium on Applied, Computing, pp. 1641–1648 (2014)

21. Hohenberger, S., Ferrara, A.L., Green, M., Pedersen, M.Ø.: Practical short signature batch verification. In: Fischlin, M. (ed.) CT-RSA 2009. LNCS, vol. 5473, pp. 309–324. Springer, Heidelberg (2009)

22. Fiat, A., Shamir, A.: How to prove yourself: practical solutions to identification and signature problems. In: Odlyzko, A.M. (ed.) CRYPTO 1986. LNCS, vol. 263, pp. 186–194. Springer, Heidelberg (1987)

23. Franklin, M., Zhang, H.: Unique group signatures. In: Foresti, S., Yung, M., Martinelli, F. (eds.) ESORICS 2012. LNCS, vol. 7459, pp. 643–660. Springer, Heidelberg (2012)

24. Furukawa, J., Imai, H.: An efficient group signature scheme from bilinear maps. IEICE Trans. **89–A**(5), 1328–1338 (2006)

25. Granger, R., Kleinjung, T., Zumbrägel, J.: Breaking '128-bit secure' supersingular binary curves. In: Garay, J.A., Gennaro, R. (eds.) CRYPTO 2014, Part II. LNCS, vol. 8617, pp. 126–145. Springer, Heidelberg (2014)

26. Groth, J.: Fully anonymous group signatures without random oracles. In: Kurosawa, K. (ed.) ASIACRYPT 2007. LNCS, vol. 4833, pp. 164–180. Springer, Heidelberg (2007)

27. Groth, J., Sahai, A.: Efficient non-interactive proof systems for bilinear groups. In: Smart, N.P. (ed.) EUROCRYPT 2008. LNCS, vol. 4965, pp. 415–432. Springer, Heidelberg (2008)

28. Hwang, J.Y., Chen, L., Cho, H.S., Nyang, D.: Short dynamic group signature scheme supporting controllable linkability. IEEE Trans. Inf. Forensics Secur. **10**(6), 1109–1124 (2015)

29. Hwang, J.Y., Lee, S. Chung,, B.-H., Cho, H.S., Nyang, D.: Short group signatures with controllable linkability. In: LightSec, pp. 44–52 (2011)

30. Hwang, J.Y., Lee, S., Chung, B.-H., Cho, H.S., Nyang, D.: Group signatures with controllable linkability for dynamic membership. Inf. Sci. **222**, 761–778 (2013)

31. Isern-Deyà, A.P., Rotger, L.H., Payeras-Capellà, M., Puigserver, M.M.: On the practicability of using group signatures on mobile devices,: implementation and performance analysis on the android platform. Int. J. Inf. Sec. **14**(4), 335–345 (2015)

32. Kiayias, A., Tsiounis, Y., Yung, M.: Traceable signatures. In: Cachin, C., Camenisch, J.L. (eds.) EUROCRYPT 2004. LNCS, vol. 3027, pp. 571–589. Springer, Heidelberg (2004)

33. Kiayias, A., Yung, M.: Secure scalable group signature with dynamic joins and separable authorities. IJSN **1**(1/2), 24–45 (2006)

34. Langlois, A., Ling, S., Nguyen, K., Wang, H.: Lattice-based group signature scheme with verifier-local revocation. In: Public Key Cryptography, pp. 345–361 (2014)

35. Libert, B., Peters, T., Yung, M.: Group signatures with almost-for-free revocation. In: Safavi-Naini, R., Canetti, R. (eds.) CRYPTO 2012. LNCS, vol. 7417, pp. 571–589. Springer, Heidelberg (2012)

36. Libert, B., Peters, T., Yung, M.: Scalable group signatures with revocation. In: Pointcheval, D., Johansson, T. (eds.) EUROCRYPT 2012. LNCS, vol. 7237, pp. 609–627. Springer, Heidelberg (2012)

37. Libert, B., Peters, T., Yung, M.: Short group signatures via structure-preserving signatures: standard model security from simple assumptions. In: Gennaro, R., Robshaw, M. (eds.) CRYPTO 2015. LNCS, vol. 9216, pp. 296–316. Springer, Heidelberg (2015)

38. Libert, B., Vergnaud, D.: Group signatures with verifier-local revocation and backward unlinkability in the standard model. In: Garay, J.A., Miyaji, A., Otsuka, A. (eds.) CANS 2009. LNCS, vol. 5888, pp. 498–517. Springer, Heidelberg (2009)

39. Malina, L., Vives-Guasch, A., Castellà-Roca, J., Viejo, A., Hajny, J.: Efficient group signatures for privacy-preserving vehicular networks. Telecommun. Syst. **58**(4), 293–311 (2015)

40. Mamun, M.S.I., Miyaji, A.: Secure VANET applications with a refined group signature. In: PST, pp. 199–206 (2014)

41. Nakanishi, T., Fujiwara, T., Watanabe, H.: A linkable group signature and its application to secret voting. JIP **40**(7), 3085–3096 (1999)
42. Nakanishi, T., Funabiki, N.: Verifier-local revocation group signature schemes with backward unlinkability from bilinear maps. In: Roy, B. (ed.) ASIACRYPT 2005. LNCS, vol. 3788, pp. 533–548. Springer, Heidelberg (2005)
43. Nakanishi, T., Funabiki, N.: A short verifier-local revocation group signature scheme with backward unlinkability. In: Yoshiura, H., Sakurai, K., Rannenberg, K., Murayama, Y., Kawamura, S. (eds.) IWSEC 2006. LNCS, vol. 4266, pp. 17–32. Springer, Heidelberg (2006)
44. Ohtake, G., Fujii, A., Hanaoka, G., Ogawa, K.: On the theoretical gap between group signatures with and without unlinkability. In: Preneel, B. (ed.) AFRICACRYPT 2009. LNCS, vol. 5580, pp. 149–166. Springer, Heidelberg (2009)
45. Sakai, Y., Schuldt, J.C.N., Emura, K., Hanaoka, G., Ohta, K.: On the security of dynamic group signatures: preventing signature hijacking. In: Public Key Cryptography, pp. 715–732 (2012)
46. Sánchez, A.H., Rodríguez-Henríquez, F.: NEON implementation of an attribute-based encryption scheme. In: Jacobson, M., Locasto, M., Mohassel, P., Safavi-Naini, R. (eds.) ACNS 2013. LNCS, vol. 7954, pp. 322–338. Springer, Heidelberg (2013)
47. Unterluggauer, T., Slamanig, D., Spreitzer, R.: Adding controllable linkability to pairing-based group signatures for free. In: Chow, S.S.M., Camenisch, J., Hui, L.C.K., Yiu, S.M. (eds.) ISC 2014. LNCS, vol. 8783, pp. 388–400. Springer, Heidelberg (2014)
48. Wu, Q., Domingo-Ferrer, J., González-Nicolás, Ú.: Balanced trustworthiness, safety, and privacy in vehicle-to-vehicle communications. IEEE T. Veh. Technol. **59**(2), 559–573 (2010)
49. Yang, L., Tang, S., Yang, G.: A novel group signature scheme based on MPKC. In: Bao, F., Weng, J. (eds.) ISPEC 2011. LNCS, vol. 6672, pp. 181–195. Springer, Heidelberg (2011)
50. Zavattoni, E., Perez, L.J.D., Mitsunari, S., Sánchez-Ramírez, A.H., Teruya, T., Rodríguez-Henríquez, F.: Software implementation of an attribute-based encryption scheme. IEEE Trans. Comput. **64**(5), 1429–1441 (2015)

RoadRunneR: A Small and Fast Bitslice Block Cipher for Low Cost 8-Bit Processors

Adnan Baysal[1,2]([✉]) and Sühap Şahin[2]

[1] TÜBİTAK BİLGEM, 41470 Gebze, Kocaeli, Turkey
[2] Department of Computer Engineering, Kocaeli University,
41380 Umuttepe Yerleşkesi, Kocaeli, Turkey
adnan.baysal@tubitak.gov.tr

Abstract. Designing block ciphers targeting resource constrained 8-bit CPUs is a challenging problem. There are many recent lightweight ciphers designed for better performance in hardware. On the other hand, most software efficient lightweight ciphers either lack a security proof or have a low security margin. To fill the gap, we present RoadRunneR which is an efficient block cipher in 8-bit software, and its security is provable against differential and linear attacks. RoadRunneR has lowest code size in Atmel's ATtiny45, except NSA's design SPECK, which has no security proof. Moreover, we propose a new metric for the fair comparison of block ciphers. This metric, called ST/A, is the first metric to use key length as a parameter to rank ciphers of different key length in a fair way. By using ST/A and other metrics in the literature, we show that RoadRunneR is competitive among existing ciphers on ATtiny45.

Keywords: Lightweight · Cryptography · Block cipher · Bitslice · 8-bit CPU · Wireless sensor network · ATtiny45

1 Introduction

As the price of small electronic devices decreases, notions like *ubiquitous computing, Internet of things,* and *smart buildings* become more popular each day. RFID tags and low cost 8-bit CPUs are commonly deployed in these applications. Atmel's ATtiny45, one of commonly used 8-bit CPUs, costs less than \$1 [1]. This availability and programmable nature make these CPUs a good choice for many applications such as wireless sensor networks (WSNs).

One of the main problems in such applications is the security and privacy of information shared between devices. In many applications, data is shared between the nodes and the server over the air. Hence, an attacker can possibly get private information, or even change it for her/his benefit. For this reason, it is required to use cryptographic algorithms in these applications. Since the nodes are resource constrained in terms of memory, frequency and energy, use of lightweight cryptography becomes the best option in these applications.

Block ciphers are one of the main primitives for cryptographic applications. Therefore, the design of lightweight block ciphers has attracted many researchers'

© Springer International Publishing Switzerland 2016
T. Güneysu et al. (Eds.): LightSec 2015, LNCS 9542, pp. 58–76, 2016.
DOI: 10.1007/978-3-319-29078-2_4

attention, especially in the last 10 years. There are many designs, some with innovative ideas, such as LBlock [45], LED [26], PRESENT [10], PRINCE [12], PRINTCIPHER [32], SEA [41], TEA [44], SIMON and SPECK [5], ITUbee [28], PRIDE [3], and RECTANGLE [47]. Most of these algorithms used building blocks to optimize hardware implementations. For this reason, many of these algorithms are not a good choice for software applications in 8-bit CPUs. On the other hand, some more recent designs such as ITUbee, SPECK, PRIDE, and RECTANGLE are focused on performance in software to be an alternative in low cost CPUs. Some of these recent ciphers use bitslice substitution layers (S-boxes) where Boolean operations on CPU words are used to describe the S-box. By this approach, look-up-tables can be avoided which saves code size and CPU clock cycles. Moreover, since bitslice ciphers use small S-boxes, their hardware areas are small.

Another problem in block cipher design is the comparison of efficiencies of different ciphers for an application, and sometimes for academic purposes. Each platform and application has its own constraints and a simple comparison of area or throughput values are neither enough nor fair. Formulas for ranking block ciphers using the area-speed characteristics are needed, since implementation methods affect both values.

$\frac{Throughput}{area}$ is one metric offered in [11] to make a fair comparison of block ciphers in different hardware implementation methods (serial, parallel, pipelined, *etc.*). Badel *et al.* [4] expanded this definition by considering the possibility to trade-off throughput for power in energy-critical applications. Their formula is called *Figure Of Merit* (FOM) and defined as $\frac{Throughput}{Area^2}$. This formula is further improved by Khoo *et al.* [29] by calculating throughput at the minimum round number that the cipher is secure according to a security metric, and called this comparison metric as *Figure Of Adversarial Merit* (FOAM). In their paper, this security metric is the number of active S-boxes in differential and linear trails.

In [20], a new definition of FOM for software implementations was given. In that paper, authors suggested summing each performance indicator (code size, ram size, cycle counts) divided by the minimum of that value in the compared ciphers in a weighted manner, i.e., by multiplying each indicator with its corresponding weight. In this approach, hardest part is to find reasonable and useful weights, and they selected all weights as 1. None of the metrics above use key size in their formula. Therefore, there is no fair way of comparing ciphers of different key sizes using the metrics in the literature.

1.1   Our Contribution

We designed a new lightweight block cipher, RoadRunneR, with the goal of efficiency (especially in 8-bit low cost CPUs) and provable security in terms of minimum number of active S-boxes in differential and linear trails. The cipher is especially designed to have a very low code size, while having high throughput. Simulation results showed that on ATtiny45, our cipher have the least code size among other compared lightweight ciphers, except NSA's design SPECK which has no provable security properties to determine the round number. Our preliminary cryptanalysis showed that RoadRunneR have a relatively high security margin in contrast to most lightweight ciphers. RoadRunneR has variable area-time-security trade-off characteristics with different implementation methods so that it can fit the needs of specific application it may be used in.

Moreover, we defined a new efficiency comparison metric for block ciphers which (to the best of our knowledge for the first time) takes into account the key size of the cipher. Using this metric, we could compare block ciphers with different key sizes in a fair way. To compare RoadRunneR with existing lightweight ciphers, we used this metric and the classical ones. We gave comparison results for both the original round numbers and in the round numbers as suggested in FOAM approach. We used ATtiny45 for benchmarking, since it is one of the lowest cost 8-bit CPUs and there are many recent ciphers implemented in this device in the literature.

The organization of the rest of the paper is as follows: In Sect. 2, we define our new cipher RoadRunneR and give the design criteria of it. Preliminary cryptanalysis of RoadRunneR against known attacks is presented in Sect. 3. Our new comparison metric for block ciphers is given in Sect. 4. We give performance results of RoadRunneR and compare it with existing block ciphers using our new metric and other known metrics in Sect. 5. Section 6 concludes the paper.

2   Definition and Design Rationale of RoadRunneR

In the design of RoadRunneR, our main objectives were the following:

1. Implementation efficiency in 8-bit CPUs,
2. No table and SRAM usage,
3. Low decryption overhead,
4. Provable security like in *wide trail design strategy* [17].

We could achieve these objectives as shown in the rest of the paper. Our main focus was on reducing memory. This is because low cost 8-bit CPUs have program memory of only a few kilobytes (KB). In most applications this memory is shared by some other algorithms (such as interrupt service routines) and possibly a real time operating system. So reducing memory footprint is beneficial in our target platform.

In [39], it is stated that a hardware implementation of a lightweight block cipher targeting RFID tags and WSNs should cost less than 2000 gate equivalent (GE). For software implementations there is no stated bound, but we believe that 1KB memory should not be exceeded for a lightweight block cipher implementation.

2.1   General Structure

RoadRunneR is a Feistel-type block cipher, shown in Fig. 1, with 64-bit block size and 80-bit or 128-bit key lengths. 80-bit key requires 10 rounds and 128-bit version is 12 rounds. Initial and final round whitening is used which XOR's the whitening keys (WK_0 and WK_1) to the left part of the state. There is no swap operation in the final round. Decryption uses the same round function where the order of whitening keys, round keys and constants are reversed.

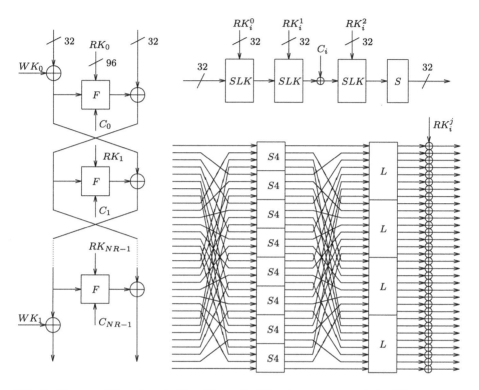

Fig. 1. Figures of functions in RoadRunneR. Feistel structure on left, F function on top right, and SLK function on bottom right.

If the state is shown as $x_0\|x_1\|\dots\|x_7$, each round function F takes most significant (leftmost) 4 bytes of the state, that is $x_0\|x_1\|x_2\|x_3$, as input data, 1-byte C_i as constant, and 96-bit round key. Output of F is XORed to $x_4\|x_5\|x_6\|x_7$. F is a 4 round substitution-permutation-network (SPN) type function as shown on top right of Fig. 1. In that figure, SLK is the consecutive application of S-box layer (S), diffusion layer (L), and key addition (K), as shown on the bottom right. The last function S is the same S-box layer in SLK. After the second SLK function, round constant is XORed to the least significant byte (rightmost byte, i.e., x_3) of the state. For round $i = 0, 1, \dots, NR - 1$, the round constant is $C_i = NR - i$, where NR is the number of rounds, and C_i is represented as 8-bit little endian integer, that is $12 = 00001100$, $11 = 00001011$, etc. Round constants prevent simple slide attacks [8] and makes the round function to be different for different rounds. 4-round SPN-like structure ensures high number of active S-boxes for an active F.

In the *SLK* function, first a bitslice S-box layer is applied on 4 words of 8 bits. This layer can be seen as parallel application of 4-bit S-boxes to the ith bit of each word, and writing the outputs to the same location (i^{th} bit) again. This is the best S-box in terms of security and efficiency (on CPUs) found in [42]. S-box layer is described in Sect. 2.2. After the S-box layer, a diffusion matrix L is applied to each byte independently to ensure diffusion inside the bits of a byte. L is designed such that it provides good diffusion and can be efficiently implemented even on the simplest CPUs. Definition and design criteria of L will be described in Sect. 2.3.

2.2   S-Box Layer

Using bitslice S-boxes has become more popular in the last 10 years, especially with the recent advances in lightweight cryptography. Block ciphers such as NOEKEON [16], SEA [41], PRIDE [3], and RECTANGLE [47] use bitslice S-boxes with different S-box layer design strategies. Bitslice S-box structure has advantage in both hardware and software implementations. In software, the permutations before and after the S-boxes disappear. In hardware, on the other hand, they can be implemented by a simple wiring which consumes no extra area. Since S-boxes of large bit size and high non-linearity have a complicated circuit representation, 3-bit and 4-bit S-boxes are used in bitslice ciphers.

In RoadRunneR, an efficient bitslice S-box is used so that it can be implemented in a small number of bit-wise operations on CPU words. The table of S-box is given below:

Input	0	1	2	3	4	5	6	7	8	9	A	B	C	D	E	F
Output	0	8	6	D	5	F	7	C	4	E	2	3	9	1	B	A

This S-box was found in [42] by a brute force search on possible assembly code combinations. The search space was restricted to 4 input words, a single temporary word, and following instructions: AND, OR, XOR, NOT, and MOV. For the best 4-bit S-boxes, maximal correlation and differential probabilities are 2^{-2}. They experimentally found that the minimum number of instructions to generate such a bitslice S-box layer is 9. The selected S-box in RoadRunneR satisfies this property. The assembly code of the S-box for Atmel's 8-bit CPU's is as follows (X0 is the most significant byte entering the S-box layer):

```
; S-box layer
mov T0,X3 ; State words : X0,X1,X2,X3
and X3,X2 ; Temporary word : T0
eor X3,X1
or  X1,X2
eor X1,X0
and X0,X3
```

```
eor X0,T0
and T0,X1
eor X2,T0
```

2.3 Diffusion Layer

After the bitslice S-box layer, we used a linear function on each byte of the state to provide diffusion inside 8-bit words. So we needed an efficient linear function operating on bytes. One classical solution for such a linear function for CPUs is using XOR of shifted and rotated values of the input word.

On ATtiny45 (and on most low cost 8-bit CPUs), there is no parametric shift or and no rotation instruction. So, to shift and/or rotate a byte for parametric values multiple cycles are necessary which consumes program memory and clock cycles. 1-bit left rotation can be done in 2 instructions if ADC instruction is used, whereas 1-bit right rotation can be done in 3 cycles using BST and BLD instructions. There is another instruction that swaps halves of a byte, which results in a 4-bit rotation.

Using these instructions, we try to build linear functions of the form $L(x) = (x \lll i) \oplus (x \lll j) \oplus (x \lll k)$ to use in RoadRunneR, where $x \lll i$ represents i-bit rotation of the CPU word x to the left. Linear layers of this form are guaranteed to be invertible and all have branch number 4. Branch number of a matrix L is defined as follows:

$$BN(L) = min_{x \neq 0}\{hw(x) + hw(L(x))\}$$

where $hw(x)$ denotes the Hamming weight of a binary vector x. This number gives the minimum number of active S-boxes in two consecutive rounds. Besides the branch number, we calculated the minimum number of active S-boxes in 4 round SPN structure of F with each L matrix candidate. Table 1 shows the best linear functions (less then 15 instructions for two matrix multiplications) found in our search:

From the Table 1, we have chosen L_1 as our diffusion layer matrix since it provides good diffusion and performance. The minimum number of differentially active S-boxes in an active F using the above linear layers is calculated in a

Table 1. Best L matrices under given constraints.

Matrix	i, j, k	# of instructions (for two matrix mult.)	Minimum # of active S-boxes in F
L_1	0,1,2	13	10
L_2	0,1,4	11	8
L_3	0,1,5	11	8
L_4	0,4,5	11	8
L_5	1,4,5	11	8

truncated manner, i.e., it is independent of the selected S-box. We could analyze this using an observation in [25] which gives:

$$\alpha = x_0 \vee x_1 \vee x_2 \vee x_3 \rightsquigarrow L[x_0] \vee L[x_1] \vee L[x_2] \vee L[x_3] = \beta \qquad (1)$$

where x_i's are 8-bit words, set bits in α and β gives the active S-box positions entering into the S-box layer and after the linear layer respectively. Since there are multiple choices for x_i's to produce the same α, some input truncated active S-box pattern will have multiple possible outputs, which we call transitions. $\alpha \rightsquigarrow \beta$ means that there is a transition from α to β. Since word size is 8 bits and there are 4 words, we could search for all possible transitions of active S-box positions while passing an SLK using an exhaustive search of 2^{32} complexity. Here we tried all possible values of $x_0\|x_1\|x_2\|x_3$ to generate $\alpha \rightsquigarrow \beta$ transitions.

Using the truncated transitions, we generated a directed graph of 256 vertices. In this graph, vertices are 8-bit numbers representing active S-box positions. If vertices α and β satisfy $\alpha \rightsquigarrow \beta$, this is shown as a directed edge from the vertex α to vertex β. Using that graph, starting from all possible vertices (except 0), we tried all possible directed paths of 4 vertices, summing the Hamming weights as the number of active S-boxes. Minimum weight in these paths give the minimum number of active S-boxes in an active F. Linear characteristics follow very similar patterns because of the definition of matrices and F function's symmetric structure.

The selected matrix have single non-trivial fixed point which is FF in hexadecimal notation. In truncated active S-box transition notation, we have the following fixed points: 77,7F,BB,BF,DD,DF,EE,EF,F7,FB,FD,FE,FF. So we can say that there are at least 6 active S-boxes whenever an analysis require to use the same active S-box positions before and after SLK.

The AVR assembly code for 2 matrix multiplication is given below. The rationale behind using two matrix multiplication is to use single cycle 16-bit copy operation MOVW on inputs of our matrix (lsb and msb denotes least and most significant bits respectively).

```
; State registers    : X0,X1
; Temporary registers : T0,T1,ZERO (value in ZERO is 0)
movw T0,X0   ; T0,T1 <- X0,X1
lsl  T0      ; msb of T0 is moved to carry flag
adc  T0,ZERO ; Since ZERO is 0, this moves msb in carry to lsb
eor  T0,X0
lsl  T0
adc  T0,ZERO
eor  X0,T0
lsl  T1
adc  T1,ZERO
eor  T1,X1
lsl  T1
adc  T1,ZERO
eor  X1,T1
```

2.4   Key Schedules

RoadRunneR can take 80-bit or 128-bit keys. RoadRunneR-80 and RoadRunneR-128 denotes 80-bit and 128-bit key versions respectively. For both key sizes, key schedules have the same simple description: Start from the beginning of the master key, whenever a new 32-bits of key material is required, continue on the master key in a circular way.

For example, if master key is 128-bit, it will be divided into 4 words of 32-bit as $A\|B\|C\|D$. Initial whitening key is A, first round key is B-C-D, second round key is A-B-C, etc. Same key words appear in the same place in a period of 4 rounds. For 80-bit key schedule, master key is divided into 5 words of 16-bit : $A\|B\|C\|D\|E$. In this nomenclature, whitening key is $A\|B$; first round key is $(C\|D)$-$(E\|A)$-$(B\|C)$; second round key is $(D\|E)$-$(A\|B)$-$(C\|D)$, etc. There is a 5-round period in this schedule, so round number is chosen as a multiple of 5. Complete list of master key words used in rounds is given in Table 2.

Table 2. Key Schedules of RoadRunneR.

80-bit key schedule		128-bit key schedule	
Master key $= A\|B\|C\|D\|E$		Master key $= A\|B\|C\|D$	
Initial whitening : $A\|B$		Initial whitening : A	
Rounds	Key words	Rounds	Key words
0, 5	$(C\|D)$-$(E\|A)$-$(B\|C)$	0, 4, 8	B-C-D
1, 6	$(D\|E)$-$(A\|B)$-$(C\|D)$	1, 5, 9	A-B-C
2, 7	$(E\|A)$-$(B\|C)$-$(D\|E)$	2, 6, 10	D-A-B
3, 8	$(A\|B)$-$(C\|D)$-$(E\|A)$	3, 7, 11	C-D-A
4, 9	$(B\|C)$-$(D\|E)$-$(A\|B)$		
Final whitening : $C\|D$		Final whitening : B	

3   Security of RoadRunneR

For the attacks on reduced round numbers, we assume that there is an initial and final whitening in reduced versions on the left hand side of the cipher, and no swap is applied in the last round. Final whitening is the next key word in the key schedule.

Whitening is only applied to left sides to prevent attackers from using known bits of the cipher's intermediate round values. There is no need to XOR whitening key on right halves to provide this property. In most of the attacks, extending the attack by even one round is not possible since this requires to search for all 128-bit keys (in 128-bit key version) because of the whitening. So, we can say that whitening keys play a crucial security role in RoadRunneR, and cannot be omitted in the attacks.

Since the key schedule uses the master key without any change while using in the rounds, we have no security claim against related key attacks. Related key attacks are easier to defend on the protocol level, and some of the lightweight ciphers do not consider this attack as well, such as PRINCE and PRIDE. Hence we used this assumption in RoadRunneR. In fact, each F can be passed with only two active S-boxes in a related key attack, with total of 24 active S-boxes. This total number may be further reduced in a more detailed analysis.

3.1 Differential and Linear Attacks

Differential attack [6] and linear attack [37] are two most successful attacks on block ciphers. RoadRunneR has provable bounds on minimum number of differentially active S-boxes, which shows that there is no useful differential characteristic for 5 rounds or more. Since the transpose of our diffusion layer have similar properties and F function have a symmetric structure, differential and linear properties (in a truncated manner) of RoadRunneR are the same. So whenever we mention active S-boxes, we mean both differentially and linearly active S-boxes.

As we have mentioned in Sect. 2.3, the minimum number of active S-boxes in an active F is 10. Note that this number is better than the value suggested by branch number, which is 8 for 4 rounds (since branch number is 4). There are 8 truncated trails of 10 and 11 active S-boxes, and all of them start with 1 active S-boxes. Moreover, the characteristics starting with the same input pattern follow the same path for round 2 and 3, that is only the last round is different for minimal weight paths. These paths are given below.

```
Weight 10:                      Weight 11:
01 --> 07 --> 1B --> 41         01 --> 07 --> 1B --> 49
02 --> 0E --> 36 --> 82         02 --> 0E --> 36 --> 92
04 --> 1C --> 6C --> 05         04 --> 1C --> 6C --> 25
08 --> 38 --> D8 --> 0A         08 --> 38 --> D8 --> 4A
10 --> 70 --> B1 --> 14         10 --> 70 --> B1 --> 94
20 --> E0 --> 63 --> 28         20 --> E0 --> 63 --> 29
40 --> C1 --> C6 --> 50         40 --> C1 --> C6 --> 52
80 --> 83 --> 8D --> A0         80 --> 83 --> 8D --> A4
```

We experimentally checked some high probability differential characteristics of F starting with one active S-box to see if the probability of characteristics and differentials are close or not. In our experiments, we did not see any significant increase in differential probability, from the theoretically calculated characteristic probability. So we assumed that each active S-box multiplies the probability with 2^{-2}, and an active F has approximately 2^{-20} probability.

We also calculated the minimum number of active S-boxes in r-round Road-RunneR for $4 \leq r \leq 6$, again in a truncated manner. This is done by an exhaustive search, thanks to the graph we mentioned in Sect. 2.3. Utilizing that graph, we could generate all possible truncated active S-box transitions on F function, together with their minimum number of active S-boxes. In our search of minimum number of active S-boxes in r-rounds RoadRunneR, we try all possible truncated input difference patterns to the cipher and follow an r-round path using branching over F and Feistel XORs, counting number of active S-boxes in all F functions. Whenever two truncated difference meet in an XOR of Feistel scheme, we tried both cases with a difference and without difference. Table 3 shows minimum number of active S-boxes for rounds from 4 up to 6, together with the percentage of active S-boxes.

Table 3. Minimum number of truncated active S-boxes for rounds.

Round	4	5	6
# of Active S-boxes	26	36	48
Percentage	20.3 %	22.5 %	25 %

Note that these bounds are better than the classical bounds on Feistel ciphers with invertible F function, which gives 2, 3 and 4 active F functions in 4, 5, and 6 consecutive rounds respectively. In that classical approach, since an active F has at least 10 active S-boxes, the bound is 20, 30 and 40 active S-boxes for 4, 5, and 6 rounds, whereas we found 26, 36, and 48 active S-boxes for these round numbers in our search. We believe that the active S-box percentage values are very good for such a lightweight linear layer. Table 3 proves that there is no useful differential characteristic (or linear trail) in 5 or more rounds of RoadRunneR, since the probability is at least 2^{-72}.

We listed all paths with minimum number of S-boxes in our search. By observing the trails, we saw that there were no clustering in best trails, i.e. no paths starting and ending with the same active S-box positions in 5 rounds. This gives confidence that characteristic and differential probabilities are very close in the whole cipher. Hence, we believe that 5 round RoadRunneR is secure against classical differential and linear attacks.

There are many attacks derived from differential attack and linear attack. Some examples are: higher order differential attack [34], boomerang attack [43], multidimensional linear attack [13], differential-linear attack [35], etc. In general, these extension attacks do not give better results then classical differential and linear attacks. We think that the same is true for RoadRunneR. Since all key material is used in the first and last rounds with the use of whitening keys, it is hard to apply 1R and 2R attacks.

3.2 Impossible Differential Attack

In impossible differential attack [7], truncated differentials with probability 1 are used to find a difference contradiction in middle rounds. This contradiction is then used to eliminate wrong keys in the extra rounds added before and after the characteristic. For Feistel ciphers, there is a generic 5 round impossible differential characteristic [31] as follows:

$$(0, \Delta\alpha) \stackrel{5}{\nrightarrow} (0, \Delta\alpha)$$

Since the round function of RoadRunneR has a four round SPN structure, we could not find impossible differential characteristic for more than 5 rounds. On the other hand, all key material is used in the first and last round when whitening keys are considered, so we believe that impossible differential attack cannot be applied to more than 6 rounds of RoadRunneR.

3.3   Integral Attack

The integral attack (or square attack) was demonstrated in [14] as a custom attack to SQUARE block cipher. It was also applied to Rijndael which become AES, and many other ciphers. In this attack, all possible values are given to specific bit blocks in the plaintext, and other bits are kept constant. After some rounds of encryption, fixed sum (generally zero) in specific ciphertext bit locations are expected.

Because of the 4 round SPN structure in F function, giving all possible values to a single S-box do not give too many rounds in an integral attack. The best attack can be achieved by 32-bit active block on the right half of the plaintexts as in the following:

$$(0, A) \rightarrow (A, 0) \rightarrow (A, A) \rightarrow (B, A) \rightarrow (?, B)$$

Here, A denotes an active 32-bit block where all possible values are seen. B is a balanced block, that is XOR sum of values are zero. An undetermined block is represented by a ? mark. This characteristic cannot be extended to more rounds. Therefore, we do not think that square attack threatens RoadRunneR for more than 6 rounds.

3.4   MITM-type Attacks

All state bits are affected by all key bits after 3 rounds of RoadRunneR encryption. Moreover, when the matching variable in a Meet-In-The-Middle (MITM) attack is selected in the right half of the state at the output of round 3, it is not possible to add even 2 rounds because of the fact that all key bits affect that variable in the decryption direction after 2 rounds. Same ideas apply for 2 rounds at the beginning and 3 rounds at the end case due to the Feistel structure. Hence, MITM attack cannot be applied to more than 4 rounds.

There are some extensions of MITM attack such as multidimensional MITM [48], Demirci-Selçuk attack [18], and MITM attacks with tabulation and differential enumeration techniques [22]. These attacks generally uses truncated differential characteristics with high probability over multiple rounds. In the case of RoadRunneR, since round function F is a 4-round SPN, we believe that these attacks are not more effective than basic MITM attack.

3.5   Side-Channel Attacks

Lightweight ciphers are vulnerable to side-channel attacks. The attacker can access low cost devices that have the secret key, and can measure encryption time, power dissipation, radiation, etc. Therefore, mechanisms to protect the cipher against such attacks may be necessary in some applications.

It is shown in [15] that ciphers with bitslice nonlinear layer are easier to defend against side-channel attacks such as differential power analysis (DPA) [33]. Since RoadRunneR has a bitslice non-linear layer, we can say that the additional overhead caused by DPA protecting mechanisms is low for our cipher.

4   A New Efficiency Metric for Block Ciphers : ST/A

In this section, we propose a new metric called ST/A, which we read as *Security times Throughput over Area*. In this new metric, we insert key size to the efficiency metric formulae since there is no fair way to compare block ciphers of different key length in the literature. We extend $\frac{Throughput}{Area}$ metric by multiplying it with the key size, so we have:

$$ST/A = \frac{KeySize \times Throughput}{Area}$$

where $KeySize$ is the bit size of key used in the cipher, $Throughput$ is given in bit-per-second, and $Area$ is gate equivalent (GE) in hardware or memory usage in software.

We inserted the key size by multiplication, hence increase in the key size increases the efficiency of a cipher. Moreover, other parameters affect the metric in a multiplicative manner. So another mathematical operation, such as addition, would have less meaning. In our metric, algorithms with equal round function and round number for different key sizes, such as PRESENT, will have better efficiency in higher key size. On the other hand, existing metrics in the literature do not differentiate these key sizes. This is an other evident that our metric makes more fair comparison even in this specific case.

In [20], the metric is calculated in an additive manner. On the other hand, all previous methods and ST/A are multiplicative, that is all performance value are multiplied. We think that multiplying is a more useful technique. For example, let E_1 and E_2 be two ciphers which will be compared. Also assume that all performance indicators are the same for both cipher except area values, where E_1 has area A and E_2 has area $2 \times A$. By the multiplication method, we can say that E_1 is two times better than E_2. In the summation case, however, even if the weights are equal, we would not have this ratio in efficiency values. Therefore, we multiply each indicator as in the classical $\frac{Throughput}{Area}$ formula (here throughput is multiplied by $\frac{1}{Area}$) in ST/A.

We believe that the throughput should be defined as in $FOAM$, but we leave this to the user of this metric. Weighting approach as in [20] can be used in ST/A by taking weights as powers of area, speed and key size values, since we use a multiplicative approach. Again, this is left to the user, and we use all powers as 1.

In Sect. 5, we use our metric for the comparison of the efficiency of some lightweight block ciphers and our new design RoadRunneR.

5   Performance Analysis

We have simulated RoadRunneR for ATtiny45 processor using AVR assembly language in Atmel Studio 6.2. Implementations are encryption only, where master key and plaintext are read from SRAM, plaintext is encrypted, and written back to the same place again. There is no SRAM usage besides master key and plaintext, so only code size is given as the area performance. Loading of key and plaintext, and storing back ciphertext is included in the single block encryption time. Various optimization methods are applied. In Table 4, we give the performance result of RoadRunneR block cipher.

Table 4. Performance values of RoadRunneR-80 and RoadRunneR-128 for different optimization methods. Compact-1 and Compact-2 are in between methods, shown as signs of possible trade-offs.

Key Size	Optimization	Code Size (Byte)	Time (cycle)
80	Area	202	3279
80	Speed	386	2091
128	Area	196	3819
128	Compact-1	228	2461
128	Compact-2	402	2171
128	Speed	502	2025

Area optimized 80-bit key version has slightly more area than 128-bit key version. This is because of the more complex key schedule in 80-bit key. Optimization column in Table 4 shows the various implementation methods we apply. Area optimization method gives the smallest code size we could achieve. This is done by extensive use of subroutines which saves program memory. Speed optimization, on the other hand, use no subroutines to avoid extra cycles required by branching to subroutines. Compact methods are described below:

– Compact-1 : This is derived from area optimized version. Some subroutines are removed and repeating codes are written for them.
– Compact-2 : Derived from speed optimized version. Key selection part in speed optimized version changed to a subroutine.

There are more trade-offs with different code size/clock cycle properties but we did not include them in the paper. From this and Table 4, we see that RoadRunneR have good throughput/area/security trade-off properties. If we start from the speed optimized version, we can reduce the area more than half and pay a speed penalty of less than half. Fastest implementation is still relatively small, and the smallest implementation is not that slow.

Comparison of RoadRunneR with some other ciphers is given in Table 5. We show four comparison metric values for each cipher. Metrics are explained below:

– T/A is the classical $\frac{Throughput}{Area}$ metric.
– T/A-FOAM is the same metric with the throughput definition in FOAM.
– ST/A is calculated by multiplying the T/A by the key size.
– ST/A-FOAM is calculated by multiplying the T/A-FOAM by the key size.

Instead of using $\frac{Throughput}{Area}$, we chose to use $Area \times Time$ product (time to produce 1 byte, i.e., Cycle/Byte) as in the comparisons in [28], which gives the same order. Here, in contrast to $\frac{Throughput}{Area}$, small values are better. We also normalize each comparison metric column for better understanding. For the normalization, we divide all numbers in the column with the smallest value in that column.

In the calculation of FOAM values, we searched for the best attack on each cipher in terms of round number, and used that as round number to calculate encryption time. This calculation done by multiplying the original encryption clock count by NR^*/NR, where NR is the original round number and NR^* is the round numbers calculated by the above idea. We do not exclude any initial setup since we do not know each implementation in detail. We also excluded related-key attacks since we have no security claim for this type of attack. For NOEKEON and SEA, we use the bounds found by the designers because of the lack of cryptanalysis in the literature on these ciphers.

In Table 5, (A) and (S) stands for area optimized and speed optimized implementations, respectively. (C1) and (C2) are compact implementations as defined previously. We write RRR as an abbreviation of RoadRunneR. We did not include SERPENT-128 and CLEFIA-128 in the list since they were far behind any of the other ciphers in the table in terms of efficiency metrics.

Table 5 shows that, the best cipher in terms of our metrics and classical metrics is SPECK family. But this family follows the Addition-Rotation-XOR (ARX) design principle and lacks the provable security properties. So, the round number selection of SPECK have no scientific rationale. Moreover, in an attack paper on Simon [38], authors claim that truncated differential characteristics to be found in the future may extend their 26 round attack to more rounds on the cipher. Therefore, if we exclude SIMON and SPECK, we have the following picture among remaining implementations:

RoadRunneR is the best algorithm in terms of code size (except speed optimized and C2 implementations) and security margin. When FOAM approach is not considered, i.e., in T/A and ST/A metrics, PRIDE outperforms all others, RoadRunneR implementations follow PRIDE. When we take into account security margins, T/A-FOAM and ST/A-FOAM metrics show that (A) and (C1) implementations have the highest rank, PRIDE and other implementations of RoadRunneR follow them. Throughput of RoadRunneR is not the best in any implementation but the fastest implementation of it has the rank 3 among 8

Table 5. Comparison of some block ciphers implemented on ATtiny45. RRR stands for RoadRunneR, (A), (S), (C1), and (C2) are implementations methods. Comparison metrics are normalized where small values are better.

Cipher	Block size	Key size	Attacked rounds	Mem. [byte]	Enc. Clks	Cyc./ Byte	T/A	T/A FOAM	ST/A	ST/A FOAM
AES [24]	128	128	7/10 [19]	1570	3159	197	11.83	12.35	11.11	12.38
PRESENT [24]	64	128	26/31 [9]	660	10792	1349	33.97	42.51	31.91	42.58
SEA [3]	96	96	72/93 [41]	386	17745	1479	21.78	25.43	27.26	33.96
NOEKEON [23]	128	128	9/12 [16]	364	23517	1470	20.41	22.84	19.17	22.88
PRINCE [3]	64	128	12/12 [27]	1108	3614	451	19.01	28.49	19.94	28.54
ITUBEE [28]	80	80	**10/20** [40]	716	2607	261	7.13	5.32	10.72	8.53
PRIDE [3]	64	128	19/20 [46]	266	1514	**189**	**1.92**	2.72	**1.80**	2.73
RRR-80 (A)	64	80	6/10	**202**	3279	410	3.16	2.83	4.75	4.53
RRR-80 (S)	64	80	6/10	386	2091	261	3.85	3.45	5.78	5.53
RRR-128 (A)	64	128	**6/12**	**196**	3819	477	3.57	**2.66**	3.35	**2.66**
RRR-128 (C1)	64	128	**6/12**	**228**	2461	308	2.68	**2.00**	2.51	**2.00**
RRR-128 (C2)	64	128	**6/12**	402	2171	271	4.16	3.10	3.91	3.11
RRR-128 (S)	64	128	**6/12**	502	2025	253	4.85	3.62	4.55	3.62
SIMON [5]	64	128	26/42 [2]	282	2000	250	2.69	2.37	2.53	2.37
SPECK [5]	64	96	18/26 [21]	182	1152	144	1.00	1.03	1.28	1.38
SPECK [5]	64	128	17/27 [21]	186	1200	150	1.06	1.00	1.00	1.00

ciphers. We think that RoadRunneR is fast enough for most applications with low cost 8-bit CPUs. Bold numbers show the best values in their column except SIMON and SPECK family. Multiple values in RoadRunneR implementations are written bold if they are better then all previous results.

6   Conclusion and Future Work

A very efficient Feistel type bitslice block cipher, RoadRunneR, with 64-bit block size and 80-bit or 128-bit key length is presented. RoadRunneR is a perfect choice for devices with very restricted memory resources and for applications requiring reasonable throughput expectations. Our cipher has a high security margin in contrast to most of other lightweight block ciphers. We simulated RoadRunneR on ATtiny45 devices by using Atmel Studio 6.2, for which there are implementation results of recent lightweight ciphers in the literature.

To compare our cipher and other ciphers with different key lengths, we proposed a new comparison metric which considers throughput, area and key size. When two ciphers of similar area and throughput values are achieved, the one with larger key size will have a higher rank in this metric. Our metric is the first one to use key length in the literature.

Implementation results show that RoadRunneR is a competitive candidate in all metrics in the literature and in our new metric. In our comparisons, only SPECK and PRIDE performed better than RoadRunneR in some metrics, but SPECK lacks a security proof and there is a 19 out of 20 round differential attack on PRIDE. In this sense, we think that RoadRunneR is a good alternative to current lightweight block ciphers.

Future Work : Methods for counting minimum number of active S-boxes in an r-round ($r > 2$) bitslice SPN cipher (like PRIDE and RECTANGLE) for larger than 8-bit word size is a challenge. If an efficient method can be found, this may be used to generate and evaluate binary matrices used in bitslice ciphers, together with their efficiency. Moreover, general frameworks for determining power weights for area, throughput, and key size (security) in ST/A for various implementation platforms is necessary. In the current state, we take all powers as 1, but some implementations may require very constrained area or time characteristics. How to find most useful powers is an open problem. We also leave efficient hardware implementations of RoadRunneR as a future work.

A   Test Vectors for 80-Bit Key Length

Plaintext	Key	Ciphertext
0000_0000_0000_0000	0000_0000_0000_0000_0000	7F0B_3486_640D_2F5E
0000_0000_0000_0002	8000_0000_0000_0000	4FA2_5EF2_64CE_C6E4
FEDC_BA98_7654_3210	0123_4567_89AB_CDEF_0123	328C_798A_0EB2_5A3B

B   Test Vectors for 128-Bit Key Length

Plaintext	Key	Ciphertext
0000_0000_0000_0000	0000_0000_0000_0000	3B07_DE72_9642_54AC
	0000_0000_0000_0000	
0000_0000_0000_0002	8000_0000_0000_0000	C168_C69A_C195_845E
	0000_0000_0000_0000	
FEDC_BA98_7654_3210	0123_4567_89AB_CDEF	D9DF_068F_5993_8882
	0123_4567_89AB_CDEF	

References

1. ATtiny45. http://www.atmel.com/devices/attiny45.aspx. Accessed 18 June 2015
2. Abed, F., List, E., Lucks, S., Wenzel, J.: Differential and linear cryptanalysis of reduced-round simon. Technical report, Citeseer (2013)
3. Albrecht, M.R., Driessen, B., Kavun, E.B., Leander, G., Paar, C., Yalçın, T.: Block ciphers – focus on the linear layer (feat. PRIDE). In: Garay, J.A., Gennaro, R. (eds.) CRYPTO 2014, Part I. LNCS, vol. 8616, pp. 57–76. Springer, Heidelberg (2014)

4. Badel, S., Dağtekin, N., Nakahara Jr., J., Ouafi, K., Reffé, N., Sepehrdad, P., Sušil, P., Vaudenay, S.: ARMADILLO: a multi-purpose cryptographic primitive dedicated to hardware. In: Mangard and Standaert [36], pp. 398–412

5. Beaulieu, R., Shors, D., Smith, J., Treatman-Clark, S., Weeks, B., Wingers, L.: The simon and speck families of lightweight block ciphers. Cryptology ePrint Archive, Report 2013/404. http://eprint.iacr.org/

6. Biham, E., Shamir, A.: Differential cryptanalysis of DES-like cryptosystems. In: Menezes, A., Vanstone, S.A. (eds.) CRYPTO 1990. LNCS, vol. 537, pp. 2–21. Springer, Heidelberg (1991)

7. Biryukov, A.: Impossible differential attack. In: van Tilborg, H.C.A. (ed.) Encyclopedia of Cryptography and Security. Springer, USA (2005)

8. Biryukov, A., Wagner, D.: Slide attacks. In: Knudsen [30], pp. 245–259

9. Blondeau, C., Nyberg, K.: Links between truncated differential and multidimensional linear properties of block ciphers and underlying attack complexities. In: Nguyen, P.Q., Oswald, E. (eds.) EUROCRYPT 2014. LNCS, vol. 8441, pp. 165–182. Springer, Heidelberg (2014)

10. Bogdanov, A.A., Knudsen, L.R., Leander, G., Paar, C., Poschmann, A., Robshaw, M.J.B., Seurin, Y., Vikkelsoe, C.: PRESENT: An ultra-lightweight block cipher. In: Paillier, P., Verbauwhede, I. (eds.) CHES 2007. LNCS, vol. 4727, pp. 450–466. Springer, Heidelberg (2007)

11. Bogdanov, A., Leander, G., Paar, C., Poschmann, A., Robshaw, M.J.B., Seurin, Y.: Hash functions and RFID tags: mind the gap. In: Oswald, E., Rohatgi, P. (eds.) CHES 2008. LNCS, vol. 5154, pp. 283–299. Springer, Heidelberg (2008)

12. Borghoff, J., et al.: PRINCE – a low-latency block cipher for pervasive computing applications. In: Wang, X., Sako, K. (eds.) ASIACRYPT 2012. LNCS, vol. 7658, pp. 208–225. Springer, Heidelberg (2012)

13. Cho, J.Y., Hermelin, M., Nyberg, K.: A new technique for multidimensional linear cryptanalysis with applications on reduced round serpent. In: Lee, P.J., Cheon, J.H. (eds.) ICISC 2008. LNCS, vol. 5461, pp. 383–398. Springer, Heidelberg (2009)

14. Daemen, J., Knudsen, L.R., Rijmen, V.: The block cipher SQUARE. In: Biham, E. (ed.) FSE 1997. LNCS, vol. 1267, pp. 149–165. Springer, Heidelberg (1997)

15. Daemen, J., Peeters, M., Van Assche, G.: Bitslice ciphers and power analysis attacks. In: Schneier, B. (ed.) FSE 2000. LNCS, vol. 1978, pp. 134–149. Springer, Heidelberg (2001)

16. Daemen, J., Peeters, M., Van Assche, G., Rijmen, V.: Nessie proposal: Noekeon (2000)

17. Daemen, J., Rijmen, V.: The wide trail design strategy. In: Honary, B. (ed.) Cryptography and Coding 2001. LNCS, vol. 2260, pp. 222–238. Springer, Heidelberg (2001)

18. Demirci, H., Selçuk, A.A.: A meet-in-the-middle attack on 8-round AES. In: Nyberg, K. (ed.) FSE 2008. LNCS, vol. 5086, pp. 116–126. Springer, Heidelberg (2008)

19. Derbez, P., Fouque, P.-A.: Exhausting demirci-selçuk meet-in-the-middle attacks against reduced-round AES. In: Moriai, S. (ed.) FSE 2013. LNCS, vol. 8424, pp. 541–560. Springer, Heidelberg (2014)

20. Dinu, D., Corre, Y.L., Khovratovich, D., Perrin, L., Großschädl, J., Biryukov, A.: Triathlon of lightweight block ciphers for the internet of things. IACR Cryptology ePrint Archive, 2015:209 (2015)

21. Dinur, I.: Improved differential cryptanalysis of round-reduced speck. Cryptology ePrint Archive, Report 2014/320 (2014). http://eprint.iacr.org/

22. Dunkelman, O., Keller, N., Shamir, A.: Improved single-key attacks on 8-round AES-192 and AES-256. J. Cryptology **28**(3), 397–422 (2015)
23. Eisenbarth, T., et al.: Compact implementation and performance evaluation of block ciphers in ATtiny devices. In: Mitrokotsa, A., Vaudenay, S. (eds.) AFRICACRYPT 2012. LNCS, vol. 7374, pp. 172–187. Springer, Heidelberg (2012)
24. Engels, S., Kavun, E.B., Paar, C., Yalçin, T., Mihajloska, H.: A non-linear/linear instruction set extension for lightweightciphers. In: Nannarelli, A., Seidel, P.-M., Tang, P.T.P. (eds.) 21st IEEE Symposium on Computer Arithmetic, ARITH 2013, Austin, TX, USA, 7–10 April 2013, p. 67–75. IEEE ComputerSociety (2013)
25. Grosso, V., Leurent, G., Standaert, F.-X., Varıcı, K.: LS-designs: bitslice encryption for efficient masked software implementations. In: Cid, C., Rechberger, C. (eds.) FSE 2014. LNCS, vol. 8540, pp. 18–37. Springer, Heidelberg (2015)
26. Guo, J., Peyrin, T., Poschmann, A., Robshaw, M.J.B.: The LED block cipher. In: Preneel, B., Takagi, T. (eds.) CHES 2011. LNCS, vol. 6917, pp. 326–341. Springer, Heidelberg (2011)
27. Jean, J., Nikolic, I., Peyrin, T., Wang, L., Wu, S.: Security analysis of prince. Cryptology ePrint Archive, Report 2015/372 (2015). http://eprint.iacr.org/
28. Karakoç, F., Demirci, H., Karakoç, A.E.: ITUbee: a software oriented lightweight block cipher. In: Avoine, G., Kara, O. (eds.) LightSec 2013. LNCS, vol. 8162, pp. 16–27. Springer, Heidelberg (2013)
29. Khoo, K., Peyrin, T., Poschmann, A., Yap, H.: FOAM: searching for hardware-optimal SPN structures and components with a fair comparison. IACR Cryptology ePrint Archive, 2014:530 (2014)
30. Knudsen, L.R. (ed.): FSE 1999. LNCS, vol. 1636. Springer, Heidelberg (1999)
31. Knudsen, L.R.: The security of feistel ciphers with six rounds or less. J. Cryptology **15**(3), 207–222 (2002)
32. Knudsen, L.R., Leander, G., Poschmann, A., Robshaw, M.J.B.: PRINTcipher: a block cipher for IC-printing. In: Mangard and Standaert [36], pp. 16–32
33. Kocher, P.C., Jaffe, J., Jun, B.: Differential power analysis. In: Wiener, M. (ed.) CRYPTO 1999. LNCS, vol. 1666, pp. 388–397. Springer, Heidelberg (1999)
34. Lai, X.: Higher order derivatives and differential cryptanalysis. In: Blahut, R.E., Costello Jr., D.J., Maurer, U., Mittelholzer, T. (eds.) Communications and Cryptography. The Springer International Series in Engineering and Computer Science, vol. 276, pp. 227–233. Springer, US (1994)
35. Langford, S.K., Hellman, M.E.: Differential-linear cryptanalysis. In: Desmedt, Y.G. (ed.) CRYPTO 1994. LNCS, vol. 839, pp. 17–25. Springer, Heidelberg (1994)
36. Mangard, S., Standaert, F.-X. (eds.): CHES 2010. LNCS, vol. 6225. Springer, Heidelberg (2010)
37. Matsui, M.: Linear cryptanalysis method for DES cipher. In: Helleseth, T. (ed.) EUROCRYPT 1993. LNCS, vol. 765, pp. 386–397. Springer, Heidelberg (1994)
38. Mourouzis, T., Song, G., Courtois, N., Christofii, M.: Advanced differential cryptanalysis of reduced-round simon64/128 using large-round statistical distinguishers. Cryptology ePrint Archive, Report 2015/481 (2015). http://eprint.iacr.org/
39. Saarinen, M.-J.O., Engels, D.W.: A do-it-all-cipher for RFID: design requirements (extendedabstract).IACR Cryptology ePrint Archive, 2012:317 (2012)
40. Soleimany, H.: Self-similarity cryptanalysis of the block cipher itubee. IET Inf. Secur. **9**(3), 179–184 (2014)
41. Standaert, F.-X., Piret, G., Gershenfeld, N., Quisquater, J.-J.: SEA: a scalable encryption algorithm for small embedded applications. In: Domingo-Ferrer, J., Posegga, J., Schreckling, D. (eds.) CARDIS 2006. LNCS, vol. 3928, pp. 222–236. Springer, Heidelberg (2006)

42. Ullrich, M., De Canniere, C., Indesteege, S., Küçük, Ö., Mouha, N., Preneel, B.: Finding optimal bitsliced implementations of 4× 4-bit s-boxes. In: SKEW Symmetric Key Encryption Workshop, Copenhagen, Denmark, pp. 16–17 (2011)
43. Wagner, D.: The boomerang attack. In: Knudsen [30], pp. 156–170
44. Wheeler, D.J., Needham, R.M.: TEA, a tiny encryption algorithm. In: Preneel, B. (ed.) FSE 1994. LNCS, vol. 1008. Springer, Heidelberg (1995)
45. Wu, W., Zhang, L.: LBlock: a lightweight block cipher. In: Lopez, J., Tsudik, G. (eds.) ACNS 2011. LNCS, vol. 6715, pp. 327–344. Springer, Heidelberg (2011)
46. Yang, Q., Hu, L., Sun, S., Qiao, K., Song, L., Shan, J., Ma, X.: Improved differential analysis of block cipher PRIDE. In: Lopez, J., Wu, Y. (eds.) ISPEC 2015. LNCS, vol. 9065, pp. 209–219. Springer, Heidelberg (2015)
47. Zhang, W., Bao, Z., Lin, D., Rijmen, V., Yang, B., Verbauwhede, I.: RECTANGLE: A bit-slice ultra-lightweight block cipher suitable for multiple platforms. IACR Cryptology ePrint Archive, 2014:84 (2014)
48. Zhu, B., Gong, G.: Multidimensional meet-in-the-middle attack and its applications to KATAN32/48/64. Crypt. Commun. **6**(4), 313–333 (2014)

PUF-Based Mutual Multifactor Entity and Transaction Authentication for Secure Banking

Amanda C. Davi Resende$^{(\boxtimes)}$, Karina Mochetti, and Diego F. Aranha

Institute of Computing, University of Campinas (UNICAMP), Campinas, Brazil
amanda@lasca.ic.unicamp.br, {mochetti,dfaranha}@ic.unicamp.br

Abstract. In this work we propose a protocol combining a Physical Unclonable Function (PUF) with Password-based Authenticated Key Exchange (PAKE). The resulting protocol provides mutual multifactor authentication between client and server and establishes a session key between the authenticated parties, important features that were not found simultaneously in the literature of PUF-based authentication. The combination can be adapted to support a panic password which allows the client to notify the server in case of emergency. Moreover, a novel protocol for two-factor transaction authentication is proposed. This ensures that only parties authenticated in the current session can realize valid bank transactions.

Keywords: PUF · PAKE · Multifactor authentication · Secure banking

1 Introduction

One of the main concerns in modern cryptography is that one or both communicating parties can prove its identity to the other party. *Authentication* protocols can be used for this purpose and generally depend on the knowledge of a long cryptographic key of exclusive possession by the legitimate holders. For this reason, it is common to employ a device to store this key securely, since human memory, in most cases, is unable to memorize it without errors. Protocols for Password-based Authenticated Key Exchange (PAKE) relax this requirement to the extent that they require the knowledge of a much shorter key (*password*).

Authentication protocols can be applied to several scenarios, ranging from simply obtaining access to a computer, to securing a bank transaction. The applicability of these protocols in the banking environment is extremely important, since many features are provided to the client via the Internet and ATMs, in which the bank primarily needs to confirm the authenticity of the client's identity. Conversely, the client must verify the authenticity of the bank's identity before providing credentials or sharing financial information. In practice, most

The authors thank Intel Labs for funding the project *"Physical Unclonable Functions for SoC Devices"* in which scope this work was conducted.

© Springer International Publishing Switzerland 2016
T. Güneysu et al. (Eds.): LightSec 2015, LNCS 9542, pp. 77–96, 2016.
DOI: 10.1007/978-3-319-29078-2_5

banking security solutions for client authentication involve a token producing one-time passwords generated by a synchronized timer and/or some keyed function. Server authentication is performed in parallel, through certificates in the SSL/TLS protocol. The main limitations of these client-side solutions are vulnerability against reverse engineering for key extraction, lack of challenge-response mechanisms, and difficult integration with other authentication factors. In this work, we argue that exploring unpredictable physical effects improves security by removing the need to explicitly store secrets that may leak or be captured by an adversary.

Several works in the literature employ Physical Unclonable Functions (PUF) [1,2] for constructing leakage-resilient block ciphers [3], performing device authentication [4], generating cryptographic keys [5], among others. Some works aim to replace the possession of a long-term cryptographic key with a PUF in authentication protocols. Delvaux et al. [6] recently reviewed lightweight authentication protocols and presented desirable requirements and attacks against many protocols in this solution space. Tuyls and Škorić [7] proposed a PUF-based protocol for authentication in banking applications with establishment of a session key. However, this protocol is not secure against server impersonation attacks in a realistic adversarial model, in which the adversary has physical access to the PUF, as shown by Busch et al. [8]. In Sect. 3, we show that the correction proposed by Busch et al. [8] for the Tuyls and Škorić protocol [7] still retains the vulnerability against server impersonation. Another work by Frikken et al. [9] employs a zero-knowledge proof of possession of a PUF for client authentication through a bank-issued device and an additional password. Besides not establishing a session key and offering only client authentication, instead of mutual authentication, this protocol is also vulnerable to offline dictionary attacks, as discussed in Sect. 3. As a result, these protocols cannot be considered secure for a realistic attacker, who has temporary possession of the PUF and colludes with an attacker able to monitor network traffic between client and server.

This paper proposes PUF+PAKE, a secure protocol resulting from the combination between PUF and PAKE. This combination is sound, because the PAKE only requires knowledge of a small shared password, and the PUF output is usually not large enough to be comparable to a cryptographic key. The general construction uses the PUF output as the shared password required by the PAKE, ensuring that the shared session key produced by the PAKE will only be available under possession of the PUF, and improving leakage resistance by eliminating any long-term secrets stored explicitly. The protocol is also protected against dictionary offline attacks by employing the PAKE. In particular, the session key can be used to protect subsequent communications involving financial information of the client. In particular, our protocols provably satisfy the following security requirements: (i) no long-term secret needs to be stored; (ii) a user should be unable to successfully authenticate without his/her device; (iii) a stolen device cannot be used to impersonate the user; (iv) and the protocol must have protection of additional credentials against offline attacks, a property hard to obtain with a lightweight protocol. The contributions of this paper are:

– A server impersonation attack against the Busch *et al.* protocol [8] which shows that the correction suggested by the authors for the protocol by Tuyls and Škorić [7] is not sufficient. This is a new attack not discussed in previous work.
– Dictionary attacks against the protocol proposed by Frikken *et al.* [9] that depend only on the temporary possession of the PUF and observation of a single trace of client-server communication.
– A protocol combining PUF and PAKE for mutual multifactor[1] (using the output of the PUF and the user's password) authentication and session key establishment between authenticated parties. The protocol combines several important features present in other protocols but that were not found together in previous protocols and offers an interesting security trade-off when compared to related work: lower resistance against internal agents, but enhanced security against dictionary attacks. The proposed solution is particularly applicable to the banking sector, where clients are already used to have an additional authentication device. Current devices could then be augmented with a PUF to provide multifactor authentication based on both computational and physical assumptions.
– Formal security analysis of the protocol, considering standard security notions for authenticated key exchange.
– An adaptation of the proposed protocol to allow the client to notify the server in case of emergency.
– A novel protocol for two-factor authentication of bank transactions, requiring knowledge of the session key and a fresh proof of possession for the PUF as authentication factors.

This paper is organized as follows. In Sect. 2, we present the definitions used during the development of this work. In Sect. 3, we show attacks against two known protocols. The proposed protocol and its formal security analysis are described in Sects. 4 and 5, respectively. Section 6 presents a simple adaptation of the protocol to support panic passwords. Section 7 presents our PUF-based solution for transaction authentication and its security analysis. Finally, in Sect. 8, we present the conclusions and point out directions for future work.

2 Preliminary Definitions

2.1 Physical Unclonable Functions

A Physical Unclonable Function [1,2] is usually implemented through an unpredictable physical effect intrinsically linked to each individual instantiation. By assumption, PUFs cannot be easily duplicated or manipulated without changing their behavior considerably. Despite the existence of PUFs with certain security properties being contested in the literature [10–12], our work depends on a suitable choice of a PUF that satisfies rigorous security properties. Although PUF

---

[1] We consider any additional credential as another *authentication factor* (such as biometric information).

behavior may be influenced by environmental factors, such as changes in the temperature, we argue that *there is a good PUF candidate* that can be made reliable enough for actual deployment [13]. In this work, we do not specify a PUF to not lose generality and for simplifying the security analysis. Notice that a strong PUF natively supporting a physically complex challenge-response mechanism is required.

Since these physical effects are rarely completely stable, a PUF can generate slightly different outputs for queries with the same input at two distinct points of time. This noisy aspect hinders the direct use of PUFs in cryptographic applications, but fuzzy extractors [14] enable the conversion of PUF outputs to a close-to-uniform distribution of binary strings. A fuzzy extractor is a pair of probabilistic procedures to generate ($Gen : \{0,1\}^n \to \{0,1\}^\ell \times \{0,1\}^*$) and reproduce ($Rep : \{0,1\}^n \times \{0,1\}^* \to \{0,1\}^\ell$) PUF outputs, where the generation process produces auxiliary information ω for which its output can be recovered with the *Rep* procedure. More formally, we fix a (m, ℓ, t, ϵ)-fuzzy extractor equipped with these procedures that are able to receive any distribution of inputs d with min-entropy m and generate $(r, \omega) \leftarrow Gen(d)$ with statistical difference between (r, ω) and $(\mathbb{U}_\ell, \omega)$ at most negligible ϵ. The correctness property requires the *Rep* procedure to exactly reproduce $r \leftarrow Rep(d', \omega)$ when $dist(d, d') \leq t$.

Given its unpredictable behavior, PUFs can be mathematically modeled as a function $PUF : \{0,1\}^m \to \{0,1\}^n$, for which one can define the following response game against a polynomial adversary $\mathcal{A}$ [9]:

- **Phase 1**: The adversary $\mathcal{A}$ requests and receives responses (r_i, ω_i) for any PUF challenge d_i of its choice.
- **PUF challenge**: $\mathcal{A}$ chooses a PUF challenge d not queried previously and receives auxiliary information ω produced by $Gen(PUF(d))$, but not its output.
- **Phase 2**: $\mathcal{A}$ can do more requests for the PUF for any other PUF challenges different from d.
- **Responde**: Eventually, $\mathcal{A}$ outputs its guess r' for $r = Rep(PUF(d), \omega)$.

The adversary $\mathcal{A}$ wins if $r = r'$. For an unpredictable PUF, $\mathcal{A}$ has the winning probability $Adv_{\mathcal{A}}^{PUF}(\ell) = Pr[r = r']$ as a negligible function of the security parameter ℓ. For the *PUF response game* above, a decisional version can be defined as the *PUF response indistinguishability game* as follows [9]:

- **Enroll**: $\mathcal{A}$ executes the enrollment phase for any value d_i of its choice, receiving the corresponding ω_i. Define the set of such pairs (d_i, ω_i) as $\mathcal{W}$.
- **Phase 1**: $\mathcal{A}$ requests and receives PUF responses r_i for any $(d_i, \omega_i) \in \mathcal{W}$ of its choice.
- **PUF challenge**: $\mathcal{A}$ chooses a PUF challenge d that has been queried during the **Enroll** phase but not in **Phase 1**. A random bit b is chosen. If $b = 0$, $\mathcal{A}$ receives $r = Rep(PUF(d), \omega)$, where $(d, \omega) \in \mathcal{W}$, otherwise it receives a string uniformly chosen from $\{0,1\}^\ell$.
- **Phase 2**: $\mathcal{A}$ is allowed to query the PUF for challenges in $\mathcal{W}$ other than (d, ω).
- **Response**: Eventually, $\mathcal{A}$ outputs a bit b'.

The adversary $\mathcal{A}$ wins if $b = b'$. Let $Adv_{\mathcal{A}}^{PUF-ind} = Pr[b = b']$ be the probability of $\mathcal{A}$ winning the game. It is assumed that $Adv_{\mathcal{A}}^{PUF-ind}(\ell) - \frac{1}{2}$ is also negligible.

2.2   Password-Based Authenticated Key Exchange

A Password-based Authenticated Key Exchange protocol establishes a shared key over an insecure channel depending only on a small shared secret, called a *password*. This is a very useful feature because an extra device is not required for storing a long cryptographic key, but only the ability of human memory to store a short secret.

The first PAKEs arised in the 90s, with the Diffie-Hellman Encrypted Key Exchange (DH-EKE) protocol in 1992 [15] and the Simple Password Exponential Key Exchange (SPEKE) protocol in 1996 [16]. More recently, an important PAKE was proposed as the AuthA protocol [17] that provides the same security properties of previous protocols, but is simpler, has a lower cost of communication and is more versatile. Other PAKE protocols can be found in the literature [18,19], with some based on the AuthA protocol [20,21]. In this paper, we employ a simplified variant of a AuthA protocol [20,22] as choice of PAKE for the purpose of illustration, but any secure PAKE protocol can be used instead.

Semantic Security. Protocols are subject to various attacks, because the message exchanges occur over an insecure channel. The information transmitted is subject to various types of threats such as eavesdropping and tampering. A malicious agent can eavesdrop honest conversation between two entities and record all exchanges of messages for later impersonating one of the two parties. This type of attack is called a *replay* or *repetition attack*.

One way to avoid this type of attack is to ensure that the protocols provide the property of *freshness*. This property ensures that the messages probably belong to the current execution, and do not constitute repetitions of previous messages exchanged in some other honest execution. The freshness property can be obtained in various ways, such as the use of clocks like in the Kerberos authentication system [23,24] or the use of challenges-response operations [25].

Challenge-response mechanisms are commonly used because they do not require clock synchronization between the entities making them robust and popular in cryptographic protocol design. In this method, an entity A sends a random value (challenge) to an entity B and requires this value to be in the next message (response) received from B, and *vice versa*. The challenge must be protected so that it can only be read by the legitimate recipient. This can be done in several ways [16,18,20]. For example, the client can choose a random value $x \in [1, q-1]$ where q is the size of a finite cyclic group $\mathbb{G}$, compute the value of g^x for a generator $g \in \mathbb{G}$ and send it to the server, which in turn, chooses a random value $y \in [1, q-1]$, computes g^y, encrypts the result using a shared secret and sends the result to the client. Afterwards, each party verifies implicitly if the other party received the correct nonce.

Authentication. One of the goals of authenticated key exchange protocols is to ensure the authentication property, which guarantees that the shared cryptographic key is obtained only by parties that satisfy the authentication requirements. The probability of an adversary $\mathcal{A}$ to impersonate the client or the server in a protocol run P is denoted by $Adv_{\mathcal{A},P}^{m-auth}(\ell)$ and thus, the protocol P is said to be *secure* if this probability is negligible in the security parameter ℓ.

3   Protocol Vulnerabilities

In this section we present a dictionary attack against the protocol proposed by Frikken *et al.* [9], which depends only on the temporary possession of the PUF and observation of a single trace of client/server communication. We also present a server impersonation attack against the protocol proposed by Busch *et al.* [8], which shows that the correction suggested by the authors is insufficient. Due to space constraints, we omit the protocol descriptions and refer the reader to the original versions [8,9], conserving most of the notation for compatibility.

3.1   Robust Authentication Using PUFs [9]

In their work, Frikken *et al.* [9] implement client authentication through a bank-issued device and an additional password. They employ a zero-knowledge proof of possession of an integrated PUF (I-PUF), assumed to be inseparably bound to a chip able to perform computation [26]. The protocol does not provide mutual authentication between client and server, and does not establish a session key.

Since the challenge c is fixed, the PUF challenge $d = H(H(c\|pwd), g, P)$ is also fixed, for some auxiliary information P. With possession of the PUF, the adversary computes a set $\mathcal{R}$ of values g^{r_i} corresponding to the PUF challenges $d_i = H(H(c\|pwd_i), g, P)$, where pwd_i is a candidate password (a dictionary attack). Observe that the I-PUF assumption does not allow the attacker to obtain the responses r_i directly, but the result of the computation g^{r_i}, similar to the one performed during the enrollment phase, could be captured without the client's knowledge. Afterwards, the adversary replays to the client the challenge c, the group description $\langle \mathbb{G}_q, q \rangle$, auxiliary information P and nonce N observed in a previous honest communication. The user then sends $(H(c\|pwd), \langle \mathbb{G}_q \rangle, q, P, N)$ to the device that computes $d = H(H(c\|pwd), g, P)$ and executes the *Rep* procedure to obtain r. The device chooses a random value $v \in \mathbb{Z}_q$ and computes $t = g^v$. Following the protocol, the device computes $c = H(g, g^r, t, N)$ and $w = v - c'r \mod q$, and returns c' and w to the client, which sends these values to the adversary. The adversary then computes a set $\mathcal{T}$ of values $t_i = g^w g^{r_i c'}$, because he knows the values of g, w, c', and if $c' = H(g, g^{r_i}, t_i, N)$ for some value of i, learning therefore the user password if $pwd = pwd_i$.

Furthermore, an insider who steals the authentication records in this protocol [9] recovers the value g^r for some user, being able to mount an offline attack by obtaining to the device and making queries to the PUF with several challenges $d_i = H(H(c\|pwd_i), g, P)$ in hope of receiving $g^{r_i} = g^r$ as response.

This observation directly contradicts a security claim against insider attacks stated in the Abstract and Introduction of the paper [9].

3.2 Strong Authentication with PUFs [8]

Tuyls and Škorić proposed a lightweight PUF-based authentication protocol [7] providing session key establishment, but without a security analysis. This protocol is divided into two parts: the first is called the enrollment phase, in which an identifier ID_{PUF} is assigned to the PUF, a random sequence rd is chosen, and a set of challenges $\mathcal{C}$ is created. Then for each challenge $c_i \in \mathcal{C}$, the output s_i and auxiliary information ω_i are generated, forming the sets $\mathcal{S}$ and $\mathcal{W}$, respectively. The memory of the card is initialized with ID_{PUF}, $n = 0$ (number of previous authentication attempts), $m = rd$; and the server stores ID_{PUF}, $n = 0$, $m' = rd$ and $\{\mathcal{C}, \mathcal{W}, \mathcal{S}\}$ in a database.

In [8], Busch *et al.* suggested a different attacker model, introducing physical control of the PUF and of its respective reader to the attacker for a short time. This type of attacker is quite realistic in an authentication setting, for example, in the situation where the employee of a business establishment takes the client's credit card away from the client's view for billing. During this time the employee (adversary) can read data stored in the card memory or perform some queries to obtain challenge-response pairs. Under this attacker model, an attack where the adversary $\mathcal{A}$ can impersonate the server by first choosing a small number of challenges $\mathcal{C}^*$ and computing their respective responses $\mathcal{R}^*$. Afterwards, $\mathcal{A}$ reads the identifier ID_{PUF}, the usage counter n and the current hash value $h^n(m)$ that are stored on the memory of card. With this information, the adversary can compute the value $M^* = h^{n-n^*}(m)$ for $n^* > n$, since the counter n and the hash value $m = h(m)$ are directly stored in memory. Then $\mathcal{A}$ calculates $K_1^* = h(M^*||ID_{PUF})$, generates a random nonce β^* and chooses a challenge $c_i^* \in \mathcal{C}^*$ to generates its respective output s_i together with auxiliary information ω_i. Then $\mathcal{A}$ computes a MAC on $(\alpha||c_i^*||\omega_i^*||\beta^*)$ using the key K_1^*, encrypts the MAC with K_1^* and sends $Enc_{K_1^*}[(\alpha||c_i^*||\omega_i^*||\beta^*)||MAC_{K_1^*}(\alpha||c_i^*||\omega_i^*||\beta^*)]$ to the reader. The reader subsequently calculates $K_1 = (m||ID_{PUF})$, decrypts $Enc_{K_1^*}[(\alpha||c_i^*||\omega_i^*||\beta^*)||MAC_{K_1^*}(\alpha||c_i^*||\omega_i^*||\beta^*)]$ and verifies if the MAC is valid. Thus, since the MAC and decrypted nonce α are valid, the protocol does not abort with an error condition and a symmetric key K^* (respectively K) is established between the reader and the adversary, proving that the adversary can impersonate the server with success.

In order to mitigate this problem, the authors propose the use of Bloom filters [27] or hash trees [28] for storing the subset of challenges which were initially queried by the server in the card memory. This storage is done compactly and does not allow an adversary with limited computational power to gain useful information about the challenges. We shall see now that the additional storage overhead imposed on the client does not solve the vulnerability against server impersonation. Consider an adversary $\mathcal{A}$ who has access to the credit card including the PUF only once. With access to the card, $\mathcal{A}$ can read from the card's memory the identity ID_{PUF}, the usage counter n and the current value of hash of m. Then, the adversary establishes a honest connection with the server to determine α^*, n^*, ID_{PUF}, $Enc_{K_1^*}[T^*||MAC_{K_1^*}(T^*)]$, where $T^* = \alpha^*||c_i'^*||\omega_i^*||\beta^*$. Thus, $\mathcal{A}$ can find the challenge as follows: $\mathcal{A}$ calculates the value of $M^* = h^{n-n^*}(m)$, which is possible, because $\mathcal{A}$ has the usage counter n and the value of $m = H(m)$, computes $K_1^* = h(M^*||ID_{PUF})$ and can thus decrypt $Enc_{K_1^*}[T^*||MAC_{K_1^*}(T^*)]$. With the value of T^*, the adversary can obtain the c_i and ω_i that were used in the eavesdropped conversation. With a valid challenge c_i and its corresponding auxiliary information ω_i, the adversary can impersonate the server successfully in the same way as Busch et al. [8].

This attack works because the client does not verify the reuse of the same c_i. For this "verification" to work, the client must remove each c_i used from the card's memory from either the Bloom filter $\mathcal{B}$ or the hash tree, introducing additional complexity and storage costs [29].

4   PUF+PAKE Protocol

The protocol presented in this section uses the combination of a PUF with a PAKE. The main idea is to use the PUF output as the shared password required by the PAKE. This protocol is divided into two phases: enrollment and authentication. In the enrollment phase, the server uses the PUF to generate tuples (c_i, ω_i, s_i) that will be used during the authentication phase. At this stage the server obtains a challenge d_i generated from a nonce c_i concatenated with the user's password pwd, and then uses the PUF output as input in the generation process Gen, presented in the Sect. 2.1, to obtain the output s_i and auxiliary information ω_i that are stored along with c_i. Notice that other authentication factors can be concatenated to c_i as input to the PUF, as suggested by Frikken et al. [9]. The server discards the tuple (c_i, s_i, ω_i) after using it in an authentication attempt.

The authentication phase is composed of three steps. In the first step, a shared secret is reproduced (which is the output of the PUF queried with the challenge d_i) between client and server. In the second step, a PAKE protocol satisfying the semantic secutity (freshness) and authentication properties is used to establish a new session key. Finally, in the third step, an additional key confirmation step is executed for ensuring mutual authentication, following the generic transform [17].

4.1   Enrollment Phase

The enrollment phase of a client's device $\mathcal{D}$, performed according to Fig. 1, is a step where the server generates and stores challenges for a client and their corresponding responses. We consider $\mathcal{N}$ as a set of nonces $c_i \in \{0,1\}^{128}$, H as a hash function and the notation $c_i \xleftarrow{R} \mathcal{N}$ indicates that c_i was sampled randomly from a set $\mathcal{N}$. We assume that this phase is **physically secured**, because in banking applications there is a trust relationship between client and bank, and

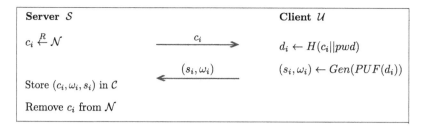

Fig. 1. Physically secure enrollment phase performed to generate a tuple $(c_i, s_i, \omega_i) \in \mathcal{C}$.

the client can participate in this phase in person. Each iteration of the enrollment phase generates a tuple (c_i, s_i, ω_i) in $\mathcal{C}$.

4.2 Authenticated Key Exchange Phase

During the authentication, generation and verification of the session key are performed as in Fig. 2. As mentioned before, this phase is divided into three steps, so the role of each feature, the PUF, the PAKE and the server authentication can be clear. The first part reproduces the value K_i and K'_i used in the combination between PUF and PAKE, in which the server randomly chooses a tuple from set $\mathcal{C}$, assigns s_i as value of his key K_i, sends c_i and ω_i to the client, which in turn,

Server $\mathcal{S}$		Client $\mathcal{U}$ I - PUF
$(c_i, \omega_i, s_i) \overset{R}{\leftarrow} \mathcal{C}$	$\xrightarrow{\quad c_i, \omega_i \quad}$	$d_i \leftarrow H(c_i\|pwd)$
$K_i \leftarrow s_i$		$r_i \leftarrow PUF(d_i)$
		$K'_i \leftarrow Rep(r_i, \omega_i)$
		II - PAKE
$y \overset{R}{\leftarrow} [1, q-1]$		$x \overset{R}{\leftarrow} [1, q-1]$
$Y \leftarrow g^y$	$\xleftarrow{\quad \mathcal{U}, X \quad}$	$X \leftarrow g^x$
$Y^* \leftarrow E_{K_i}(Y)$	$\xrightarrow{\quad \mathcal{S}, Y^* \quad}$	$Y' \leftarrow D_{K'_i}(Y^*)$
$K_\mathcal{S} \leftarrow X^y$		$K_\mathcal{U} \leftarrow (Y')^x$
$H(Auth) \overset{?}{=} H(H_1(\mathcal{U}\|\mathcal{S}\|X\|Y\|K_\mathcal{S}))$	$\xleftarrow{\quad H(Auth) \quad}$	$Auth \leftarrow H_1(\mathcal{U}\|\mathcal{S}\|X\|Y'\|K_\mathcal{U})$
$sk_\mathcal{S} \leftarrow H_0(\mathcal{U}\|\mathcal{S}\|X\|Y\|K_\mathcal{S})$		$sk_\mathcal{U} \leftarrow H_0(\mathcal{U}\|\mathcal{S}\|X\|Y'\|K_\mathcal{U})$
		III - Confirmation
$Auth \leftarrow H_1(\mathcal{U}\|\mathcal{S}\|X\|Y\|K_\mathcal{S})$	$\xrightarrow{\quad Auth \quad}$	$Auth \overset{?}{=} H_1(\mathcal{U}\|\mathcal{S}\|X\|Y'\|K_\mathcal{U})$
Remove (c_i, ω_i, s_i) from $\mathcal{C}$		

Fig. 2. Authenticated key exchange phase, divided into three parts, where we use the secure PAKE protocol.

employs the PUF and password to generate the value for key K_i'. Notice that for the protocol to be performed successfully, K_i must be equal to K_i'.

The second part is flexible and can be performed by any secure PAKE [15,16,20]. In Fig. 2, we use an One-Encryption Key Exchange protocol (OEKE) [20,22], which is a simplified variant of the PAKE protocol proposed by Bellare *et al.* [17] with slight adaptations. This PAKE protocol has proofs of semantic security and authentication properties [20,22], the two necessary requirements for a PAKE protocol to be considered secure. Client authentication happens in this stage.

The third part is also flexible and there are other choices of protocols for key confirmation, as discussed by Jablon [16]. In this part, server authentication occurs and, hence, the mutual authentication between client and server is established. Functions H_0, H_1 represent cryptographic hash functions that can be constructed from a hash function H with different prefixes and E, D represent the encryption and decryption functions of an authenticated symmetric primitive (such as AES-GCM [30]), respectively.

5   Security

At any instant of time, the adversary does not have simultaneous access to all authentication factors, otherwise an attack becomes trivial. Thus, the adversary is unable to capture K_i directly. In order to prevent progressively leaking K_i by continuous interaction, a different tuple in $\mathcal{C}$ is used in each authentication attempt. We assume the bank has enough capacity for storing thousands of nonces c_i, and corresponding responses s_i with auxiliary information ω_i. This is different from other works that assume the existence of a I-PUF [26]. In this case, communication between the PUF and the chip is inaccessible to an attacker and thus cannot be tampered with.

Accordingly, we consider that the adversary $\mathcal{A}$ has temporary access to the PUF when he can perform a limited number of queries to build a set of PUF challenge-response pairs. If the number of authentication attempts is exceeded, the server can impose a limit of time that prevents an online exhaustive search attack in the password without blocking completely the client/server. The adversary also has access to network traffic between the client and server, corresponding to successful authentication attempts.

5.1   Security Intuition

We analyze three scenarios in which the attacker tries to impersonate the client and the server.

Adversary does not have Access to the PUF and to the Password. In this scenario the adversary does not have access to PUF at any moment and does not know the client's password. The adversary only has access to previous honest communication traffic between the client and server.

– **Client and Server**: Since the PAKE is secure and satisfies the freshness property, the probability of an adversary impersonating the client or the server is the same probability as guessing K_i. For this to work, the adversary must be able to guess the response generated by the PUF, which happens with negligible probability, following Sect. 2.1.

Adversary does have Access to the PUF, but does not Know the Password. This scenario is the most realistic for authentication, where the adversary has access to the PUF for a limited time but does not have knowledge of the client's password *pwd*.

– **Client and Server**: The adversary is able to impersonate the client successfully if he can guess the user's password. The probability for the adversary to impersonate the server successfully is considered negligible either if the distribution of passwords is nearly uniform or if there is a limited number of unsuccessful authentication attempts. Notice that the PAKE requires each authentication to involve interaction between client and server, allowing the client and the server to limit the number of unsuccessful attempts. Additionally, recall that the probability distribution of passwords is usually far from uniform, due to the fact that some passwords are commonly chosen and prone to dictionary attacks.

Adversary does not have Access the PUF, but has Access to the Password. In this case the adversary cannot obtain PUF responses, but knows the client's password.

– **Client and Server**: For the adversary to impersonate the client or the server, he needs to guess the output K_i of the PUF under input d_i. The probability of the adversary guessing this value is negligible, according to Sect. 2.1.

5.2   Formal Analysis

A protocol for authenticated key exchange must satisfy two security notions: semantic security (also called freshness property in this context) and the authentication property. The first security notion ensures that the protocol produces a new shared cryptographic key as result. The second security notion ensures that the shared cryptographic key is obtained only for parties who meet certain authentication requirements.

Theorem 1. *The combined PUF+PAKE protocol using a semantically secure PAKE protocol remains semantically secure under the assumptions of the PAKE protocol and assuming a close to uniform statistical distribution of the PUF outputs.*

Proof. A PAKE protocol is semantically secure given a set of computational assumptions and uniformly random choice of a shared password. A PUF modeled as an unpredictable function postprocessed by a fuzzy extractor satisfies this requirement. Therefore, the combined construction only transfers the semantic security and other security properties from the PAKE protocol to the PAKE+PUF protocol under the same computational assumptions that guarantee the semantic security of the PAKE protocol isolated.

Theorem 2. *A polynomial adversary with access to the PUF (with security parameter ℓ) has negligible probability of success in the PUF+PAKE authentication protocol for a previous user enrollment, assuming that H is a random oracle, the PAKE protocol satisfies the property of authentication and passwords are chosen from a set large enough for the probability of guessing to be also negligible.*

Proof. This security reduction is an adaptation of Theorem 1 as seen in the work from [9]. Assuming that an adversary $\mathcal{A}$ with non-negligible success probability exists for the authentication property, we construct an adversary $\mathcal{B}$ for the PUF indistinguishability using $\mathcal{A}$ as a black box. The adversary $\mathcal{B}$ chooses a random challenge c and a random password pwd, computes $d = H(c\|pwd)$ and chooses d as his PUF challenge for the game of indistinguishability. The adversary $\mathcal{B}$ receives a pair (r_b, ω) determined by the random bit b such that $r_0 = Rep(PUF(d), \omega)$ and r_1 is randomly chosen; and instantiates the adversary $\mathcal{A}$ with values (c, ω) giving oracle access to H and PUF. To simulate the random oracle H, $\mathcal{B}$ creates a set of tuples initialized as $H_S = (c\|pwd, h)$ for a randomly chosen value h. When $\mathcal{A}$ queries the oracle with input x, $\mathcal{B}$ verifies if a pair (x, y) already exists in H_S and returns y, otherwise adds (x, h') to set H_S and returns the randomly chosen value h' as result. To simulate the PUF for a query (d', ω'), $\mathcal{B}$ checks if $d = d'$ and returns FAIL if positive. Otherwise, $\mathcal{B}$ returns $(r', \omega') = Gen(d')$ as a result. Thus, $\mathcal{A}$ has a view indistinguishable from the real protocol and eventually produces a proof of authentication for the possibly shared key. If this proof of authentication is correct, $\mathcal{B}$ returns 0 as a result, or an random bit b' otherwise.

First, let's analyze the probability $\Pr[b = b']$. Let F be the event that $\mathcal{B}$ returns FAIL. This event occurs with only negligible probability, since it requires that the adversary $\mathcal{A}$ guess the password pwd or the PUF challenge d to query the PUF. One can divide the remaining case $\Pr[b = b'|\overline{F}]$ for the two values of b:

$$\Pr[b = b'|\overline{F}] = \frac{1}{2}\Pr[b = b'|\overline{F}, b = 0] + \frac{1}{2}\Pr[b = b'|\overline{F}, b = 1].$$

Let G be the event that $\mathcal{A}$ produces a correct proof of authentication. We condition both of the above cases on G. For the case $b = 1$:

$$\Pr[b = b'|\overline{F}, b = 1] = \Pr[b = b'|\overline{F}, b = 1, G]\Pr[G|\overline{F}, b = 1] + \Pr[b = b'|\overline{F}, b = 1, \overline{G}]\Pr[\overline{G}|\overline{F}, b = 1].$$

We have that $\Pr[b = b'|\overline{F}, b = 1, G] = 0$, because $b = 0$ for the event G; $\Pr[b = b'|\overline{F}, b = 1, \overline{G}] = \frac{1}{2}$, because $b = 1$ occurs with 50 % for the event $\overline{G}$, and $\Pr[G|\overline{F}, b = 1]$ is a negligible function by the security of the PAKE protocol. Hence, for some negligible function $\lambda(\ell)$:

$$\Pr[b = b'|\overline{F}, b = 1] > \frac{1}{2} - \lambda(\ell).$$

The case $b = 0$ is similar:

$$\Pr[b = b'|\overline{F}, b = 0] = \Pr[b = b'|\overline{F}, b = 0, G]\Pr[G|\overline{F}, b = 0] + \Pr[b = b'|\overline{F}, b = 0, \overline{G}]\Pr[\overline{G}|\overline{F}, b = 0].$$

Here, $\Pr[b = b'|\overline{F}, b = 0, G] = 1, \Pr[b = b'|\overline{F}, b = 0, \overline{G}] = \frac{1}{2}$ and $\Pr[G|\overline{F}, b = 0] > \frac{1}{f(\ell)}$ for some polynomial f, by the assumption that $\mathcal{A}$ breaks the authentication property with non-negligible probability. Therefore:

$$\Pr[b = b'|\overline{F}, b = 0] > \frac{1}{f(\ell)} + \frac{1}{2} \cdot \left(1 - \frac{1}{f(\ell)}\right) = \frac{1}{2} + \frac{1}{2f(\ell)}.$$

Substituting the terms, we have:

$$\Pr[b = b'|\overline{F}] > \frac{1}{2}\left(\frac{1}{2} + \frac{1}{2f(\ell)}\right) + \frac{1}{2}\left(\frac{1}{2} - \lambda(\ell)\right).$$

In summary, if we have $\Pr[b = b'|\overline{F}] - \frac{1}{2}$ non-negligible then, $\Pr[b = b'] - \frac{1}{2}$ is also non-negligible and the attacker $\mathcal{A}$ must exist, contradicting the hypothesis that the PAKE protocol is secure.

5.3 Checklist Analysis

Delvaux *et al.* [6] were the pioneers in enumerating a set of ten requirements that PUF-based protocols should possess. In the following, we do a brief analysis about how our protocol fits into each one these requirements.

1. **Complete Specification**: The PUF+PAKE protocol has a complete unambiguous specification with graphical representation of both enrollment and authentication phases, showing details of all computations and exchanged messages between client and server. Also, we loosely recommend a PUF candidate [13], noting that the protocol can be used with any PUF satisfying the security properties.
2. **Leakage Resilience**: The PUF+PAKE protocol does not impose secure data storage on the client, hence, leakage of information does not occur. Data is only stored at server-side in a non-volatile memory that is assumed secure.
3. **Able to Handle Noisiness**: The PUF+PAKE protocol handles noisiness and also non-uniform distribution of PUF outputs using a fuzzy extractor, as discussed in Sect. 2.1.
4. **Counteracting Strong PUF Modeling Attacks**: The adversary is unable to capture PUF challenges, because the challenges d_i are not transmitted or stored in the server. The challenges are correctly generated only if the adversary knows the user's password. Hence, collecting pairs (d_i, s_i) for mounting machine learning modeling attacks requires physical access to the PUF.
5. **Strong PUF**: The PUF+PAKE protocol requires a strong PUF providing a large set of challenges. Hence, we can use any PUF that has response space expansion.

6. **Low-Cost and Resource-Constrained**: The PUF+PAKE protocol only requires symmetric primitives and few public key operations. The latter can be instantiated with elliptic curves to benefit from efficient implementations and reduced parameter sizes.
7. **Easy-to-Instantiate**: The PUF+PAKE protocol is easy-to-instantiate because we designed the protocol to not depend on a specific PUF, but any PUF that satisfies the security requirements.
8. **Resistance Against Protocols Attacks**: The PUF+PAKE protocol has a formal analysis of security (Sect. 5.2) and no attacks are currently known.
9. **Scalability:** In banking applications, identification is easy and clients provide the bank branch and account number before performing the authentication protocol.
10. **On the Mutual Authentication Order**: In PUF+PAKE client authentication happens first, because in banking applications client impersonation is more common. Changing the order of the messages at the end of the second part (PAKE) is enough to adapt the protocol for applications in which the server authenticates first.

5.4   Comparison

Considering the scenarios discussed in Sect. 5.1 the protocol developed by Frikken *et al.* [9] has the same security properties as the protocol proposed in this paper, with a notable exception when the adversary has temporary access to the PUF, but does not know the user's password. In the PUF+PAKE protocol, the adversary successfully impersonates the client or the server under these circumstances with negligible probability for each authentication attempt. In Sect. 3.1, we presented a server impersonation attack that allows the server to discover the user password with higher probability. This happens because the adversary only needs to impersonate the server one time to check if the user password is included in the set of candidate passwords queried through the PUF and the remaining work can be done offline. The PAKE in our protocol forces the adversary to impersonate the client/server to check a single password candidate per authentication attempt, further allowing either the client or the server to monitor the malicious behavior of the other party. Comparing our protocol to Frikken *et al.* provides an interesting security trade-off: while our protocol provides stronger resistance against dictionary attacks, an insider attack is easier to mount in PUF+PAKE because the PUF response is stored in the server.

Delvaux *et al.* [6] present many attacks against lightweight authentication protocols. Our attack in Sect. 3.2 against the protocol proposed by Tuyls and Škorić [7] is new, and illustrates the inherent limitations of lightweight protocols for our target application. In short, lightweight protocols are not designed to receive and protect additional credentials (multifactor feature) against offline attacks. For attaining this goal, more computationally expensive protocols forcing client-server interaction in every authentication attempt are needed.

6   Emergency

Panic passwords are mechanisms that allow users to use a special kind of password, called *panic password*, to signal the server (or any other communicant party) that his password is being inserted as a result of coercive action [31]. They are also known as help passwords or codes in the literature. A popular example of the use of panic passwords was employed in older versions of the RSA SecurID device [32]. This device is intended to perform two-factor user authentication for accessing network resources using both a personal identification number and a one-time password generated by the token.

The protocol shown in Fig. 2 can easily support panic passwords, by using an adaptation of a known technique [9]. There are two valid passwords for each user, both with a fixed-length shared prefix (pwd_1) and distinct suffixes that indicate normal situation (pwd_2) and emergency (pwd_3). Let pwd^* represent one of the two valid suffixes. The server is able to distinguish between the two situations by checking what session key was derived by the protocol execution. The enrollment phase undergoes some changes and proceeds as shown in Fig. 3.

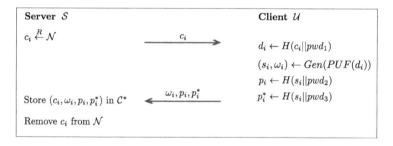

Fig. 3. Physically secure panic enrollment phase performed to generate a tuple $(c_i, \omega_i, p_i, p_i^*) \in \mathcal{C}^*$.

In the authentication phase, the roles for the client and server are reversed in the illustrative PAKE, which causes no security impact when the generic transformation of mutual authentication is applied [17]. This reversion is needed to transfer the encryption step to the client, which will send the encryption under one of the two possible keys, indicating normal or emergency situation. The server can then decrypt the received message and check what kind of situation the next message from the client corresponds.

When the server detects an emergency situation, it executes the protocol normally, so that the adversary does not notice that the panic password has been used, therefore, both executions must be *indistinguishable*. In this case, the server can send a signal to the authorities, warning that something suspicious is happening or even limit the amount of money available for withdrawal.

In most cases, when there is no emergency situation, the server continues normally and sends its message to mutual authentication. The resulting protocol is described in Fig. 4. Naturally, when notification of emergency is desirable, all clients in any situation should use the adjusted protocol so that normal instances of the protocol have the same communication pattern as emergency situations. The formal analysis of security of this variant follows directly from the formal analysis of the Sect. 5.2, since only simple modifications were required in the protocol.

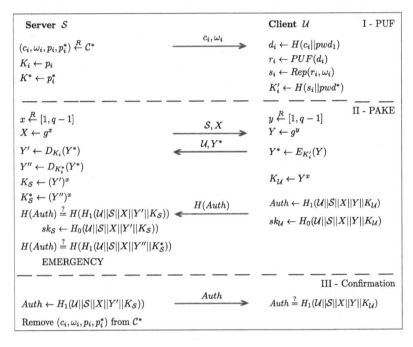

Fig. 4. Authenticated key exchange phase with support for panic passwords, where pwd^* represent one of the two valid suffixes (normal (pwd_2) or emergency (pwd_3)) situation).

7 Transaction Authentication Protocol

In banking applications, ensuring that both parties, server and client, are authenticated in the beginning of a session is not enough. It is also important to ensure that the client remains connected and with access to the authentication factors at the time when transactions are performed. Protocols with this feature are called transaction authentication protocols. The Fig. 5 shows our transaction authentication protocol, to be executed for each new transaction in a session. The protocol is linked to the PUF+PAKE protocol shown in Sect. 4, since the same session key is used here (sk_S and $sk_\mathcal{U}$) to ensure that the transaction is indeed occurring in the current session. For this reason, it is a two-factor transaction authentication protocol, implicitly authenticating participation in the current session and access to the previously enrolled PUF.

The protocol is performed as follows: first, the client encrypts the transaction data T with the session key $(sk_\mathcal{U})$ and then sends it to the server. The server then decrypts the transaction with its session key $(sk_\mathcal{S})$, randomly chooses a tuple on the set $\mathcal{C}$ and generates a new key K_j based on the concatenation of the PUF output (for a new nonce c_j and consequently a new d_j to the client) and the session key. The server then chooses a 4-digit one-time password z, that is concatenated with T' as $(z\|T')$ and then encrypted using K_j, and sent together with the nonce c_j and the auxiliary information ω_j. The client compares the received transaction data with the requested transaction, and if positive calculates the value of K'_j using the PUF, his password pwd and the session key $sk_\mathcal{U}$. Then, the client decrypts the message Z^* and returns the decrypted one-time password for verification[2]. Finally, the server remove the tuple (c_i, ω_i, s_i) from $\mathcal{C}$.

To reduce the size of $\mathcal{C}$, one can employ the same tuple (c_i, ω_i, s_i) on all transactions in the same session, one for entity authentication and another for transaction authentication. Because of this, only two tuples of $\mathcal{C}$ are necessary per session. In the Fig. 5, E and D are defined as previously.

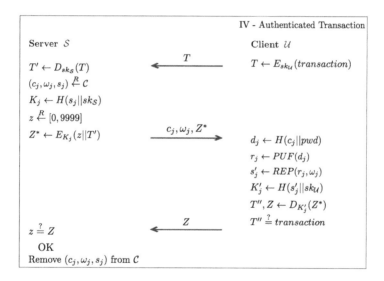

Fig. 5. Transaction authentication protocol using the same tuple (c_i, ω_i, s_i) on all transactions in the same session.

7.1   Security Analysis

The security analysis is restricted to the scenario where the adversary does not have access to the PUF. Consider that the PUF+PAKE protocol was performed

---

[2] This is the only user interaction with the protocol, besides making the transaction request. The other operations are done by *software*.

successfully and securely, and consequently the session key is only known by authenticated parties. Assume that the adversary does not have access to the PUF and/or user's password at any moment. Otherwise, and if the adversary had authenticated successfully in the PUF+PAKE protocol, an attack is trivial. The adversary thus only has access to previous traffic of honest communications between the client and server.

For an adversary to impersonate the client successfully, he would have to guess the values of $sk_{\mathcal{U}}$ (client's session key) and the output of the PUF for the challenge d_j that can only be computed if the adversary knows the client's password. As the PUF+PAKE protocol is secure, the advantage of the adversary in guessing $sk_{\mathcal{S}}$ is negligible and the probability of guessing the output of the PUF, according to Sect. 2.1, is also negligible. Thus, the advantage of the adversary successfully impersonating the client is negligible.

8   Conclusions and Future Work

In this paper, we proposed a flexible authentication protocol based on a combination of PUF with PAKE that provides mutual authentication between the client and the server establishing a session key, some of the main features for a useful authentication protocol. This protocol can be used in various environments, for example authentication in banking applications, in which the session key can be used to authenticate subsequent transactions or protect financial information in transit. In particular, the PUF+PAKE combination improves the state of the art of authentication solutions based on PUFs, according to the formal analysis presented. Additionally, a variant of the protocol is proposed to support panic passwords for emergency situations where the client is compelled to deliver the PUF and reveal his password, and a two-factor authentication solution for transaction authentication is discussed. We also presented server impersonation attacks on two PUF-based authentication protocols proposed in the literature, motivating the need for mutual authentication in such applications.

For future work, we plan to develop an alternate protocol that provides security against both insider agents and offline dictionary attacks, satisfying both of the security properties. Finally, it is important to implement the proposal with a real PUF candidate for obtaining performance/reliability measures and studying its practical feasibility.

References

1. Pappu, R., Recht, B., Taylor, J., Gershenfeld, N.: Physical one-way functions. Science **97**, 2026–2030 (2002)
2. Gassend, B., Clarke, D., van Dijk, M., Devadas, S.: Silicon physical random functions. In: Proceedings of the 9th ACM Conference on Computer and Communications Security (CCS 2002), pp. 148–160. ACM (2002)
3. Armknecht, F., Maes, R., Sadeghi, A.-R., Sunar, B., Tuyls, P.: Memory leakage-resilient encryption based on physically unclonable functions. In: Matsui, M. (ed.) ASIACRYPT 2009. LNCS, vol. 5912, pp. 685–702. Springer, Heidelberg (2009)

4. Suh, G.E., Devadas, S.: Physical unclonable functions for device authentication and secret key generation. In: Proceedings of the 44th Annual Design Automation Conference (DAC 2007), pp. 9–14. ACM (2007)
5. Maes, R., Van Herrewege, A., Verbauwhede, I.: PUFKY: a fully functional PUF-based cryptographic key generator. In: Prouff, E., Schaumont, P. (eds.) CHES 2012. LNCS, vol. 7428, pp. 302–319. Springer, Heidelberg (2012)
6. Delvaux, J., Gu, D., Peeters, R., Verbauwhede, I.: A Survey on Lightweight Entity Authentication with Strong PUFs. COSIC Internal Report (2015). http://www.cosic.esat.kuleuven.be/publications/article-2497.pdf
7. Tuyls, P., Škorić, B.: Strong authentication with physical unclonable functions. In: Petković, M., Jonker, W. (eds.) Security, Privacy, and Trust in Modern Data Management Data-Centric Systems and Applications, pp. 133–148. Springer, Heidelberg (2007)
8. Busch, H., Katzenbeisser, S., Baecher, P.: PUF-based authentication protocols – revisited. In: Youm, H.Y., Yung, M. (eds.) WISA 2009. LNCS, vol. 5932, pp. 296–308. Springer, Heidelberg (2009)
9. Frikken, K.B., Blanton, M., Atallah, M.J.: Robust authentication using physically unclonable functions. In: Samarati, P., Yung, M., Martinelli, F., Ardagna, C.A. (eds.) ISC 2009. LNCS, vol. 5735, pp. 262–277. Springer, Heidelberg (2009)
10. Maes, R.: An accurate probabilistic reliability model for silicon PUFs. In: Bertoni, G., Coron, J.-S. (eds.) CHES 2013. LNCS, vol. 8086, pp. 73–89. Springer, Heidelberg (2013)
11. Helfmeier, C., Boit, C., Nedospasov, D., Seifert, J.-P.: Cloning physically unclonable functions. In: International Symposium on Hardware-Oriented Security and Trust (HOST 2013), pp. 1–6. IEEE, June 2013
12. Katzenbeisser, S., Kocabaş, U., Rožić, V., Verbauwhede, I., Sadeghi, A.-R., Wachsmann, C.: PUFs: myth, fact or busted? a security evaluation of physically unclonable functions (PUFs) cast in silicon. In: Prouff, E., Schaumont, P. (eds.) CHES 2012. LNCS, vol. 7428, pp. 283–301. Springer, Heidelberg (2012)
13. Holcomb, D.E., Fu, K.: Bitline PUF: building native challenge-response PUF capability into any SRAM. In: Batina, L., Robshaw, M. (eds.) CHES 2014. LNCS, vol. 8731, pp. 510–526. Springer, Heidelberg (2014)
14. Dodis, Y., Reyzin, L., Smith, A.: Fuzzy extractors: how to generate strong keys from biometrics and other noisy data. In: Cachin, C., Camenisch, J.L. (eds.) EUROCRYPT 2004. LNCS, vol. 3027, pp. 523–540. Springer, Heidelberg (2004)
15. Bellovin, S.M., Merritt, M.: Encrypted key exchange: password-based protocols secure against dictionary attacks. In: Proceedings of the 1992 IEEE Computer Society Symposium on Research in Securityand Privacy, pp. 72–84. IEEE, May 1992
16. Jablon, D.P.: Strong password-only authenticated key exchange. ACM SIGCOMM Comput. Commun. Rev. **26**, 5–26 (1996)
17. Bellare, M., Rogaway, P.: The AuthA Protocol for Password-based Authenticated Key Exchange, Technical report, Citeseer (2000)
18. Boyko, V., MacKenzie, P.D., Patel, S.: Provably secure password-authenticated key exchange using Diffie-Hellman. In: Preneel, B. (ed.) EUROCRYPT 2000. LNCS, vol. 1807, pp. 156–171. Springer, Heidelberg (2000)
19. Katz, J., Ostrovsky, R., Yung, M.: Efficient password-authenticated key exchange using human-memorable passwords. In: Pfitzmann, B. (ed.) EUROCRYPT 2001. LNCS, vol. 2045, pp. 475–494. Springer, Heidelberg (2001)

20. Bresson, E., Chevassut, O., Pointcheval, D.: Proof of security for password-based key exchange (IEEE P1363 AuthA Protocol and Extensions). ACMCCS **3**, 241–250 (2003)

21. Abdalla, M., Catalano, D., Chevalier, C., Pointcheval, D.: Efficient two-party password-based key exchange protocols in the UC framework. In: Malkin, T. (ed.) CT-RSA 2008. LNCS, vol. 4964, pp. 335–351. Springer, Heidelberg (2008)

22. Bresson, E., Chevassut, O., Pointcheval, D.: Security proofs for an efficient password-based key exchange. In: Proceedings of the 10th ACM Conference on Computer and Communications Security (CCS 2003), pp. 241–250. ACM (2003)

23. Miller, S.P., Neuman, B.C., Schiller, J.I., Saltzer, J.H.: Kerberos Authentication and Authorization System. In: Project Athena Technical Plan, Citeseer (1987)

24. Steiner, J.G., Neuman, B.C., Schiller, J.I.: Kerberos: an authenticationservice for open network systems. In: USENIX Winter, pp. 191–202 (1988)

25. Lam, K.-Y., Gollmann, D.: Freshness assurance of authentication protocols. In: Deswarte, Y., Eizenberg, G., Quisquater, J.-J. (eds.) ESORICS 1992. LNCS, vol. 648, pp. 261–271. Springer, Heidelberg (1992)

26. Tuyls, P., Batina, L.: RFID-tags for anti-counterfeiting. In: Pointcheval, D. (ed.) CT-RSA 2006. LNCS, vol. 3860, pp. 115–131. Springer, Heidelberg (2006)

27. Bloom, B.H.: Space/time trade-offs in hash coding with allowable errors. Commun. ACM **13**, 422–426 (1970)

28. Merkle, R.C.: Protocols for public key cryptosystems. In: IEEE Symposium on Security and Privacy, vol. 1109, pp. 122–134 (1980)

29. Fan, L., Cao, P., Almeida, J., Broder, A.Z.: Summary cache: a scalable wide-area web cache sharing protocol. IEEE/ACM Trans. Network. (TON) **8**, 281–293 (2000)

30. Dworkin, M.J.: SP 800-38D. Recommendation for block cipher modes ofoperation: Galois/Counter Mode (GCM) and GMAC (2007). http://csrc.nist.gov/publications/nistpubs/800-38D/SP-800-38D.pdf

31. Clark, J., Hengartner, U.: Panic passwords: authenticating under duress. In: Proceedings of the 3rd Conference on Hot Topics in Security (HOTSEC2008). USENIX Association, Berkeley, pp. 8:1–8:6 (2008)

32. Popp, N., Bajaj, S., Hallam-Baker, P.: Hybrid authentication. US Patent App. 10/864,501, January 2005

On Lightweight Security Enforcement in Cyber-Physical Systems

Yanjiang Yang[1]([✉]), Jiqiang Lu[1], Kim-Kwang Raymond Choo[2],
and Joseph K. Liu[3]

[1] Institute for Infocomm Research, Singapore, Singapore
{yyang,jlu}@i2r.a-star.edu.sg
[2] School of Information Technology and Mathematical Sciences,
University of South Australia, Adelaide, Australia
raymond.choo@fulbrightmail.org
[3] Faculty of Information Technology, Monash University, Melbourne, Australia
joseph.liu@monash.edu

Abstract. Cyber-physical systems (CPS) are a key component in industrial control systems (ICS), which are widely used in the critical infrastructure sectors. The increasing reliance on CPS, however, affords exploitative opportunities for malicious actors targeting our critical infrastructure. The real-time requirement of control systems, coupled with the deployment of resource-constrained field devices, complicate efforts to secure our critical infrastructure. A key technical limitation for security solutions is that they should be lightweight. While lightweight cryptography is useful to some extent, enforcement of asymmetric key cryptographic primitives in control systems is known to be problematic. In this paper, we suggest investigating the enforcement of lightweight security solutions in ICS from a different perspective. Rather than focusing on designing lightweight (individual) cryptographic primitives, we propose taking a whole-of-system approach to (1) achieve system/collective lightweightness, (2) outsource expensive computations from resource-constrained field devices to neighboring devices and equipments that have more computational capacity, and (3) selectively protect critical data (partial/selective protection of Data of Interest).

1 Introduction

Cyber-physical systems (CPS) are engineered systems where the computer-based subsystem controls and monitors the field devices (which form the physical subsystem). Field devices provide measurements and operational data to the computer-based control subsystem. CPS form the core of industrial control systems (ICS), which are the backbone of many aspects of the critical infrastructure sectors, particularly in technologically advanced countries. Examples of critical infrastructure sectors include the 16 critical infrastructure sectors identified by the United States Department of Homeland Security (http://www.dhs.gov/critical-infrastructure-sectors).

© Springer International Publishing Switzerland 2016
T. Güneysu et al. (Eds.): LightSec 2015, LNCS 9542, pp. 97–112, 2016.
DOI: 10.1007/978-3-319-29078-2_6

There are two broad categories of ICS, namely: distributed control systems (DCS) and supervisory control and data acquisition (SCADA) systems [48]. DCS are generally used in a small geographic area, such as a single power generation plant. SCADA systems, on the other hand, are typically deployed in a much larger, geographically dispersed area, such as a power grid. While both categories differ in scale and complexity, DCS and SCADA perform similar control and data collection functionalities. Figure 1 shows the basic architecture of a SCADA system – the control center commands and monitors the remote field devices through communication networks, and the field devices send measurements/operational data back to the control center.

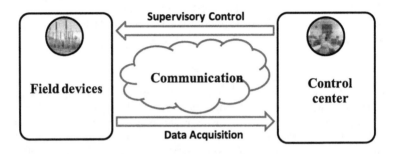

Fig. 1. Basic architecture of SCADA

ICS (and CPS) will be increasingly open, coordinated, distributed, and interconnected. Laplante, Michael and Voas [33] remarked that "providing assurance that critical infrastructures and the information infrastructure on which they rely are trustworthy is challenging [due to their] interdependence when they are integrated vertically (such as the electric power grid in North America) or horizontally (as with emergency services relying on transportation systems) into systems of systems". Therefore, guaranteeing the security of ICS (and CPS) is of paramount importance [30,40,43].

There have been recent incidents of ICS being reportedly targeted by both cyber criminals and nation state actors. One of the most high-profile incidents is Stuxnet - a malware targeting SCADA systems in Iran's nuclear facilities. Subsequent investigations indicated that this attack was the work of the United States and Israel [44]. Unsurprisingly, critical infrastructure resilience and protection have been identified by countries, such as Australia and United States, as national security priorities [14,15].

Cardenas et al. [8] outlined the various challenges in enforcing security measures in ICS. For example, ICS needs to be able to send commands to field devices in real-time to carry out critical functions. It is also essential to guarantee the real-time acquisition of the field data by the control system for monitoring purposes. Therefore, security solutions for ICS must be efficient, and satisfy the real-time requirement. However, field devices (e.g. sensors, actuators, valves, switches, and brakes) and equipments used in such a setting are typically resource constrained (e.g. computation, communication and storage). In addition, field devices are usually operated through remote terminal units (RTUs) and programmable logic controllers (PLCs) at the field. Both RTU and PLC are microprocessor-controlled electronic devices that act as the interface between the field devices and the control system. Although RTUs and PLCs are typically equipped with industry-grade processors and installed with several MBs of memory, these devices do not have the computational capacity necessary for running full-fledged security solutions without affecting performance.

Security solutions for ICS must be *lightweight*, and a natural solution is to use cryptographic primitives which provide fundamental security features, such as confidentiality, authenticity, and non-repudiation. Considerable research efforts have been expended in designing lightweight cryptographic primitives, both symmetric (see [2, 4, 20–22, 27, 28, 47]) and asymmetric (see [16, 18, 23, 29, 34–38]), suitable to be deployed in systems, such as ICS. The design of lightweight cryptographic primitives typically involves tradeoffs among security, cost, and performance [41]. A good design would strike a fine balance among these three metrics, and at the same time fulfill the needs of the underlying application.

1.1   Contributions

While advocating the ongoing study of (monolithic) lightweight cryptographic primitives, we propose to investigate lightweight security enforcement in ICS from a broader perspective. More specifically, rather than solely focusing on individual cryptographic primitives, we posit that it is also important to achieve "system/collective lightweightness" without compromising on either security or efficiency. To achieve this aim, we make the following propositions.

1. Proposition 1 (System/Collective Lightweightness): We consider cryptographic primitives collectively, seeking to understand lightweightness beyond individual cryptographic primitives. The rationale is that cryptographic primitives are not deployed in isolation and they are interconnected to attain certain functionalities. Therefore, rather than seeking to achieve the lightweightness of individual primitives, it would be more sensical to aim at achieving system lightweightness.
2. Proposition 2 (Outsourcing of Expensive Computations): To achieve lightweight security enforcement, we need to leverage the architecture of the underlying control system(s). In particular, this idea relates to offloading computationally expensive security enforcement workload from the resource-constrained devices to more powerful devices or equipments in the vicinity. In a SCADA system, for example, there is usually a slave workstation performing local control/monitoring and data collection in a geographic area. Such a slave workstation is a potential powerful-device candidate to the resource-constrained devices within its territorial area.
3. Proposition 3 (Selective Protection of Data of Interest): The data sent from the side of field devices to the control subsystem may be large in quantity; if protected (e.g. encrypted) in entirety, then it may fail to meet the real-time

requirement of the underlying system. To alleviate this problem, we suggest a partial protection strategy, e.g., instead of encrypting all data needed to be communicated, the field devices can choose certain segments of the data (Data of Interest) to encrypt while leaving the remaining data unprotected. The objective of the partial protection strategy is to reduce the number of security enforcement operations (e.g. encryption) to be committed by the field devices, so as to attain better system performance.

1.2 Organization

The remaining of the paper is organized as follows. Section 2 reviews related work. In Sects. 3, 4 and 5, we discuss in detail our approaches/strategies mentioned above for security enforcement in CPS, respectively. Section 6 concludes the paper.

2 Related Work

Historically, ICS, such as SCADA, were stand-alone systems and not connected to the Internet. Such systems are typically designed to achieve reliability and performance, rather than security. Increasingly, ICS are connected to corporate networks and the Internet. Consequently, they are being exposed to threats and vulnerabilities that they are ill-equipped to protect against. This situation is exacerbated by the fact that ICS is now tightly integrated into business and economic processes [42].

In recent years, the research and practitioner communities and international organizations (e.g. American Gas Association, National Institute of Standards and Technology, Centre for the Protection of National Infrastructure, North American Electric Reliability Corporation, International Electrotechnical Commission, and IEEE) have published international standards, guidelines, and best practices, in an attempt to secure ICS, particularly for the critical infrastructure sectors. The majority of existing international standards provide guidance on general security protection for ICS, and we refer the interested reader to [10,25,46] for an overview and comparative studies of existing standards and initiatives.

Wright et al. [51] proposed a low latency Cyclic Redundancy Checks (CRC) mechanism to ensure the integrity of SCADA communications, which was included in the first draft of AGA standard [1]. This scheme was later found to be vulnerable by Wang et al. [48]. Wang et al. [48] then presented a suite of security mechanisms for SCADA, which include point-to-point secure channels, authenticated broadcast channels, and authenticated emergency channels. These mechanisms were built on symmetric key cryptographic primitives.

It is not a surprise that symmetric key cryptographic primitives have been proposed to protect control systems, as symmetric key cryptographic primitives achieve better performance relative to asymmetric key cryptographic primitives. Further, *lightweight* symmetric key cryptographic primitives have also been the subject of research inquiry. For example, the international standard, ISO/IEC 29192-2 [28], recommends two lightweight block ciphers, while ISO/IEC 29192-5 is an on-going initiative in standardizing lightweight cryptographic hash functions. A number of lightweight cryptographic primitives suitable for resource-constrained wireless sensors have also been presented, such as the block ciphers Katan & Kantan [9], Kline [20], Led [22], Piccolo [47], Prince [4], and Simon & Speck [7]. A benchmarking exercise was undertaken in [19], which reported performance (on certain resource-constrained device) of several lightweight block ciphers. Additional specially-crafted lightweight hash functions include Quark [2], Keccak [32] and LHash [53].

Symmetric key cryptographic primitives may have better performance, but they alone are not adequate for security enforcement in ICS. In a typical system, we would require both symmetric and asymmetric cryptographic primitives to achieve the necessary security. For example, asymmetric cryptographic primitives can address the shortcomings of symmetric key cryptographic primitives, such as scalability in key establishment, and provision of non-repudiation. In a number of studies, researchers have attempted to deploy asymmetric key cryptography in ICS for sectors, such as smart grid (see [3,17,39,52]), and on resource-constrained devices (see [5,11,54]). In addition, three entity authentication mechanisms using asymmetric key cryptographic primitives [35] were standardized in ISO/IEC 29192-4 (Information technology – Security techniques – Lightweight cryptography – Part 4: Mechanisms using asymmetric techniques).

Despite these initiatives, designing lightweight cryptographic primitives suitable for real-world ICS deployment remains a research challenge, mainly due to the operational challenges in such an environment. This is a gap that we aim to address in this paper. We are partly inspired by the concept of computation outsourcing – resource-constrained devices utilizing computational resources from other powerful machines, such as cloud servers, for computationally expensive operations [12,24,50]. Therefore, in this paper, we explore the feasibility of such an approach in achieving lightweight implementation of asymmetric key cryptographic primitives in ICS by leveraging the underlying architecture.

3   System/Collective Lightweightness

Existing efforts focus on designing individual lightweight cryptographic primitives. This is necessary, but alone cannot provide a comprehensive solution. In practice, to realize a certain security functionality, several cryptographic primitives are required. For example, an entity authentication protocol often involves both asymmetric key primitive (e.g. digital signature and asymmetric encryption), and symmetric key primitives (e.g. hash function and pseudo-random function) [13].

Therefore, in our first approach to achieve lightweight security enforcement in ICS, we consider cryptographic primitives collectively. In signcryption, for example, the encryptor uses a public key encryption scheme followed by a digital signature scheme. This allows the encryptor to trivially achieve non-repudiation, confidentiality and integrity. Signcryption is intended as a more effective alternative to the combination of public key encryption and digital signature schemes.

Proposition 1. *In addition to achieving lightweightness of individual crypto-graphic primitives, system designer should attempt to achieve system/collective lightweightness.*

We use a lightweight implementation of crypto-GPS [29] as an example to explain Proposition 1. The crypto-GPS offers a range of parameters for different security-performance trade-offs. The example we are using, adapted from [41], is about the implementation of an elliptic curve-based variant of crypto-GPS. This particular implementation generates smaller keysizes.

Figure 2 describes the implementation, where h denotes the length of the hash function, HASH.

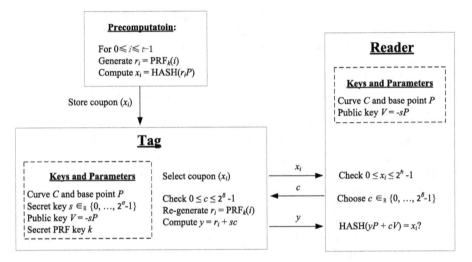

Fig. 2. Lightweight implementation of crypto-GPS

The implementation is discussed in the context of a RFID Tag and a Reader. To achieve a lightweight implementation, several optimization measures are taken. The first is a storage-computation trade-off that uses t coupons; each consists of a pair $(r_i; x_i)$ for $1 \leq i \leq t$. These coupons are stored on the Tag before deployment. The on-tag computation is, therefore, reduced to $y = r_i + (s \cdot c)$, where c is a challenge of δ bits long provided by the Reader and s is a σ-bit secret that is stored on the Tag.

The second optimization measure is the Low Hamming Weight challenge. Specifically, to avoid the computationally expensive $(\sigma \times \delta)$-bit multiplication, the multiplication is "transformed" into a series of simple additions. To do this, we would need to transform the challenge c into a Low Hamming Weight (LHW) challenge, such that at least $\sigma - 1$ zero bits are between two subsequent 1 bits. When using binary representations of the multiplicands, it is easy to see that multiplications can be performed using the basic Shift-And-Add multiplication algorithm[1]. Therefore, a multiplication operation can be reduced to simple shifting and addition operations.

A compact encoding of the Low Hamming Weight challenge represents the third optimization. The basic idea is that since the challenge is sparse (most of the bits are zeros), it is possible to use less bits to encode the original challenge. Indeed, the encoding scheme in [41] allows one to use only 40 bits to encode the 848-bit challenge c.

To achieve a security level of 80 bits, Poschmann [41] uses the following parameters:

- $\sigma = |s| = 160$, and
- a challenge c of length $\delta = |c| = 848$ with a Hamming weight of 5.

These parameters enable crypto-GPS to achieve a soundness level equivalent to a probability of impersonation of 2^{-32}.

We acknowledge the effectiveness of the above discussed optimization measures. However, in the context of our proposed Proposition 1, the above implementation fails to consider the hash function, HASH. In fact, the hash function directly relates to the soundness of the protocol. We remark that with a soundness level of 2^{-32}, it is actually wasteful to use regular hash function with a digest size of 128 bits, 160 bits or more. A hash function with a smaller digest size could suffice to meet the soundness level of 2^{-32}. In addition, hash functions with small digest sizes are much easier to be designed efficiently. This is evident from the observation that ISO/IEC 29192-5 standardizes lightweight hash functions of 80 or 128 bits, but lightweight hash functions of 160 bits and above are still not achieveable.

In this particular case, the choice of HASH does not affect the performance of Tag. However, the choice of HASH has an impact on the Reader's performance, which matters in a real-world ICS deployment. For example, a server may need to simultaneously authenticate a large number of resource-constrained field devices. We also remark that to achieve an optimal level of system/collective lightweightness, further fine-tuning and better integration of the cryptographic primitives are required. This, however, may have the undesirable effect of invalidating existing security proof for the cryptographic primitives. Therefore, extra caution must be taken when investigating the security of the collective cryptographic primitives, to ensure that the system/collective lightweightness does not come at the price of a weaken or invalid security guarantee.

4   Outsourcing of Expensive Computations

Our second approach in achieving lightweight security enforcement in ICS is to allow resource-constrained devices (e.g. field devices, RTUs and PLCs) to

---

[1] If a bit of the input challenge c is 0, then the multiplicand s is shifted to the left by one position. Otherwise (i.e. the bit of the input challenge c is 1), the multiplicand s is shifted to the left and the result is added (with carry) to the multiplicand s.

outsource expensive computations to other devices or equipments. It is realistic to find such powerful devices or equipments in an ICS.

Figure 3 illustrates a simple SCADA system, where the control center commands multiple geographically dispersed subordinate control centers. In each subordinate control center, there is often one or more SCADA slave workstations performing local control/monitoring over the field devices within its territory. The slave workstations can serve as powerful devices to which the field devices can outsource their computations.

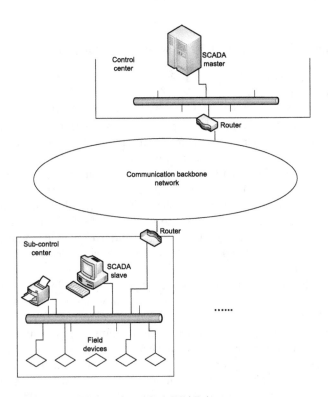

Fig. 3. A typical SCADA system

Proposition 2. *To make security enforcement operations affordable, resource-constrained field devices should attempt to offload expensive computation operations to neighboring devices and equipments that have more computational capacities (hereafter, referred to as computation servers).*

It is important to note that for security reason, resource-constrained devices should not simply place full trust on the computation servers. In other words, appropriate trust assumptions need to be made in the context of the particular application. These computation servers may be subject to cyberattacks, or targeted by disgruntled employees - for example, in the case of the Australian Maroochy water hacking incident[2].

Outsourcing of Modular Exponentiations. We use asymmetric key primitives as an example to explain Proposition 2. We know that modular exponentiation is the fundamental operation in asymmetric key primitives, for example, in RSA-, discrete-logarithm- and ECC-based cryptography. It is, thus, highly desirable to have ways to outsource modular exponentiation, which would address the main challenge in using asymmetric key cryptographic primitives in ICS.

There have been some preliminary attempts to outsource modular exponentiation in the context of cloud computing (i.e. the cloud acts as computation servers) - see [12,24,31,50]. In existing literature, a computation server is assumed not to be fully trusted, and it may deviate from the protocol by deducing additional information from the data given by the user or dishonestly providing the user with the wrong computation output. Thus, the main security requirements are to ensure the *privacy of the user's secret input* and to ensure the *checkability of the server's output*. The formalization of these security requirements is discussed in [24].

In general, three types of modular exponentiations are to be considered, namely: public-base & private-exponent, private-base & public-exponent, and private-based & private-exponent. These modular exponentiation types are useful in practice, depending on the specific cryptographic primitives being used. For instance, Schnorr signature is public-base & private-exponent outsourcing, while RSA blind signature involves private-base & private-exponent outsourcing.

Shortcomings of Existing Schemes. We now summarize the key shortcomings of the existing modular exponentiation outsourcing literature. Due to these shortcomings, existing schemes are unlikely to be suitable for real-world deployment, although it also implies that there are research opportunities in this area.

To better convey our ideas, we refer to the scheme proposed by Kiraz and Uzunkol [31]. This scheme appears to be one of the most efficient solutions to outsourcing of modular exponentiation currently. In particular, the main algorithm of the scheme (cf. Algorithm 1) invokes a sub-algorithm SubAlg, which allows the client to outsource the computation of modular exponentiation g^z to the computation server. Note that neither the base g nor the exponent z are necessarily private in this sub-algorithm, and the main objective of the algorithm is to achieve adjustable checkability, governed by c_1 and c_2 which are small numbers. For the reader's convenience, we list the SubAlg algorithm from [31] in Fig. 4. Let G be a multiplicative group (it could be a modular group or an elliptic curve group), and m be the order of G; $\mathsf{Exp}(a, u)$ denotes an algorithm

---

[2] This infamous incident highlighted the reality of the inadequate security and vulnerability of SCADA systems and ICS. The accused person, a disgruntled employee, allegedly issued radio commands to the sewage equipment, which resulted in 800,000 L of raw sewage to spill out into local parks and rivers, killing marine life. The accused person was sentenced to two years' imprisonment. Subsequent appeal to the Australian High Court was unsuccessful - see *R v Boden [2002] QCA 164*.

EnSubAlg:
Input: (z, g, c) - where $z \in \mathbb{Z}/m\mathbb{Z}, g \in G$, $c \in \mathbb{N}$ is an arbitrary small number
Output: $g^z \in G$

Precomputation: computes and stores the following quantities, which are re-usable:

- $(s, g^s) \in \mathbb{Z}/m\mathbb{Z} \times G$
- $(t_1, t_1^{-1}, g^{t_1}), (t_2, t_2^{-1}, g^{t_2}) \in (\mathbb{Z}/m\mathbb{Z})^2 \times G$
- $I = \{1, \cdots, c\}, I^{-1} = \{1^{-1}, \cdots, c^{-1}\} \subseteq \mathbb{Z}/m\mathbb{Z}$

---

1. Picks a random number $c_1, c_2 \in I$, and the corresponding $c_1^{-1}, c_2^{-1} \in I^{-1}$, where $c_1 \neq c_2$.
2. Computes $z_1 \leftarrow (z - s) \cdot c_1^{-1}$ and $z_2 \leftarrow (-z + 2s) \cdot c_2^{-1}$.
3. Runs
   (a) $Z_1 \leftarrow \mathsf{Exp}(z_1.t_1^{-1}, g^{t_1})$.
   (b) $Z_2 \leftarrow \mathsf{Exp}(z_2.t_2^{-1}, g^{t_2})$.
4. Verifies $Z_1^{c_1} \cdot Z_2^{c_2} \overset{?}{=} g^s$, and returns $Z_1^{2c_1} \cdot Z_2^{c_2}$.

Fig. 4. The SubAlg algorithm in [31]

through which the Client queries $a \in \mathbb{Z}/m\mathbb{Z}, u \in G$ to the computation server, who returns u^a to the Client. In addition, c is a small number, determining the level of checkability.

1. The majority of existing literature use two or more computation servers, and to the best of our knowledge, the only schemes using one single computation server were those proposed in [31,50]. This highlights the challenges in designing schemes that use only one server, although one-server scheme is more suitable and preferable for practical deployment.
2. Existing schemes are not shown to achieve full checkability. More specifically, in these schemes, when given the computation output returned by the computation server(s), the resource-constrained client device can only detect with a certain probability whether the output is genuine or not, with respect to its secret input. As far as we know, the best result on verifiability is the work described in [31], which achieves *adjustable verifiability* of $1 - \frac{1}{c_1 c_2}$ in Fig. 4. That is, a malicious computation server has to correctly guess the values of c_1 and c_2 in order to cheat the Client. Thus the probability of the computation server's success in cheating is $\frac{1}{c(c-1)}$, and in turn the checkability is $1 - \frac{1}{c_1 c_2}$. For example, if $c = 4$, then the scheme has a checkability of $11/12$. Checkability is an important property to attain in practice; thus, full checkability is an open problem for future research.
3. We observe that all existing schemes consist of a pre-computation step, which involves multiple modular exponentiations, e.g. g^s, g^{t_1}, g^{t_2} in Fig. 4. In other words, outsourcing of one (online) modular exponentiation comes at the cost

of several precomputed modular exponentiations. These precomputed modular exponentiations are often one-use only. That is, for each outsourcing session, a different set of precomputed modular exponentiations are needed. We believe that this invocation of modular exponentiations, although assumed to be precomputed, is not satisfactory in practice. It is better to avoid having pre-computed modular exponentiations; or if it is unavoidable, ways should be explored to reuse these precomputed modular exponentiations. Reusable precomputed quantities would be less problematic in practice, as they can be preinstalled on resource-constrained devices (e.g. as regular secrets). In Fig. 4, g^s is one-use, while g^{t_1}, g^{t_2} can be used multiple times. We leave the avoidance of (one-use) pre-computed modular exponentiations as an open problem.

5   Selective Protection of Data of Interest

In a cyber-physical system such as SCADA, the field devices need to send measurement/operational data back to the control subsystem at fixed time intervals or responding to the data acquisition requests from the control subsystem. The data to be communicated uplink may be large in quantity. If a field device protects all the data (e.g. encrypts the data), then it may still fail the real-time requirement of the underlying system, even in the case where the above two strategies are in place.

To alleviate this problem, we propose another proposition which is a partial protection strategy – instead of putting all data to be communicated under protection, the field devices can choose certain critical segments of the data to encrypt while leaving non-critical data unprotected, in an attempt to minimize the overhead incurred due to data protection. We call the critical data to be protected *Data of Interest* (DoI).

Proposition 3. *Depending on applications, data sent by the field devices could be classified as critical or non-critical with respective to the sensitivity of the data. Whenever possible, it should choose to protect the critical data (referred to as Data of Interest) only, which could enormously improve the system performance by reducing the overhead due to security enforcement.*

For this strategy to be implemented, it is important to differentiate critical and non-critical data. Sometimes, it may even be required to deliberately reformat the data to make the differentiation possible. Suppose that the field devices in a cyber-physical system sent to the control subsystem their sensed temperature data at a fixed time interval – a possible strategy is to partition the time into *epochs*, where each epoch consists of a definite number of intervals; for each epoch, only the actual temperature reading for the first interval of the epoch needs to be sent in an encrypted form, while for each subsequent interval, the difference between the actual reading and the first reading is sent unprotected. The control subsystem can certainly recover those readings with the first reading in its possession, while for eavesdroppers they cannot deduce the actual readings of any time interval without the knowledge of the first reading. It is apparent that such a partial protection approach greatly reduces the number of protection enforcement computations.

When the protection mechanism is encryption, the partial protection approach is quite similar to Selective Encryption for multimedia content, such as image and video [26,45,49]. For an image or a video frame, a large amount of redundancy exists in the content. It was, thus, found that complete encryption is unnecessary and a waste of resources, and it suffices to encrypt only the partial yet significant data that can reconstruct the image or the video frame. Selective encryption generally has much faster performance than complete encryption because of the reduced encryption workload. In the same vein, selective encryption of DoI in CPS promises the same advantage. However, data in a cyber-physical system may not offer obvious redundancy, and it is crucial to identify the DoI of a specific cyber-physical system. Furthermore, it is equally important to ensure that the redundant data (unprotected) does not lead to the compromise of the system' security.

Finally, the downlink communications from the control subsystem to the field devices in CPS mostly comprise control or data acquisition instructions. These instructions are normally short or have special format. Format preserving encryption [6], thus, seems a suitable tool for encrypting the download communications. Studying format preserving encryption, which is lightweight and affordable to field devices in CPS, will be another interesting research topic.

6 Conclusion

The diversity of cyberthreats and threat actors necessitates ongoing efforts to secure our critical infrastructure and the underlying systems (e.g. CPS). Although we may never be able to completely eradicate cyberattacks targeting our CPS, we should aim to maintain persistent pressure on criminals and actors with malicious intent to safeguard our cyber and national interests [15].

In this paper, we proposed three general approaches to achieve lightweight security enforcement in industrial control systems (ICS). In the first approach, we explained how we should seek to achieve system/collective lightweightness (i.e. efficiency) by considering cryptographic primitives collectively, rather than individually. In the second approach, we sought to leverage the architecture of ICS and offload computationally expensive operations from resource-constrained field devices to neighboring powerful devices or equipments (e.g. SCADA slave workstations). We also highlighted three key limitations in existing outsourcing of modular exponentiation literature. In the third approach, we suggested partially protecting data of interest while without compromising the security guarantee, in order to reduce the security enforcement workload as much as possible.

Future work will include materializing and applying these general approaches to developing concrete techniques that are applicable to real world CPS. It includes conducting extensive security testing and validation under controlled and reproducible conditions, such as in a testbed environment simulating emergency services alarm management system (in the emergency sector), traffic light and railway control systems (in the transport sector), water pump system (in the water sector), electric grid system (in the energy sector), and centrifuge system which is the target of the Stuxnet malware.

Acknowledgment. This work was supported by the National Research Foundation (NRF), Prime Minister's Office, Singapore, under its National Cybersecurity R&D Programme (Award No. NRF2014NCR-NCR001-31) and administered by the National Cybersecurity R&D Directorate.

References

1. AGA Report No. 12 (2004): Cryptographic Protection of SCADA Communications:General Recommendations, Draft 2, 2004. The Draft 3 is available for purchage at http://www.aga.org/
2. Aumasson, J., Henzen, L., Meier, W., Naya-Plasencia, M.: Quark: a lightweight hash. J. Cryptology **26**(2), 313–339 (2013)
3. Baek, J., Vu, Q.H., Liu, J.K., Huang, X., Xiang, Y.: A secure cloud computing based framework for big data information management of smart grid. IEEE Trans. Cloud Comput. **3**(2), 233–244 (2015)
4. Borghoff, J., et al.: PRINCE – a low-latency block cipher for pervasive computing applications. In: Wang, X., Sako, K. (eds.) ASIACRYPT 2012. LNCS, vol. 7658, pp. 208–225. Springer, Heidelberg (2012)
5. Bichsel, P., Camenisch, J., Gro, T., Shoup, V.: Anonymous credentials on a standard java card. In: Proceedings of ACM Conference on Computer and Communication Security, CCS 2009, pp. 600–610 (2009)
6. Bellare, M., Ristenpart, T., Rogaway, P., Stegers, T.: Format-Preserving Encryption. https://eprint.iacr.org/2009/251.pdf
7. Beaulieu, R., Shors, D., Smith, J., Treatman-Clark, S., Weeks, B., Wingers, L.: The SIMON and SPECK Families of Lightweight Block Ciphers. https://eprint.iacr.org/2013/404.pdf
8. Cardenas, A., Amin, S., Sinopoli, B., Giani, A., Perrig, A., Sastry, S.: Challenges for securing cyber physical systems. In: Proceedings of Workshop on Future Directions in Cyber-Physical Systems Security, DHS (2009)
9. De Cannière, C., Dunkelman, O., Knežević, M.: KATAN and KTANTAN — a family of small and efficient hardware-oriented block ciphers. In: Clavier, C., Gaj, K. (eds.) CHES 2009. LNCS, vol. 5747, pp. 272–288. Springer, Heidelberg (2009)
10. Carlson, R., Dagle, J., Shamsuddin, S., Evans, R.: A Summary of Control System Security Standards Activities in the Energy Sector, Office of Electricity Delivery and Energy Reliability U.S. Department of Energy (2005)
11. Camenisch, J., Herreweghen, E.V.: Design and implementation of the idemix anonymous credential system. In: Proceedings of ACM Conference on Computer and Communication Security, CCS 2002 (2002)
12. Chen, X., Li, J., Ma, J., Tang, Q., Lou, W.: New algorithms for secure outsourcing of modular exponentiations. In: Foresti, S., Yung, M., Martinelli, F. (eds.) ESORICS 2012. LNCS, vol. 7459, pp. 541–556. Springer, Heidelberg (2012)
13. Choo, K.-K.R.: Secure Key Establishment. Springer, Heidelberg (2009)
14. Choo, K.-K.R.: The cyber threat landscape: challenges and future research directions. Comput. Secur. **30**(8), 719–731 (2011)

15. Choo, K.-K.R.: A conceptual interdisciplinary plug-and-play cyber security framework. ICTs and the Millennium Development Goals: A United Nations Perspective, pp. 81–99. Springer, New York (2014)

16. Chow, S.M., Liu, J.K., Zhou, J.: Identity-based online/offline key encapsulation and encryption. In: Proceedings of ACM Symposium on Information, Computer and Communications Security, ASIACCS 2011, pp. 52–60 (2011)

17. Chu, C., Liu, J.K., Wong, J.W., Zhao, Y., Zhou, J.: Privacy-preserving smart metering with regional statistics and personal enquiry services. In: Proceedings of ACM Symposium on Information, Computer and Communications Security, ASIACCS 2013, pp. 369–380 (2013)

18. Chu, C., Liu, J.K., Zhou, J., Bao, F., Deng, R.H.: Practical ID-based encryption for wireless sensor network. In: Proceedings of ACM Symposium on Information, Computer and Communications Security, ASIACCS 2010, pp. 337–340 (2010)

19. Eisenbarth, T., et al.: Compact implementation and performance evaluation of block ciphers in ATtiny devices. In: Mitrokotsa, A., Vaudenay, S. (eds.) AFRICACRYPT 2012. LNCS, vol. 7374, pp. 172–187. Springer, Heidelberg (2012)

20. Gong, Z., Nikova, S., Law, Y.W.: KLEIN: a new family of lightweight block ciphers. In: Juels, A., Paar, C. (eds.) RFIDSec 2011. LNCS, vol. 7055, pp. 1–18. Springer, Heidelberg (2012)

21. Guo, J., Peyrin, T., Poschmann, A.: The PHOTON family of lightweight hash-functions. In: Rogaway, P. (ed.) CRYPTO 2011. LNCS, vol. 6841, pp. 222–239. Springer, Heidelberg (2011)

22. Guo, J., Peyrin, T., Poschmann, A., Robshaw, M.: The LED block cipher. In: Preneel, B., Takagi, T. (eds.) CHES 2011. LNCS, vol. 6917, pp. 326–341. Springer, Heidelberg (2011)

23. Girault, M., Poupard, G., Stern, J.: On the fly authentication and signature schemes based on groups of unknown order. J. Cryptology 19(4), 463–487 (2006)

24. Hohenberger, S., Lysyanskaya, A.: How to securely outsource cryptographic computations. In: Kilian, J. (ed.) TCC 2005. LNCS, vol. 3378, pp. 264–282. Springer, Heidelberg (2005)

25. Igure, V., Laughter, S., Williams, R.: Security issues in SCADA networks. Comput. Secur. 25, 498–506 (2006)

26. Lian, S., Sun, J., Wang, Z.: Quality analysis of several typical MPEG video encryption algorithms. J. Image Graph. 9(4), 483–490 (2004)

27. ISO/IEC 18033-3: Information technology – Security techniques – Encryption algorithms – Part 3: Block ciphers

28. ISO/IEC 29192-2: Information technology – Security techniques – Lightweight-cryptography – Part 2: Block ciphers

29. ISO/IEC 29192-4: Information technology – Security techniques – Lightweight-cryptography – Part 4: Mechanisms using asymmetric techniques

30. Kravets, K.: Feds: Hacker Disabled Offshore Oil Plaforms' Leak-Detection System, 18 March 2009. http://www.wired.com/threatlevel//03/feds-hacker-dis/

31. Kiraz, M., Uzunkol, O.: Efficient and Verifiable Algorithms for Secure Outsourcing of Cryptogrpahic Computations. https://eprint.iacr.org/2014/748.pdf

32. Kavun, E.B., Yalcin, T.: A lightweight implementation of keccak hash function for radio-frequency identification applications. In: Ors Yalcin, S.B. (ed.) RFIDSec 2010. LNCS, vol. 6370, pp. 258–269. Springer, Heidelberg (2010)

33. Laplante, P., Michael, B., Voas, J.: Cyberpandemics: history, inevitability, response. IEEE Secur. Priv. 7(1), 63–67 (2009)

34. Liu, J.K., Baek, J., Zhou, J.: Online/offline identity-based signcryption revisited. In: Lai, X., Yung, M., Lin, D. (eds.) Inscrypt 2010. LNCS, vol. 6584, pp. 36–51. Springer, Heidelberg (2011)
35. Liu, J.K., Baek, J., Zhou, J., Yang, Y., Wong, J.W.: Efficient online/offline identity-based signature for wireless sensor network. Int. J. Inf. Sec. **9**(4), 287–296 (2010)
36. Liu, J.K., Au, M.H., Susilo, W., Zhou, J.: Online/offline ring signature scheme. In: Qing, S., Mitchell, C.J., Wang, G. (eds.) ICICS 2009. LNCS, vol. 5927, pp. 80–90. Springer, Heidelberg (2009)
37. Liu, J.K., Chu, C.K., Zhou, J.: Identity-based server-aided decryption. In: Parampalli, U., Hawkes, P. (eds.) ACISP 2011. LNCS, vol. 6812, pp. 337–352. Springer, Heidelberg (2011)
38. Liu, J.K., Zhou, J.: An efficient identity-based online/offline encryption scheme. In: Abdalla, M., Pointcheval, D., Fouque, P.-A., Vergnaud, D. (eds.) ACNS 2009. LNCS, vol. 5536, pp. 156–167. Springer, Heidelberg (2009)
39. Molina-Markham, A., Danezis, G., Fu, K., Shenoy, P., Irwin, D.: Designing privacy-preserving smart meters with low-cost microcontrollers. In: Keromytis, A.D. (ed.) FC 2012. LNCS, vol. 7397, pp. 239–253. Springer, Heidelberg (2012)
40. NERC-CIP. Critical Infrastructure Protection, North American Electric Reliability Corporation (2008). http://www.nerc.com/cip.html
41. Poschmann, A.: Lightweight Cryptography: Cryptographic Engineering for A Pervasive World, Ph.D. Thesis (2009)
42. Ralston, A., Graham, H., Patel, C.: Literature Review of Security, Risk Assessment of SCADA, DCS Systems, Technical report. http://www.cs.dlouisville.edu/facilities/ISLab/tech/ISRL-TR-06-01.pdf
43. Stouffer, K., Falco, J., Kent, K.: Guide to Supervisory Control and Data Acquisition (SCADA) and Industrial Control Systems Security. NIST SP 800–82 (2006)
44. Sanger, D.: Confront and Conceal: Obama's Secret Wars and Surprising Use of American Power. Crown, NY (2012)
45. Shahid, Z., Chaumont, M., Puech, W.: Fast protection of H.264/AVC by selective encryption of CAVLC and CABAC for I and P frames. IEEE Trans. Circ. Syst. Video Technol. **21**(5), 565–576 (2011)
46. Sommestad, T., Ericsson, N., Nordlander, J.: SCADA system cyber security: a comparison of standards. In: Proceedings of IEEE Power and Energy Society General, pp. 1–8 (2010)
47. Shibutani, K., Isobe, T., Hiwatari, H., Mitsuda, A., Akishita, T., Shirai, T.: *Piccolo*: an ultra-lightweight blockcipher. In: Preneel, B., Takagi, T. (eds.) CHES 2011. LNCS, vol. 6917, pp. 342–357. Springer, Heidelberg (2011)
48. Wang, Y.: sSCADA: securing SCADA infrastrcture communications. Int. J. Commun. Netw. Distrib. Syst. **6**(11), 59–78 (2011)
49. Wang, Y., O'Neill, M., Kurugollu, F.: A tunable encryption scheme and analysis of fast selective encryption for CAVLC and CABAC in H.264/AVC. IEEE Trans. Circ. Syst. Video Technol. **23**(9), 1476–1490 (2013)
50. Wang, Y., Wu, Q., Wong, D.S., Qin, B., Chow, S.S.M., Liu, Z., Tan, X.: Securely outsourcing exponentiations with single untrusted program for cloud storage. In: Kutyłowski, M., Vaidya, J. (eds.) ESORICS 2014, Part I. LNCS, vol. 8712, pp. 326–343. Springer, Heidelberg (2014)
51. Wright, A.K., Kinast, J.A., McCarty, J.: Low-latency cryptographic protection for SCADA communications. In: Jakobsson, M., Yung, M., Zhou, J. (eds.) ACNS 2004. LNCS, vol. 3089, pp. 263–277. Springer, Heidelberg (2004)

52. Wan, Z., Wang, G., Yang, Y., Shi, S.: SKM: scalable key management for advanced metering infrastructure in smart grids. IEEE Trans. Industr. Electron. **61**(12), 7055–7066 (2014)
53. Wu, W., Wu, S., Zhang, L., Zou, J., Dong, L.: LHash: a lightweight hash function. In: Lin, D., Xu, S., Yung, M. (eds.) Inscrypt 2013. LNCS, vol. 8567, pp. 291–308. Springer, Heidelberg (2014)
54. Yuen, T.H., Zhang, Y., Yiu, S.M., Liu, J.K.: Identity-based encryption with post-challenge auxiliary inputs for secure cloud applications and sensor networks. In: Kutyłowski, M., Vaidya, J. (eds.) ESORICS 2014, Part I. LNCS, vol. 8712, pp. 130–147. Springer, Heidelberg (2014)

Implementation Challenges

Fast Software Implementation of QUARK on a 32-Bit Architecture

Roberto Cabral$^{(\boxtimes)}$ and Julio López$^{(\boxtimes)}$

Institute of Computing, University of Campinas, 1251 Albert Einstein,
Cidade Universitária, Campinas, Brazil
{rbcabral,jlopez}@ic.unicamp.br

Abstract. Secure applications for the Internet of Things (IoT) are constantly increasing and many of them require some lightweight cryptographic algorithms. Most lightweight cryptographic algorithms were not designed to be efficient in software platforms. As a result the throughput in software of these algorithms is low on recent IoT devices. In this paper we present optimization techniques for improving the software implementation of the QUARK functions. QUARK is a family of lightweight hash functions that is efficient in hardware but its design was not oriented for software platforms. We obtained a reduction on the number of binary operations required in each iteration of QUARK, and by computing in parallel some internal functions we achieved a further speed up. In addition, we also present the results of our optimized implementations of S-QUARK and D-QUARK on the 32-bit Intel Galileo platform.

Keywords: Hash functions · Lightweight cryptography · QUARK family · Fast software implementation · Intel Galileo

1 Introduction

Hash functions are used in several security applications like generation and verification of digital signatures, key derivation, pseudo-random number generation, and so forth. Hash functions map an arbitrary-size bit string to a fixed-length bit string commonly known as a *message digest* or *hash value*.

The large growth of System on Chip (SoC) devices aimed at the Internet of Things (IoT) has increased the need of lightweight cryptographic algorithm implementations for resource-constrained devices. On those scenarios, the software implementations should be fast, compact, low-power and secure against side channel attacks. For the past few years, strong candidates of lightweight hash

The authors were partially supported by Intel Labs University Research Office.
The first author was partially supported by CNPq, Bolsista de Desenvolvimento Tecnológico em TICs do CNPq - Nível F.
The second author was partially supported by a research productivity scholarship from CNPq Brazil.

© Springer International Publishing Switzerland 2016
T. Güneysu et al. (Eds.): LightSec 2015, LNCS 9542, pp. 115–130, 2016.
DOI: 10.1007/978-3-319-29078-2_7

functions have appeared, such as PHOTON [11], QUARK [3], SPONGENT [6], among others.

QUARK was proposed by Aumasson, Henzen, Meier and Naya-Plasencia [3]. This family of lightweight hash function has high performance in hardware; however its design was not oriented for a software implementation, as it was noted by its authors.

Related Works. For platforms that do not have a dedicated hardware implementation of hash algorithms, the only option is to implement in software a hash algorithm that takes advantage of the instruction set of the processor. In recent years, cryptographic lightweight functions have been implemented in software for an 8-bit microcontroller; in [4] it was shown a software implementation of the lightweight hash functions QUARK, PHOTON and SPONGENT for 80 and 112 bit security levels and in [9] it was shown a software implementation of lightweight block ciphers. For 32-bit architectures there are just few optimized implementations of lightweight hash functions; in [12] is given a table-based implementation of PHOTON is given for five different security levels.

Our Contribution. In this work, we faced the challenge to optimize the QUARK algorithm for a software implementation; to achieve this, we rewrite the internal functions in order to make them more suitable to a software implementation, reducing the number of binary operations by about 25 %. We present some techniques that enable a software implementation with a high speedup and a small code size on a 32-bit architecture. In particularly, we show the performance for the recent platform Intel Galileo. The proposed techniques can also be used on 8 or 16-bit architectures.

2   Description of QUARK

The family of lightweight hash functions QUARK was firstly presented in [3] and further it was published an extended version in 2013 [1], where the parameter n was added to address a flaw in the initial analysis.

2.1   Sponge Function

The sponge function is a generalization of the concept of cryptographic hash function, since it takes an input bit stream of any length and produces an output bit stream of any desired length [5]. The structure of the sponge function can be seen in Fig. 1. The family QUARK uses the sponge construction and a permutation function P, which will be defined in Sect. 2.2.

The sponge function, given in Fig. 1, operates on a state of $b = r + c$ bits. The value r is the *bitrate* and the value c is the *capacity*. The state of b bits is defined as $S = (S_0, \ldots, S_{b-1})$, where S_0 is the most significant bit and S_{b-1} is the least significant bit.

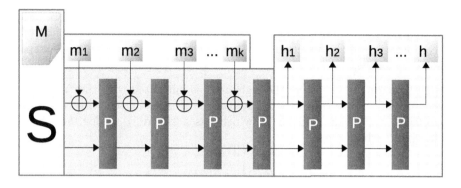

Fig. 1. Sponge construction [5].

Given an initial state of b bits[1] S and a message M, the message is padded to ensure that the size of the message be a multiple of r. Thereafter, the message is processed in two phases:

1. **Absorption.** The message is divided into k blocks of r bits $(m_1, \ldots, m_k)$. Then, in each iteration is performed an XOR operation between the block of the message and the first r bits of the current state. After that, the state will be processed by the permutation function P.
2. **Squeezing.** The first r bits from the state are used as output; if the digest size is bigger than r the state is processed through a permutation function again and the first r bits are concatenated with the previous r bits; this process is repeated until all the n bits required are squeezed.

In the absorbing phase of the QUARK family, the message blocks are XORed to the last r bits of the internal state, instead of the first. According to [1], this provides a better diffusion than if the first r bits were used, because differences introduced in the last bits remain in the register, while those in the first quickly disappear due to the bit shifts. In the squeezing phase, digest bits are also extracted from the last r bits of the state. According to [1], the motivation is simple: these are the last bits computed by the permutation; extracting from the first bits would make the computation of the last rounds useless.

2.2   The Permutation Function P

The design of the permutation function P was inspired by the Grain stream cipher [13] and the KATAN block cipher [8]. Internally, the function P is composed of three Feedback Shift Register (FSR), being one of them linear (L) and the other two nonlinear (X and Y); these FSRs use the update functions p, f and g, defined in Appendix A.

---

[1] The state of each instance of QUARK is initialized with the first b bits of the SHA-256 digest of their name.

The permutation function P is the critical function in terms of performance of the algorithm; its input is a state of b bits and its output is the state updated. The computation of the function $P(S)$ can be divided into three basic steps, described as follows:

1. **Initialization:** In this step, the register X is initialized with the "most significant half" of the state S and the register Y is initialized with the "least significant half". The register L, which has a size of $q = \lceil \log 4b \rceil$ bits, is initialized with all ones.
$$S = X \| Y.$$
$$L = (1, 1, \ldots, 1).$$

2. **Update:** In each iteration, the i-th bit of X, Y and L, denoted by X_i, Y_i and L_i, is updated as follows:
$$X_i = f(X) \oplus h(X, Y, L) \oplus Y_i.$$
$$Y_i = g(Y) \oplus h(X, Y, L).$$
$$L_i = p(L).$$

3. **Output:** After the update step, the output is the state S, which is composed of the values of X and Y, where $X = (S_0 \ldots S_{\frac{b}{2}-1})$ is the most significant half of S and $Y = (S_{\frac{b}{2}} \ldots S_{b-1})$ is the least significant half of S.

In Fig. 2 it is shown how the state is updated. The permutation function P runs $4b$ iterations and in each iteration only two bits of the state are updated.

Algorithm 1. Permutation Function P

Input: State S of b bits.
Output: State updated S'.

1: $X = (S_0, \ldots, S_{(b/2)-1})$
2: $Y = (S_{b/2}, \ldots, S_{b-1})$
3: **for** j = 0 **to** 7 **do**
4:     **for** i = 0 **to** $(4b/8) - 1$ **do**
5:         $h' = h(X, Y, L)$
6:         $X_i = f(X) \oplus h' \oplus Y_i$
7:         $Y_i = g(Y) \oplus h'$
8:         $L_{i \bmod q} = p(L)$
9:     **end for**
10: **end for**
11: $(S'_0, \ldots, S'_{(b/2)-1}) = X$
12: $(S'_{b/2}, \ldots, S'_{b-1}) = Y$
13: **return** S'.

The LFSR L is deterministic, so it can be precomputed. The steps used to compute the permutation function P can be seen in Algorithm 1. The functions p, f, g and h of the QUARK family are defined for every QUARK instance in Appendix A.

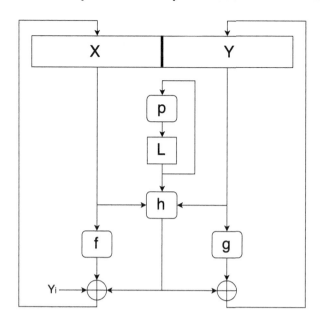

Fig. 2. Diagram of the permutation function P.

2.3 QUARK Family

There are three different flavors of the QUARK family: U-QUARK, D-QUARK and S-QUARK. Each one has different values of bitrate (r), capacity (c), digest (n), and functions f, g and h. The parameters of each one are shown in Table 1.

Table 1. Parameters of the QUARK family.

Instance	Security level	Bitrate (r)	Capacity (c)	Rounds $(4b)$	Digest (n)	Parallelism degree
U-QUARK	64	8	128	544	136	8
D-QUARK	80	16	160	704	176	8
S-QUARK	112	32	224	1024	256	16

The functions f and g are the same for each instance of the QUARK family, but with different indexes. On the other hand, the function h is different for each instance of QUARK.

3   Algorithmic Optimizations

In each iteration of the permutation function P, 13 bits of the vectors X and Y are used as input of the functions f and g. These functions are performed $4b$

times in each call of the permutation function P and the computation of them requires 100 binary operations (58 AND's and 42 XOR's); thus, an optimization in these functions will have a high impact on the whole computation.

We observed that the number of binary operations required to compute the functions f and g can be simplified using some algebraic properties. Since the functions f and g of all instances of QUARK process the same binary operations, we will present the optimized version of these functions just for the S-QUARK algorithm.

By optimizing these functions, the number of binary operations required for evaluating them was reduced to 32 AND's, 38 XOR's and 4 NOT's; this implies a saving of 26 % on the number of binary operations. The optimized functions f and g are shown in Functions 1 and 2, respectively.

Optimized Function f: Given a 128-bit vector X, the function f returns one bit, computed as:

$$
\begin{aligned}
f(X) = {} & X_0 \oplus X_{16} \oplus X_{26} \oplus X_{39} \oplus X_{52} \oplus X_{61} \oplus X_{69} \oplus X_{84} \oplus X_{94} \oplus X_{97} \\
& \oplus X_{103}(X_{111}\neg(X_{28}X_{39}) \oplus X_{97}(X_{84} \oplus X_{69}(X_{61} \oplus X_{84}X_{111}))) \\
& \oplus X_{52}(X_{16}X_{84}X_{111} \oplus X_{39}X_{61}\neg(X_{16}X_{28} \oplus X_{69}X_{84}X_{97})) \\
& \oplus X_{16}X_{28} \oplus X_{61}X_{69} \oplus X_{103}.
\end{aligned} \tag{1}
$$

Optimized Function g: Given a 128-bit vector Y, the function g returns one bit, computed as:

$$
\begin{aligned}
g(Y) = {} & Y_0 \oplus Y_{13} \oplus Y_{30} \oplus Y_{37} \oplus Y_{56} \oplus Y_{65} \oplus Y_{69} \oplus Y_{79}Y_{92} \oplus Y_{96} \\
& \oplus Y_{101}(Y_{109}\neg(Y_{28}Y_{37}) \oplus Y_{96}(Y_{79} \oplus Y_{69}(Y_{65} \oplus Y_{79}Y_{109}))) \\
& \oplus Y_{56}(Y_{13}Y_{79}Y_{109} \oplus Y_{37}Y_{65}\neg(Y_{13}Y_{28} \oplus Y_{69}Y_{79}Y_{96})) \\
& \oplus Y_{13}Y_{28} \oplus Y_{65}Y_{69} \oplus Y_{101}.
\end{aligned} \tag{2}
$$

For each instance of the QUARK family, the function h can also be optimized by simplifying the binary operations. We obtain a reduction of about 25 % on the number of instructions for the function h. The optimized functions h for U-QUARK, D-QUARK and S-QUARK are shown in Functions 3, 4 and 5, respectively.

Optimized U-QUARK h: Given two 68-bit vectors X and Y and a constant vector L, the function h returns one bit, computed as:

$$
\begin{aligned}
h(X, Y, L) = {} & X_1 \oplus Y_2 \oplus X_4 \oplus Y_{10} \oplus X_{31} \oplus Y_{43} \oplus X_{56} \oplus L_0 \oplus X_{25} \oplus Y_{59} \\
& \oplus X_{25}(L_0 \oplus Y_3 X_{46}) \oplus X_{55}(Y_3 \vee X_{46} \oplus Y_{59}) \\
& \oplus Y_{59}(X_{46}(Y_3 \oplus L_0 X_{25})).
\end{aligned} \tag{3}
$$

Optimized D-QUARK h: Given two 88-bit vectors X and Y and a constant vector L, the function h returns one bit, computed as:

$$
\begin{aligned}
h(X, Y, L) = {} & X_1 \oplus Y_2 \oplus X_5 \oplus Y_{12} \oplus X_{40} \oplus Y_{55} \oplus X_{72} \oplus L_0 \oplus Y_{24} \oplus Y_{61} \\
& \oplus X_{48} \oplus X_{35} \oplus X_{35}(L_0 \oplus Y_4 X_{57}) \oplus Y_{79} \oplus X_{68}(Y_4 \vee X_{57} \oplus Y_{79}) \\
& \oplus Y_{79}(X_{57}(Y_4 \oplus L_0 X_{35})).
\end{aligned} \tag{4}
$$

Optimized S-QUARK h**:** Given two 128-bit vectors X and Y and a constant vector L, the function h returns one bit, computed as:

$$h(X, Y, L) = X_1 \oplus Y_3 \oplus X_7 \oplus Y_{18} \oplus X_{58} \oplus Y_{80} \oplus X_{105} \oplus L_0 \oplus Y_{34} \oplus Y_{71}$$
$$\oplus X_{90} \oplus Y_{91} \oplus X_{47} \oplus X_{47}(L_0 \oplus Y_8 X_{72}) \oplus Y_{111}$$
$$\oplus X_{100}(Y_8 \vee X_{72} \oplus Y_{111}) \oplus Y_{111}(X_{72}(Y_8 \oplus L_0 X_{47})). \qquad (5)$$

The computation of the permutation function P with the new functions f, g and h uses approximately 25 % less binary operations. These optimizations directly affect the software implementation, allowing a gain of efficiency and code size of approximately 20 % and 10 %, respectively, as it will be shown in Sect. 4.4.

4   Implementation

In this section we will describe our software implementation of Algorithm 1 on the Intel Galileo Platform. We will present the main features of the Galileo architecture, the optimization techniques for S-QUARK and D-QUARK and the results. Our codes were written using the programming language C.

4.1   Galileo Architecture

Galileo is a microcontroller board based on the Intel Quark SoC X1000 processor, that is a 32-bit processor designed for lower power consumption. It is x86 compatible with Pentium opcode instructions but implements features like ACPI (Advanced Configuration and Power Interface) and includes several interfaces that provide connections with external peripherals. Intel Quark is the first Intel initiative to merge into the "Internet of Things" (IoT) and the wearable market [14].

The Intel Quark SoC X1000 has eight 32-bit general purpose registers named EAX, EBX, ECX, EDX, ESI, EDI, EBP and ESP [15]. This processor can not perform out-of-order processing, but has two pipelines for executing instructions and under certain conditions can execute two consecutive instructions simultaneously by an instruction pairing mechanism described in [10].

The main features of the processor Quark SoC X1000 are: a frequency of 400 MHz, single core, 32-bit Intel Pentium instructions set, 16 KB of L1 cache, 512 KB on-die of SRAM and 256 MB of DRAM.

4.2   S-QUARK

Each call to the permutation function P of S-QUARK corresponds to 1024 calls to the functions f, g and h. Our first optimization to implement S-QUARK in software was to process groups of consecutive bits (words) instead of scattered bits.

The S-QUARK algorithm allows a parallelization degree of 16 [1], that is, it is possible to compute the first 16 rounds without data dependency. This feature of the algorithm allows us to join blocks of 16 bits and work on them. Thus, after organizing the input bits, we can process 16 rounds of functions f and g in parallel.

Working with blocks of 16 bits enables an implementation in software using 16-bit registers, since operations on words are faster than operations on scattered bits. Benefiting of this characteristic of the algorithm, we can join blocks of 16 bits to be executed by the function f, and analogously by the function g. However, even with this optimization, we are not taking advantage of the 32 bits available on Galileo platform, since we are only processing 16 bits at a time.

Analyzing the functions f and g we realized that they are symmetric, in the sense that they perform the same operations on a different data set. Thus, the second optimization was to use the upper part of a 32-bit register to process the function f while in parallel computing the function g in the lower part. This allows us to join the functions f and g in a new function u, defined in Function 6, which receives as input 13 words of 32 bits (t) and return one word of 32 bits. We will use a vector of 13 words of 32 bits $t = [t_0, t_1, \ldots, t_{12}]$ to represent the input of the function u.

Function u: Given a vector of 13 words of 32 bits t, the function u computes a 32-bit value as follows:

$$u(t) = t_0 \oplus t_2 \oplus t_3 \oplus t_4 \oplus t_5 \oplus t_6 \oplus t_7 \oplus t_8 \oplus t_1 \oplus t_9 \oplus t_{10}(t_{11} \neg (t_{12}t_4)$$
$$\oplus t_9(t_8 \oplus t_7(t_6 \oplus t_8 t_{11}))) \oplus t_5(t_2 t_8 t_{11} \oplus t_4 t_6 \neg (t_2 t_{12} \oplus t_7 t_8 t_9))$$
$$\oplus t_2 t_{12} \oplus t_6 t_7 \oplus t_{10}. \tag{6}$$

In Fig. 3 we can see the initial state of each one of the 13 words needed to perform the first round of the function u; in the following rounds the value of the bits in each word t will be the bit index added by 16 modulo 128; for instance, the t_0 in the subsequent step will be composed of the values X_{16} to X_{31} in the higher part and Y_{16} to Y_{31} in the lower part. On other hand, the word t_{11} will have the values X_{127} to X_{14} in the higher part and Y_{125} to Y_{13} in the lower part. This optimization allows us to take advantage of the 32 bits available on the Galileo architecture.

Given two vectors X and Y of 128 bits, we use 8 words of 32 bits (x_0 to x_3 and y_0 to y_3) to store X and Y. The amount of work employed to organize the words in Fig. 3 varies according to the position of the involved bits; for example, to initialize t_0 the processing is very simple, we only need to zero-out the lower part of x_0 and perform an XOR with the result of a 16-bit left shift of word y_0. However, for other words the initialization could be more complex; for instance, the word t_5 joins bits from x_1, x_2, y_1 and y_2. The steps for computing t_5 are shown below:

$$aux_1 = (x_1 \ll 16) \oplus (x_2 \gg 16);$$
$$aux_2 = (y_1 \ll 16) \oplus (y_2 \gg 16);$$
$$t_5 = ((aux_1 \ll 4) \wedge \texttt{0xFFFF0000}) \oplus ((aux_2 \gg 8) \wedge \texttt{0x0000FFFF});$$

$t_0 =$	$X_0, \ldots\ldots\ldots\ldots\ldots, X_{15}$	$Y_0, \ldots\ldots\ldots\ldots\ldots, Y_{15}$
$t_1 =$	$X_{94}, \ldots\ldots\ldots\ldots\ldots, X_{109}$	$Y_{30}, \ldots\ldots\ldots\ldots\ldots, Y_{45}$
$t_2 =$	$X_{16}, \ldots\ldots\ldots\ldots\ldots, X_{31}$	$Y_{13}, \ldots\ldots\ldots\ldots\ldots, Y_{28}$
$t_3 =$	$X_{26}, \ldots\ldots\ldots\ldots\ldots, X_{41}$	$Y_{92}, \ldots\ldots\ldots\ldots\ldots, Y_{107}$
$t_4 =$	$X_{39}, \ldots\ldots\ldots\ldots\ldots, X_{54}$	$Y_{37}, \ldots\ldots\ldots\ldots\ldots, Y_{52}$
$t_5 =$	$X_{52}, \ldots\ldots\ldots\ldots\ldots, X_{67}$	$Y_{56}, \ldots\ldots\ldots\ldots\ldots, Y_{71}$
$t_6 =$	$X_{61}, \ldots\ldots\ldots\ldots\ldots, X_{76}$	$Y_{65}, \ldots\ldots\ldots\ldots\ldots, Y_{80}$
$t_7 =$	$X_{69}, \ldots\ldots\ldots\ldots\ldots, X_{84}$	$Y_{69}, \ldots\ldots\ldots\ldots\ldots, Y_{84}$
$t_8 =$	$X_{84}, \ldots\ldots\ldots\ldots\ldots, X_{99}$	$Y_{79}, \ldots\ldots\ldots\ldots\ldots, Y_{94}$
$t_9 =$	$X_{97}, \ldots\ldots\ldots\ldots\ldots, X_{112}$	$Y_{96}, \ldots\ldots\ldots\ldots\ldots, Y_{111}$
$t_{10} =$	$X_{103}, \ldots\ldots\ldots\ldots\ldots, X_{118}$	$Y_{101}, \ldots\ldots\ldots\ldots\ldots, Y_{116}$
$t_{11} =$	$X_{111}, \ldots\ldots\ldots\ldots\ldots, X_{126}$	$Y_{109}, \ldots\ldots\ldots\ldots\ldots, Y_{124}$
$t_{12} =$	$X_{28}, \ldots\ldots\ldots\ldots\ldots, X_{43}$	$Y_{28}, \ldots\ldots\ldots\ldots\ldots, Y_{43}$

Fig. 3. Initialization of the words $t_0, \ldots, t_{12}$ used as input of the first round of function u on S-QUARK algorithm.

Once the functions f and g were optimized, the next step is to optimize the implementation of the function h. The S-QUARK allows us to join blocks of 16 bits, as is shown in Table 1; however, since we have a 32-bit register machine, the implementation would be wasting half of the available bits.

Unlike f, the function h is not symmetric and therefore we can not use the previous optimization. Analyzing the inputs, we realized that 14 from the 17 inputs allow a parallelism of degree 32. This allows us to split the function h into two functions h_1 and h_2, where $h(X, Y, L) = h_1(X, Y, L) \oplus h_2(X, Y, L)$. The function h_1 processes 32 bits, where the first 16 bits will be used on the i-th iteration and the last 16 bits will be used on the $(i +1)$-th iteration. The function h_2 processes 16 bits and it is computed at each iteration. The functions h_1 and h_2 are defined in Functions 7 and 8, respectively.

Function h_1: Given two vectors X and Y of 128 bits and one vector of constants L, the output of the function h_1 is:

$$h_1(X, Y, L) = X_1 \oplus Y_3 \oplus X_7 \oplus Y_{18} \oplus X_{58} \oplus Y_{80} \oplus L_0 \oplus Y_{34} \oplus Y_{71}$$
$$\oplus X_{90} \oplus Y_{91} \oplus X_{47} \oplus X_{47}(L_0 \oplus Y_8 X_{72}). \tag{7}$$

Function h_2: Given two vectors X and Y of 128 bits and one vector of constants L, the output of the function h_2 is:

$$h_2(X, Y, L) = X_{105} \oplus Y_{111} \oplus X_{100}(Y_8 \vee X_{72} \oplus Y_{111})$$
$$\oplus Y_{111}(X_{72}(Y_8 \oplus L_0 X_{47})). \tag{8}$$

Algorithm 2. S-QUARK Optimized

Input: State S of 256 bits.
Output: State S'.

1: $x_0 = (S_0, \ldots, S_{31})$, $x_1 = (S_{32}, \ldots, S_{63})$;
2: $x_2 = (S_{64}, \ldots, S_{95})$, $x_3 = (S_{96}, \ldots, S_{127})$;
3: $y_0 = (S_{128}, \ldots, S_{159})$, $y_1 = (S_{160}, \ldots, S_{191})$;
4: $y_2 = (S_{192}, \ldots, S_{223})$, $y_3 = (S_{224}, \ldots, S_{255})$;
5: **for** j = 0 **to** 7 **do**
6:    **for** i = 0 **to** 3 **do**
7:      Compute the input values of u, h_1 and h_2
8:      $aux_1 = (x_i \oplus y_i) \wedge \text{0xFFFF0000}$
9:      $aux_1 = aux_1 \oplus u(t)$
10:     $aux_2 = h1(x, y, l)$
11:     $aux_3 = h2(x, y, l)$
12:     $aux_3 = aux_2 \oplus aux_3$
13:     $aux_3 = (aux_3 \wedge \text{0xFFFF0000}) \oplus (aux_3 \ggg 16)$
14:     $aux_1 = aux_1 \oplus aux_3$
15:     Compute the input values of u and h_2
16:     $aux_4 = (x_i \oplus y_i) \lll 16$
17:     $aux_4 = aux_4 \oplus u(t)$
18:     $aux_3 = h2(x, y, l)$
19:     $aux_3 = aux_2 \oplus aux_3$
20:     $aux_3 = (aux_3 \wedge \text{0x0000FFFF}) \oplus (aux_3 \lll 16)$
21:     $aux_2 = aux_4 \oplus aux_3$
22:     $x_i = x_i \oplus ((aux_1 \wedge \text{0xFFFF0000}) \oplus (aux_2 \ggg 16))$
23:     $y_i = y_i \oplus ((aux_1 \lll 16) \oplus (aux_2 \wedge \text{0x0000FFFF}))$
24:    **end for**
25: **end for**
26: $(S'_0, \ldots, S'_{31}) = x_0$, $(S'_{32}, \ldots, S'_{63}) = x_1$, $(S'_{64}, \ldots, S'_{95}) = x_2$
27: $(S'_{96}, \ldots, S'_{127}) = x_3$, $(S'_{128}, \ldots, S'_{159}) = y_0$, $(S'_{160}, \ldots, S'_{191}) = y_1$
28: $(S'_{192}, \ldots, S'_{223}) = y_2$, $(S'_{224}, \ldots, S'_{255}) = y_3$
29: **return** S'.

For the computation of h_1 and h_2 we need to precompute the 17 inputs; however we do not need keep all the 17 inputs saved, since most of them will be used only once, so this allows us to compute the value on the fly. Thus, the number of words required can be decreased from 17 to 5. The optimized version of algorithm S-QUARK is shown in Algorithm 2.

4.3   D-QUARK

The same techniques applied to S-QUARK implementation can be also applied to D-QUARK. However, the level of their parallelism is different, the S-QUARK algorithm allows to process 16 bits concurrently, while D-QUARK can handle only 8 bits in parallel.

Using the same techniques of Sect. 4.2, we organize the words t_0 to t_{12} as follows: the bits to compute the function f are on the first 8 bits of the lower part of the register and on the next 8 bits are the necessary bits to perform the function g. Thereafter, we can perform the algorithm using 16-bit register and with a level of parallelism of 8.

The version that processes 8 bits at the same time and uses 16-bit registers has a good efficiency when compared to the reference version[2]. However, this version does not use all the processing power available in the architecture, since we are using only 16 of the 32 bits available.

Analyzing the D-QUARK functions we realized that is possible to use the same techniques used in the implementation of the function h on the S-QUARK for the functions f and g; this is possible because from the 13 inputs of both, 12 inputs have a level of parallelism of 16. Thus, we can split f and g into two smaller functions, $f(X) = f_1(X) \oplus f_2(X)$ and $g(Y) = g_1(Y) \oplus g_2(Y)$.

By taking advantage of the symmetry of the functions f_1 and g_1, they can be joined into a function u_1, which receives 13 words of 32 bits as input and outputs 32 bits, where the first 16 bits are used on the i-th iteration and the remaining bits are used on the $(i+1)$-th iteration. The remaining processing is computed by the function u_2. The functions u_1 and u_2 are defined as follows:

Function u_1: Given a vector of 13 words of 32 bits t, the function u_1 computes a 32-bit output as follows:

$$u_1(t) = t_0 \oplus t_2 \oplus t_4 \oplus t_5 \oplus t_6 \oplus t_7 \oplus t_8 \oplus t_9 \oplus t_{10} \oplus t_6(t_7 \oplus (t_{10}t_7t_9)$$
$$\oplus (t_5t_4)\neg(t_{12}t_2 \oplus t_9t_8t_7)) \oplus (t_{12}t_2) \oplus (t_{10}t_9t_8). \qquad (9)$$

Function u_2: Given a vector of 13 words of 32 bits t, the function u_2 computes a 32-bit output as follows:

$$u_2(t) = t_{11} \wedge t_{10}(\neg(t_4t_{12}) \oplus (t_7t_9t_8)) \oplus (t_8t_5t_2). \qquad (10)$$

Using this optimization we can take advantage, in most of the time, of the power processing of the 32-bit machine. The initial state of each one of the 13 words needed to perform the first round of the functions u_1 and u_2 is shown in Fig. 4. From these words, only t_{11} needs to be computed at each iteration to be used in the function u_2 in the next round; in Fig. 5 is shown the 32 bits of t_{11} on the $(i+1)$-th iteration.

The function h of D-QUARK uses the same optimization used in the function h of S-QUARK, processing 16 bits in each iteration.

4.4   Performance Results

In this section we describe the performance results of our implementations[3]. The target machine used was the 32-bit Intel Galileo using the compiler i586-poky-linux-uclibc-gcc (GCC) 4.7.2.

---

[2] The reference code is available in [2] and has not any optimization.
[3] Our implementations are available in https://github.com/rbCabral/QUARK_32bits.

$t_0 =$	$X_0, \ldots\ldots\ldots\ldots, X_{15}$	$Y_0, \ldots\ldots\ldots\ldots, Y_{15}$	
$t_1 =$	$X_{64}, \ldots\ldots\ldots\ldots, X_{79}$	$Y_{20}, \ldots\ldots\ldots\ldots, Y_{35}$	
$t_2 =$	$X_{11}, \ldots\ldots\ldots\ldots, X_{26}$	$Y_9, \ldots\ldots\ldots\ldots, Y_{24}$	
$t_3 =$	$X_{18} \ldots\ldots\ldots\ldots, X_{33}$	$Y_{63}, \ldots\ldots\ldots\ldots, Y_{78}$	
$t_4 =$	$X_{27}, \ldots\ldots\ldots\ldots, X_{42}$	$Y_{25}, \ldots\ldots\ldots\ldots, Y_{40}$	
$t_5 =$	$X_{36}, \ldots\ldots\ldots\ldots, X_{51}$	$Y_{38}, \ldots\ldots\ldots\ldots, Y_{53}$	
$t_6 =$	$X_{42}, \ldots\ldots\ldots\ldots, X_{57}$	$Y_{44}, \ldots\ldots\ldots\ldots, Y_{59}$	
$t_7 =$	$X_{47}, \ldots\ldots\ldots\ldots, X_{62}$	$Y_{47}, \ldots\ldots\ldots\ldots, Y_{62}$	
$t_8 =$	$X_{58}, \ldots\ldots\ldots\ldots, X_{73}$	$Y_{54}, \ldots\ldots\ldots\ldots, Y_{69}$	
$t_9 =$	$X_{67}, \ldots\ldots\ldots\ldots, X_{82}$	$Y_{67}, \ldots\ldots\ldots\ldots, Y_{82}$	
$t_{10} =$	$X_{71}, \ldots\ldots\ldots\ldots, X_{86}$	$Y_{69}, \ldots\ldots\ldots\ldots, Y_{84}$	
$t_{11} =$	$X_{79}, \ldots\ldots, X_{86}, 0, \ldots, 0$	$Y_{78}, \ldots\ldots, Y_{85}, 0, \ldots, 0$	
$t_{12} =$	$X_{19}, \ldots\ldots\ldots\ldots, X_{34}$	$Y_{19}, \ldots\ldots\ldots\ldots, Y_{34}$	

Fig. 4. Initialization of the words $t_0, \ldots, t_{12}$ used as input of the first round of function u_1 on D-QUARK algorithm.

$t_{11} =$	$0, \ldots, 0, X_{87}, \ldots\ldots, X_6$	$0, \ldots, 0, Y_{86}, \ldots\ldots, Y_5$

Fig. 5. Word t_{11} on the $(i+1)$-th iteration.

Table 2. Performance of C-Code reference using the optimized functions.

Function	Optimization flag O2		Optimization flag Os	
	Size code	Cycles per byte	Size code	Cycles per byte
S-QUARK$_{ref}$	2000	78370	1602	88778
*S-QUARK$_{ref}$	1808	61650	1469	70816

In Table 2 is shown the performance results of the C-code reference when only the algorithmic optimization of Sect. 3 were applied. In the first row, we have the C-code (S-QUARK$_{ref}$) provided by the authors in [2] and in the next row we have the same code using the optimized functions presented in Sect. 3, called (*S-QUARK$_{ref}$). The use of this optimization allows us to reduce in about 10 % the code size and 20 % the number of cycles per byte.

In Table 3 are shown the code size and the cycles per byte of the lightweight hash functions for 112-bit security level with the optimization flags -O2 or -O3 (the fastest) and -Os. The **S-QUARK$_{opt}$ is the implementation of Algorithm 2, *S-QUARK$_{opt}$ is also an implementation of Algorithm 2, but with the loop unrolled, PHOTON-224 is a table-based implementation from the authors available in [12] and SPONGENT-224 is a reference implementation from the authors available in [7]. The fastest implementation is the PHOTON-224 compiled with -O3, but for achieving that performance it needs a storage of 13450 bytes. On the other hand, our *S-QUARK$_{opt}$ implementation compiled with -O3 was 2.3× slower than PHOTON-224, but with a code size 5.3× smaller. Using the compiler flag -Os (for size code optimization), our *S-QUARK$_{opt}$ was the fastest and most compact implementation.

Table 3. Performance of hash function at 112-bit security level.

Function	Optimization flag O2–O3		Optimization flag Os	
	Size code	Cycles per byte	Size code	Cycles per byte
*S-QUARK$_{opt}$	2518	5671	2107	5832
**S-QUARK$_{opt}$	7078	5138	3298	8015
PHOTON-224	13450	2366	2612	7678
SPONGENT-224	5030	1040014	3016	2311836

In Table 4 are shown the code size and the cycles per byte of the lightweight hash functions for 80-bit security level with the optimization flags -O2 or -O3 (the fastest) and -Os. D-QUARK$_{ref}$ is the C code reference from the authors available in [2], D-QUARK$_{opt}$ is our implementation, PHOTON-160 is a table-based implementation from the authors available in [12] and SPONGENT-160 is a reference implementation from the authors available in [7]. The D-QUARK implementation was slower than S-QUARK implementation even with less security level, this happened because D-QUARK needs to perform the permutation function P more times than the S-QUARK, since the S-QUARK splits the message in blocks of 32 bits and the D-QUARK in blocks of 16 bits.

Table 4. Performance of hash function at 80-bit security level.

Function	Optimization flag O2–O3		Optimization flag Os	
	Size code	Cycles per byte	Size code	Cycles per byte
D-QUARK$_{ref}$	1990	102997	1592	117462
D-QUARK$_{opt}$	3326	9628	3114	10319
PHOTON-160	13795	1651	2698	12625
SPONGENT-160	4901	562337	3016	1255905

5   Conclusions

This work contributes with a fast software implementation of the QUARK family. We introduced some techniques for improving the performance of two variants of the QUARK family. In particular, for the 32-bit Intel Galileo Platform, our software implementation of S-QUARK (for 112-bit security level) and D-QUARK (for 80-bit security level) obtained a significant speedup of 15× and 10×, respectively, when compared to the reference implementation. Our techniques can also be applied to implement QUARK on 8-bit or 16-bit platforms.

Acknowledgments. This research was partially supported by Intel and CNPq. The authors would like to thank the anonymous reviewers for their helpful suggestions and comments. Additionally, they would like thank Armando Faz Hernández for his comments that greatly improved the manuscript.

A   QUARK Family

Here is presented the definition of the QUARK family and the functions p, f, g and h for each member of the family. The function p, used by L, is the same for all three instances: given a vector L, $p(L) = L_0 \oplus L_3$.

U-QUARK. It is the lightest flavor of QUARK. It was designed to provide a 136-bit hash value and has a security level of 64 bits. The functions f, g and h used in this instance are defined as follows.

Function f: Given a 68-bit vector X, the function f returns 1 bit computed as:

$$
\begin{aligned}
f(X) = &X_0 \oplus\ X_{55} \oplus X_{14} \oplus X_{21} \oplus X_{28} \oplus X_{33} \oplus X_{37} \oplus X_{45} \oplus X_{50} \oplus X_{52} \\
&\oplus X_9 X_{28} X_{45} X_{59} \oplus X_9 \oplus X_{33} X_{37} X_{52} X_{55} \oplus X_{21} X_{28} X_{33} X_{37} X_{45} X_{52} \\
&\oplus X_{55} X_{59} \oplus X_9 X_{15} X_{21} X_{28} X_{33} \oplus X_{45} X_{52} X_{55} \oplus X_{21} X_{28} X_{33} \\
&\oplus X_{37} X_{45} X_{52} X_{55} X_{59} \oplus X_{15} X_{21} X_{55} X_{59} \oplus X_9 X_{15} \oplus X_{33} X_{37}.
\end{aligned}
$$

Function g: Given a 68-bit vector Y, the function g returns 1 bit computed as:

$$
\begin{aligned}
g(Y) = &Y_0 \oplus Y_7 \oplus Y_{15} \oplus Y_{20} \oplus Y_{30} \oplus Y_{35} \oplus Y_{37} \oplus Y_{42} \oplus Y_{49} \oplus Y_{51} \\
&\oplus Y_7 Y_{30} Y_{42} Y_{58} \oplus Y_{35} Y_{37} Y_{51} Y_{54} \oplus Y_7 Y_{16} \oplus Y_{20} Y_{30} Y_{35} Y_{37} Y_{42} Y_{51} \\
&\oplus Y_{54} Y_{58} \oplus Y_{35} Y_{37} \oplus Y_7 Y_{16} Y_{20} Y_{30} Y_{35} \oplus Y_{42} Y_{51} Y_{54} \oplus Y_{20} Y_{30} Y_{35} \\
&\oplus Y_{54} \oplus Y_{37} Y_{42} Y_{51} Y_{54} Y_{58} \oplus Y_{16} Y_{20} Y_{54} Y_{58}.
\end{aligned}
$$

Function h: Given two 68-bit vectors X and Y and a constant vector L, the function h returns 1 bit computed as:

$$
\begin{aligned}
h(X, Y, L) = &L_0 \oplus X_1 \oplus Y_2 \oplus X_4 \oplus Y_{10} \oplus X_{25} \oplus X_{31} \oplus Y_{43} \oplus X_{56} \oplus Y_{59} \\
&\oplus Y_3 X_{55} \oplus X_{46} X_{55} \oplus X_{55} Y_{59} \oplus Y_3 X_{25} X_{46} \oplus Y_3 X_{46} X_{55} \\
&\oplus Y_3 X_{46} Y_{59} \oplus L_0 X_{25} X_{46} Y_{59} \oplus L_0 X_{25}.
\end{aligned}
$$

D-QUARK. D-QUARK is the intermediary version of the QUARK family. It provides a hash value of 160 bits and has 80 bits of security level. The functions f, g, and h, are defined below:

Function f: Uses the same function f of U-QUARK, but with taps, 0, 11, 18, 19, 27, 36, 42, 47, 58, 64, 67, 71, 79 instead of 0, 9, 14, 15, 21, 28, 33, 37, 45, 50, 52, 55, 59, respectively.

Function g: Uses the same function g of U-QUARK, but with taps, 0, 9, 19, 20, 25, 38, 44, 47, 54, 63, 67, 69, 78 instead of 0, 7, 15, 16, 20, 30, 35, 37, 42, 49, 51, 54, 58, respectively.

Function h: Given two 88-bit vectors X and Y and a constant vector L, the function h returns 1 bit computed as:

$$h(X,Y,L) = L_0 \oplus X_1 \oplus Y_2 \oplus X_5 \oplus Y_{12} \oplus Y_{24} \oplus X_{35} \oplus X_{40} \oplus X_{48} \oplus Y_{55}$$
$$\oplus Y_{61} \oplus Y_{79} \oplus Y_4 X_{68} \oplus X_{57} X_{68} \oplus X_{68} Y_{79} \oplus Y_4 X_{35} X_{57}$$
$$\oplus X_{72} \oplus Y_4 X_{57} X_{68} \oplus Y_4 X_{57} Y_{79} \oplus L_0 X_{35} X_{57} Y_{79} \oplus L_0 X_{35}.$$

S-QUARK. The S-QUARK is the version that provides the highest level of security in the family QUARK. It provides a hash value of 256-bits and has 112 bits of security level. Like the other versions of QUARK, it uses essentially three functions, f, g and h, which are defined below:

Function f: Uses the same function f of U-QUARK, but with taps, 0, 16, 26, 28, 39, 52, 61, 69, 84, 94, 97, 103, 111 instead of 0, 9, 14, 15, 21, 28, 33, 37, 45, 50, 52, 55, 59, respectively.

Function g: Uses the same function g of U-QUARK, but with taps, 0, 13, 28, 30, 37, 56, 65, 69, 79, 92, 96, 101, 109 instead of 0, 7, 15, 16, 20, 30, 35, 37, 42, 49, 51, 54, 58, respectively.

Function h: Given two 128-bit vectors X and Y and a constant vector L, the function h returns 1 bit computed as:

$$h(X,Y,L) = L_0 \oplus X_1 \oplus Y_3 \oplus X_7 \oplus Y_{18} \oplus Y_{34} \oplus X_{47} \oplus X_{58} \oplus Y_{71} \oplus Y_{80}$$
$$\oplus X_{90} \oplus Y_{91} \oplus X_{105} \oplus Y_{111} \oplus Y_8 X_{100} \oplus X_{72} X_{100} \oplus X_{100} Y_{111}$$
$$\oplus Y_8 X_{47} X_{72} \oplus Y_8 X_{72} X_{100} \oplus Y_8 X_{72} Y_{111} \oplus L_0 X_{47} X_{72} Y_{111}$$
$$\oplus L_0 X_{47}.$$

References

1. Aumasson, J.-P., Henzen, L., Meier, W., Naya-Plasencia, M.: Quark: a lightweight hash. J. Crypt. **26**(2), 313–339 (2013)
2. Aumasson, J.-P., Henzen, L., Meier, W., Naya-Plasencia, M.: Quark: a lightweight hash, May 2015. https://131002.net/quark/
3. Aumasson, J.-P., Henzen, L., Meier, W., Naya-Plasencia, M.: Quark: a lightweight hash. In: Mangard, S., Standaert, F.-X. (eds.) CHES 2010. LNCS, vol. 6225, pp. 1–15. Springer, Heidelberg (2010)
4. Balasch, J., et al.: Compact implementation and performance evaluation of hash functions in ATtiny devices. In: Mangard, S. (ed.) CARDIS 2012. LNCS, vol. 7771, pp. 158–172. Springer, Heidelberg (2013)
5. Bertoni, G., Daemen, J., Peeters, M., Van Assche, G.: Sponge functions. In: ECRYPT Hash Workshop, vol. 2007 (2007)

6. Bogdanov, A., Knežević, M., Leander, G., Toz, D., Varıcı, K., Verbauwhede, I.: Spongent: a lightweight hash function. In: Takagi, T., Preneel, B. (eds.) CHES 2011. LNCS, vol. 6917, pp. 312–325. Springer, Heidelberg (2011)

7. Bogdanov, A., Knežević, M., Leander, G., DenizToz, K., Verbauwhede, I., Spongent: the design space of lightweight cryptographic hashing, June 2015. https://sites.google.com/site/spongenthash/home

8. De Cannière, C., Dunkelman, O., Knežević, M.: KATAN and KTANTAN — a family of small and efficient hardware-oriented block ciphers. In: Clavier, C., Gaj, K. (eds.) CHES 2009. LNCS, vol. 5747, pp. 272–288. Springer, Heidelberg (2009)

9. Eisenbarth, T., et al.: Compact implementation and performance evaluation of block ciphers in ATtiny devices. In: Mitrokotsa, A., Vaudenay, S. (eds.) AFRICACRYPT 2012. LNCS, vol. 7374, pp. 172–187. Springer, Heidelberg (2012)

10. Fog, A.: The microarchitecture of Intel, AMD and via CPUs/An optimization guide for assembly programmers and compiler makers (2014)

11. Guo, J., Peyrin, T., Poschmann, A.: The photon family of lightweight hash functions. In: Rogaway, P. (ed.) Advances in Cryptology – CRYPTO2011. Lecture Notes in Computer Science, vol. 6841, pp. 222–239. Springer, Heidelberg (2011)

12. Guo, J., Peyrin, T., Poschmann, A., The photon family of lightweight hash functions, May 2015. https://sites.google.com/site/photonhashfunction/

13. Hell, M., Johansson, T., Maximov, A., Meier, W.: A stream cipher proposal: Grain-128. In: IEEE International Symposium on Information Theory (ISIT). Citeseer (2006)

14. Intel® corporation. Intel Quark SoC X1000 Core Developer's Manual. Number 329679–001US, October 2013

15. Ramon, M.C.: Intel Galileo and Intel Galileo Gen 2. Springer, New York (2014). http://www.springer.com/us/book/9781430268390#aboutBook

Single-Cycle Implementations of Block Ciphers

Pieter Maene[1,2]([✉]) and Ingrid Verbauwhede[1,2]

[1] Department of Electrical Engineering (ESAT), COSIC,
KU Leuven, Leuven, Belgium
{pieter.maene,ingrid.verbauwhede}@esat.kuleuven.be
[2] iMinds, Gent, Belgium

Abstract. Security mechanisms to protect our systems and data from malicious adversaries have become essential. Strong encryption algorithms are an important building block of these solutions. However, each application has its own requirements and it is not always possible to find a cipher that meets them all. This work compares unrolled combinational hardware implementations of six lightweight block ciphers, along with an AES implementation as a baseline. Up until now, the majority of such ciphers were designed for area-constrained environments where speed is often not crucial, but recently the need for single-cycle, low-latency block ciphers with limited area requirements has arisen to build security architectures for embedded systems. Our comparison shows that some designers are already on this track, but a lot of work still remains to be done.

Keywords: Block ciphers · Lightweight cryptography · Single-cycle · Synthesis

1 Introduction

Software applications have always been vulnerable to attacks from malicious actors. One research topic in the trusted computing community is Protected Module Architecture (PMAs), where applications can be automatically protected against them. For example, Intel's Software Guard Extensions (SGX) provide architectural support to isolate applications [3]. Software runs in so-called enclaves, which have special hardware features to protect code and data from unauthorised access. When sensitive data leaves or enters the enclave, it is automatically encrypted and decrypted, and this requires a fast algorithm. Finding suitable low-latency cryptographic algorithms is one of the biggest challenges when bringing these isolation techniques to area-constrained embedded systems.

As smaller silicon technology nodes make it possible to place more and more transistors on a single die, modern Systems-on-Chip (SoCs) have become many-core devices. High-bandwidth, packet-switched Networks-on-Chip (NoCs) have replaced slower buses [15]. Protection of these networks is an open research question. The underlying ideas of security mechanisms for traditional networks can be used, but will require fast and efficient cryptographic primitives.

© Springer International Publishing Switzerland 2016
T. Güneysu et al. (Eds.): LightSec 2015, LNCS 9542, pp. 131–147, 2016.
DOI: 10.1007/978-3-319-29078-2_8

In both these applications, data elements should be processed as fast as possible and it is not necessary that the cipher has high throughput. Additionally, design constraints often limit the clock frequency of these circuits. Therefore, only a limited number of cycles will be available to finish the encryption within a given delay and in some cases a single-cycle implementation will be the only alternative. One approach to achieve this, is by unrolling existing iterative block ciphers. However, this results in long combinational paths, which have a high associated delay. As will be shown in our work, they can only operate at such low clock frequencies, the operating speed of the architectures they are integrated with will be limited. Of course, introducing pipeline registers would increase the throughput and maximum clock frequency, but at the cost of additional latency. Another advantage of fully combinational implementations is that they can be easily integrated with existing designs, because of the lack of control logic.

Our work gives synthesis results for unrolled implementations of six families of lightweight ciphers, where the same approach is used for all of them. Whenever possible, algorithms are grouped by block and key size to make a fair comparison with regard to the security they offer. The different algorithms are AES [14], KATAN [16], PRESENT [8], PRINCE [11], RECTANGLE [33], SIMON [5] and SPECK [5]. These ciphers were chosen because they cover a wide range of algorithm types and possible design choices. A similar analysis was done by Knežević et al. in 2012 [23]. This paper includes some of the same ciphers, but also adds results for several recent designs that were introduced since. A short summary of the best known cryptanalysis results is given for each algorithm. Section 2 first introduces some general concepts and terminology. Synthesis results for FPGA and ASIC are given in Sect. 3. Finally, Sect. 4 compares our results, followed by a conclusion in Sect. 5.

2   Preliminaries

2.1   Block Cipher Structure

A block cipher (Definition 1 [24]) is a basic cryptographic building block offering confidentiality of data. It is used in a wide variety of applications, from protecting communication to generating pseudo-random numbers.

Definition 1. *An n-bit block cipher is a function $E : V_n \times \mathcal{K} \rightarrow V_n$, such that for each key $K \in \mathcal{K}$, $E(P, K)$ is an invertible mapping (the encryption function for K) from V_n to V_n, written $E_K(P)$. The inverse mapping is the decryption function, denoted $D_K(C)$. $C = E_K(P)$ denotes that ciphertext C results from encrypting plaintext P under K.*

Algorithm designers typically use established design techniques when creating new algorithms. Most current block ciphers are iterated ciphers (Definition 2 [24]). Feistel ciphers (Definition 3 [24]) are a special instance with a particular structure.

Definition 2. *An iterated block cipher is a block cipher involving the sequential repetition of an internal function called the round function. Parameters include the number of rounds r, the block bit-size n, and the bit-size k of the input key K from which r subkeys K_i (round keys) are derived. For invertibility (allowing unique decryption), for each value K_i the round function is a bijection on the round input.*

Definition 3. *A Feistel cipher is an iterated cipher mapping a $2t$-bit plaintext (L_0, R_0), for t-bit blocks L_0 and R_0, to a ciphertext (R_r, L_r), through an r-round process where $r \geq 1$. For $1 \leq i \leq r$, round i maps $(L_{i-1}, R_{i-1}) \xrightarrow{K_i} (L_i, R_i)$ as follows: $L_i = R_{i-1}$, $R_i = L_{i-1} \oplus f(R_{i-1}, K_i)$, where each subkey K_i is derived from the cipher key K.*

Hardware implementations of iterated block ciphers usually have logic for a single round and a controller that manages the round function iterations. Consequently, several clock cycles will be required before the result is ready. It is important to note that the number of clock cycles needed to encrypt a block is a property of the implementation. One way to reduce the number of cycles is by unrolling the iterations, and in doing so, we obtain single-cycle implementations. When all rounds are fully unrolled, this process results in the same basic structure for all of them (see Fig. 1).

It can be seen from Definition 2 that each round has two components: the key expansion and round function. The former generates the subkeys K_i based on the original key, a previous one or a combination of both. The latter transforms the input data using the key. In general, the function is identical for each round, but some algorithms introduce small variations (e.g. a different constant could be added in each round). The total number of rounds depends on the algorithm and can vary widely. An operation is sometimes applied to the plaintext before using it as an input to the first round. The last round's output can be similarly modified before using it as the ciphertext.

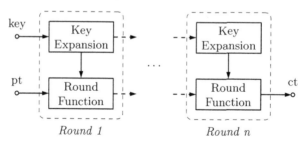

Fig. 1. Structure of unrolled block ciphers (pt: plaintext, ct: ciphertext).

2.2 Logic Depth

The logic depth [27] of a path is defined as the number of combinational gates between input and output. Since each level of the path has a specific delay associated with it, the logic depth will be linked to the latency of the circuit. However, some operations will have a longer intrinsic delay than others, so that a deep circuit of low-latency gates will have a lower delay than a shallow circuit with high-latency gates. The logic depth is a property of the implementation, which is influenced by the design.

Section 3 will give the logic depth of the critical path on FPGA for each algorithm. The critical path of a circuit is the path for which it takes the longest for the output to stabilize [28], i.e., the one with the longest delay.

2.3 Fan-Out

The fan-out denotes the number of load gates N that are connected to the output of the driving gate [28]. When the fan-out of a gate is large, it will deteriorate performance because the load on that gate will be very high. This impacts its dynamic performance and will slow down the circuit. The fan-out of a gate is influenced by the design of the algorithm and how it is implemented. Therefore, a designer should be careful not to reuse a single intermediate result in a next step too often.

3 Synthesis Results

We will now discuss the design criteria and specifications of each block cipher, as well as its most important results. The best cryptanalysis results known to us are given as well. An overview of the properties of all discussed algorithms is given in Table 1. Tables 2 and 3 give an overview of all FPGA and ASIC results respectively. A diagram of the critical path for each cipher is also given. Note that these figures do not show the algorithm's full data flow, but rather a simplified version for clarity.

The regular structure (Sect. 2.1) of block ciphers makes it possible to use a generic approach for unrolling each algorithm. Only the encryption mode of each cipher was implemented. The area cost of adding decryption will depend on the design: this requires less overhead compared to encryption for some than others. Both FPGA and ASIC results are listed, because although most real-world applications will eventually be produced as ASIC, FPGAs are sometimes introduced in products (e.g., because they can be upgraded in the field). They are also heavily used in the development of new chips.

The FPGA results were obtained after Place and Route (PAR) on a Xilinx Virtex 6 in Xilinx ISE. More specifically, the configuration of the Xilinx ML605 development board was selected (`xc6vlx240t-2ff1156`). All syntheses for ASIC were done with UMC's 0.13 μm technology in Synopsys Design Vision.

3.1 AES

In 1998, Daemen and Rijmen submitted their Rijndael algorithm [14] to the Advanced Encryption Standard (AES) competition, organised by NIST.

Table 1. Properties of all implemented algorithms.

Cipher	Key size	Block size	Rounds	Type	Characteristics
AES	128	128	10	SP Network	8-bit S-box
KATAN	80	32	254		Non-Linear Boolean Functions (AND and XOR)
		64			
PRESENT	80	64	31	SP Network	4-bit S-box
	128				
PRINCE	128	64	12	Unrolled	4-bit S-box, Matrix Layer
RECTANGLE	80	64	25	SP Network	4-bit S-box
SIMON	64	32	32	Feistel	XOR and Left Cyclic Shift
	128	64	44		
SPECK	64	32	22		XOR, Addition and Cyclic Shift
	128	64	27		

Three years later, the design won and it is now known as AES. The implementation criteria for the AES contest were high throughput, low memory requirements, and hardware and software suitability [6]. It is used for confidentiality in a wide range of applications: among others to protect Wi-Fi connections, secure web traffic, or encrypt hard drives. The Rijndael family can accommodate any block and key size from 128 to 256 bits, with steps of 32 bits. NIST fixed the block size at 128 bits, but the key size can be chosen depending on the required level of security (128, 192, or 256 bits) [26].

The algorithm has the following three basic operations: *SubBytes*, *ShiftRows* and *MixColumns*. SubBytes substitutes a state byte with the result of an S-box look-up. ShiftRows cyclically shifts the state's rows. MixColumns applies an invertible linear transformation to each column. AES was not specifically designed as a low-area or low-latency hardware cipher, but it is included here as a reference because its algorithm is well-understood and generally known.

The best known shortcut attack that works on the full versions of AES is a biclique attack from 2011 [9]. It breaks all 10 rounds of AES128 with a time complexity of $2^{126.18}$ and data complexity of 2^{88}. These numbers are still high enough to have no practical value.

Our implementation for 128-bit keys uses 8,984 LUTs and has a 24.7 ns combinational delay. On FPGA, logic is responsible for 21.94 % of the delay and routing for 78.06 %. The logic depth (Sect. 2.2) of the critical path consists of 52 levels. The S-box look-up of each round accounts for three levels, or 30 for our design (10 rounds). A diagram of the critical path for one round is shown in Fig. 2. The S-box look-up and finite field multiplication are the most

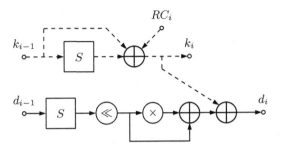

Fig. 2. Diagram of the critical of one unrolled AES round (RC_i: round constant, $\ll$: circular shift, $\times$: finite field multiplier). The dashed part is the key expansion, which does not impact the critical path.

expensive components in terms of delay. However, note that the multiplication can be implemented efficiently and without a full multiplier. Although the key expansion for each round is done in parallel with the calculations of the round itself and therefore does not appear on the critical path, it is shown to give an idea of its cost.

The big difference between the logic and routing delay has two causes. First, the main operations on the critical path are look-ups in big 8-bit S-boxes, which have long delays. They incur a total delay (both logic and routing) of 11.2 ns, or 45.24 %. Second, the input signal to each round has a large fan-out, slowing down the circuit. This is not caused by a design decision here, but rather an effect of how the S-box was synthesized.

All S-boxes were implemented with 8-bit to 8-bit Look-Up Table (LUTs). This explains the large ASIC area, because LUTs do not map well to ASIC. Note that implementations which rely on composite field arithmetic yield significantly better area results, especially in ASIC [20,29].

3.2 KATAN

De Cannière et al. designed KATAN and KTANTAN [16] to be used in RFID tags. Their goal was to build an algorithm with an efficient hardware implementation, while still achieving reasonable throughput. The family of ciphers has a fixed key size of 80 bits, but the block size is a parameter (32, 48 or 64 bits). KATAN uses a Linear Feedback Shift Register (LFSR) for the key expansion. Encryption is done by splitting the state into two parts of different length and applying a non-linear function to each in every round of the algorithm. The only difference between KATAN and KTANTAN is that the latter has a hard-coded key.

Bogdanov and Rechberger [10] first broke the KTANTAN family of ciphers with a meet-in-the-middle attack that has a time complexity of $2^{75.170}$ and data complexity of 3. So far, there are only known attacks against reduced-round versions of KATAN, the best of which is a related-key boomerang attack by Isobe et al. [21]. It breaks 174 out of 254 rounds of KATAN32 with a time complexity $2^{78.8}$ and data complexity $2^{27.6}$.

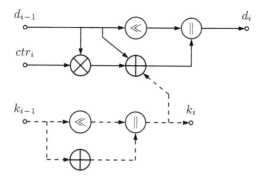

Fig. 3. Diagram of the critical path of one unrolled KATAN round (ctr_i: LFSR round counter, $\ll$: regular shift). The dashed part is the key expansion, which does not impact the critical path.

Two versions of KATAN were built: KATAN32 and KATAN64 use 32-bit and 64-bit blocks respectively. The former requires 1,064 LUTs and has a critical path of 41.2 ns. Although it has a very small area, its practical use is limited by the long delay, which is caused by the large number of rounds. The results for the latter are similar, with 2,550 LUTs and 47.3 ns. On FPGA, 91 % of the delay is caused by routing, and 9 % by logic for both variations. The logic depth consists of respectively 62 and 72 levels for the 32- and 64-bit states.

Figure 3 shows a diagram of the critical path. The signal runs in parallel through the paths with the left shift and XOR and AND gates respectively. Since it does not cost much to implement a shift in hardware, only the latter will be in the critical path. Both the key expansion and LFSR round counter (ctr_i, which is not shown) can be calculated in parallel and are therefore not part of the critical path. Although the round function has a small delay, the large number of rounds explains why a combinational implementation of the overall algorithm is slow.

The XOR gates have a 9 to 1 delay ratio. In the Virtex 6 FPGA, they are implemented with 6-input LUTs, which have a constant look-up time of 0.061 ns (the logic delay). The routing delay accounts for the time needed to get the result to the next LUT. Contrary to the constant logic delay, it varies slightly depending on the fan-out (Sect. 2.3) and placement of the design on the fabric.

3.3   PRESENT

Like KATAN (Sect. 3.2), PRESENT [8] was created as a lightweight block cipher for constrained environments. They have very similar characteristics, but PRESENT has a higher throughput with lower area. In each encryption round, the state's nibbles are run through a 4-bit S-box. This is followed by a permutation layer which moves bits to different positions. The block size is fixed at 64 bits, but both 80- and 128-bit keys can be used. The variation with 80-bit keys takes up 2,089 LUTs and has a 29.2 ns delay. The one with 128-bit keys

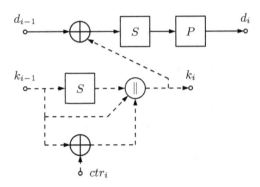

Fig. 4. Diagram of the critical path of one unrolled PRESENT round. The dashed part is the key expansion, which does not impact the critical path.

uses 2,203 LUTs and has a critical path of 32.6 ns. Increasing the key size has a small impact on area and critical path.

No known attacks break the full version of PRESENT. The best one was published by Joo Yeon Cho [13] and breaks 25 out of 31 rounds of the 80-bit variation with a time complexity of 2^{64} and data complexity of $2^{62.4}$.

On FPGA, 9.0 % of the delay is caused by logic and 91.0 % by routing for both key sizes. A diagram of the critical path for one round is shown in Fig. 4. In each round, it first passes through the XOR with the key, followed by the S-box look-up and finally the permutation layer. The latter is a very cheap operation in hardware, as it only requires reordening wires. The XOR gates have the same characteristics that were mentioned earlier, but the smaller 4-bit S-boxes have a logic and routing delay similar to other gates. The critical path of the former has a logic depth of 48 levels, while the latter comes in at 52 levels.

3.4   PRINCE

PRINCE [11] is the first lightweight block cipher design that focuses on reducing latency. Traditional block ciphers are iterated algorithms with almost identical round functions (Sect. 2.1). This similarity is a big advantage to build compact multi-cycle algorithms, but becomes problematic when the ciphertext needs to be ready in a single cycle. By deciding on an unrolled structure from the start, the design space greatly increases, as there is no need for each round to be identical. An additional requirement for PRINCE was negligible overhead for the decryption mode.

The algorithm has a symmetric design about a center matrix multiplication. Aside from the addition of the expanded key and round constants, the rounds have two basic operations: a 4-bit S-box and matrix multiplication. The latter is constructed so that every output bit is influenced by three input bits. The matrix multiplication is implemented as an XOR of the selected bits. Three different matrices are used: the construction of the symmetric matrix M' is given in the original paper. The matrix M is derived from M' by first shifting the input state

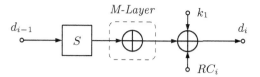

Fig. 5. Critical path diagram of one regular PRINCE round (RC_i: round constant). The dashed part is the key expansion, which does not impact the critical path.

similarly to AES' *ShiftRows* before the multiplication. Both the block and key size are fixed to 64 and 128 bits respectively. The 128-bit key input is expanded to 192 bits, so that three different 64-bit keys are available. k_0 and k'_0 are used for pre- and post-whitening respectively, and k_1 as the round subkey.

The key k_0 and a round constant are added first. Then, there are five rounds in which the S-box is applied to the state, followed by multiplication with M, and again the addition of a round constant and the key k_1 (see Fig. 5). The center part of the algorithm applies the S-box, multiplies the result with M', and applies the inverse S-box. This is followed by five inverse rounds (the order of the operations is reversed, and the inverse S-box and M^{-1} are used). The final step is again the addition of a round constant and key k'_0.

Since its publication, the resistance of PRINCE against different attacks has been investigated. The most recent ones are due to Morawiecki [25], Derbez and Perrin [17], Canteaut et al. [12] and Zhao et al. [34]. The best known attack so far is the one by Morawiecki [25]. His meet-in-the-middle approach compromises 10 out of 12 rounds with (online) time complexity 2^{68} and data complexity 2^{57}. When the reflection parameter α can be chosen, the cipher core, i.e. the algorithm without the pre- and post-whitening keys, is fully broken with a time and data complexity of 2^{41} [22].

PRINCE only needs 1,244 LUTs and has a short critical path of 16.4 ns. It first passes through the three initial XORs, which are combined in a single LUT. In the five regular rounds that follow (see Fig. 5), the S-box look-up and matrix multiplication are also synthesized to a single LUT, as well as the two remaining XORs. The signal then runs through another S-box look-up and the matrix multiplication at the center. The rest of the path is symmetric, due to the cipher's design. On FPGA, routing is responsible for 91.0 % of the delay and logic for 9.0 %, which can again be explained by the general gate characteristics given earlier. The logic depth of the critical path is 26 levels.

The absence of a complicated key expansion does not impact the critical path, as it can be processed in parallel with the data processing. This was observed for the other algorithms, where the key expansion never shows up in the critical path. However, it does lower the area requirements of the cipher.

3.5   RECTANGLE

Published in 2014, RECTANGLE [33] is the most recent cipher discussed here. It was designed to have good hardware and software performance. The round

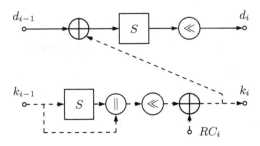

Fig. 6. Critical path diagram of one unrolled RECTANGLE round ($\ll$: circular shift, RC_i: round constant). The dashed part is the key expansion, which does not impact the critical path.

function is very simple: first, there is an XOR with the round subkey, followed by the application of a 4-bit S-box substitution to the state's columns and a cyclic shift of its rows over different offsets. The key expansion also has these two operations (the S-box is only applied to the 0th column of the key state) and the addition of a round constant, which is generated by an LFSR. The block size is fixed at 64 bits, but there are two possible key sizes (80 and 128 bits).

Since it was only published very recently, few analyses have been published on RECTANGLE. Currently, there is only one report about the variation with 80-bit keys by Shan et al. [30]. Their differential attack breaks 19 out of 25 rounds with a time complexity of $2^{67.42}$ and data complexity of 2^{62}.

The variation with 80-bit keys takes up 1,682 LUTs and has a 19.4 ns delay. The one with 128-bit keys requires 1,730 LUTs and has a critical path of 19.3 ns. Notice that the latencies for both key sizes are almost identical, confirming that the key expansion is not part of the critical path. For each round, the critical path runs through the XOR with the round key, S-box look-up and circular shift (see Fig. 6). The key expansion can be done in parallel and is only shown to give an idea of its cost. On FPGA, one LUT combines the XOR, S-box look-up, and shift. However, the synthesis cannot merge the three operations in some cases (probably due to placement constraints). The final component is the XOR with the last subkey (not shown on Fig. 6). On FPGA, 8.2 % of the delay is caused by logic and 91.8 % by routing, which is expected given the general characteristics of the gates. The logic depth of the critical path is 41 levels.

3.6   SIMON

The designers of SIMON and SPECK (Sect. 3.7) [5] focused on flexibility. Most lightweight block ciphers have a small number of possible block and key sizes. This can make it hard to find a suitable algorithm for a specific application. In contrast, the parameters of SIMON and SPECK give rise to 10 variations. The block size ranges from 32 to 128 bits and the key size from 64 to 256 bits.

SIMON is a Feistel cipher (Sect. 2.1) where the cipher's state is split in half and in each round, the upper part of the input is left unchanged and becomes

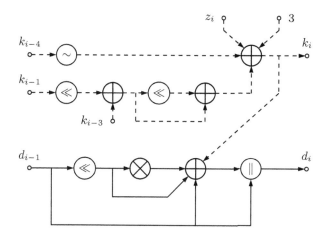

Fig. 7. Critical path diagram of one unrolled SIMON round ($\sim$: inverter, $\ll$: circular shift, z_i: bit from a predefined constant vector). The dashed part is the key expansion, which does not impact the critical path.

the lower part of the output. The round function is applied to the lower part and assigned to the upper part of the output. SIMON's round function is very straightforward: it has just three cyclic shifts, three XOR gates, and one AND gate. The key expansion is slightly more complicated, but uses similar building blocks as the round function.

SIMON and SPECK have been analysed for mathematical weaknesses using a variety of techniques [1,2,4,7,31,32], but none have broken the full cipher so far. Note that some publications are limited to a set of specific parameter pairs. The best result for SIMON 32/64 at this time is a linear super-trail attack by Ashur [4] which breaks 24 out of 32 rounds with a time complexity of $2^{63.57}$ and data complexity of $2^{31.57}$.

We implemented two parameter pairs: one with 32-bit blocks and 64-bit keys and one with 64-bit blocks and 128-bit keys. The former needs 960 LUTs and has a critical path of 20.4 ns. The latter uses 2,688 LUTs and the output is ready after 27.3 ns. The critical path runs through a circular shift, AND and XOR gate (see Fig. 7). Again, the key expansion is not part of the critical path, but is only included in the diagram to show its cost. The XOR and AND operations in each round are combined in a single LUT. On FPGA, 90 % of the delay is caused by routing and 10 % by logic for both variations, which is the ratio we've seen for the other designs as well. The logic depth of the smallest variation consists of 34 levels and 46 levels for the other one.

3.7   SPECK

SPECK was published together with SIMON (Sect. 3.6), and although both perform well in general, SIMON was optimised for hardware implementations and

SPECK for software. The state is also split in half in SPECK's design, but it is not a Feistel cipher, so both halves change in each round. The round function has even fewer operations than SIMON's, but a very important difference is that one adder is now being used. Although trivial in software, this design decision has a big impact on hardware performance, as can be seen from the results.

Of all reports on SIMON, only Biryukov et al. [7] also analysed SPECK, but improved results were obtained by Dinur [18]. The best attack breaks 14 out of 22 rounds of SPECK 32/64 with a time complexity of 2^{63} and data complexity of 2^{31}.

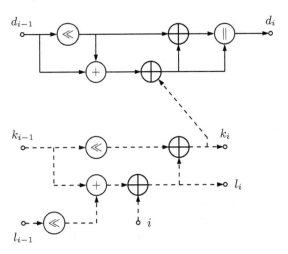

Fig. 8. Critical path diagram of one unrolled SPECK round ($\ll$: circular shift, i: round counter). The dashed part is the key expansion, which does not impact the critical path.

Implementations were built for the same two parameter pairs as were used with SIMON (Sect. 3.6). SPECK 32/64 requires 1,513 LUTs and has a 40.3 ns delay. SPECK 64/128 uses 3,594 LUTs and has a critical path of 50.3 ns. The components of the critical path differ between the rounds depending on the possible optimizations after placement. In general, it runs through the circular shift, adder chain, and finally the XOR gates (see Fig. 8). Comparing the delay for both variations, we can clearly see the impact of the adder. On FPGA, logic is responsible for 33 % and the wiring for 67 % for both variations. This is due to the adders introducing longer logic delays than the basic gates that were used in all other algorithms. The critical path of SPECK 32/64 has a logic depth of 124 levels, while SPECK 64/128 comes in at 197 levels. The total delay caused by the adders is 26.4 ns (65.53 %) and 32.8 ns (65.28 %) respectively.

4   Comparison

Table 2 summarizes all FPGA results from the previous section, grouped by block and key size. Looking at the ciphers with 32-bit blocks, SIMON 32/64 has the best performance both in terms of area and throughput. An important disadvantage are the 64-bit keys which only offer very short-term protection against small organizations [19]. While KATAN 32/80 uses stronger keys and has similar area requirements, its large number of rounds results in a long critical path.

Among the algorithms with 64-bit blocks and 80-bit keys, RECTANGLE is the smallest and has the shortest latency too. PRESENT has similar characteristics because they use the same techniques. The difference between the two is only caused by the actual S-box design and permutation layer. Although KATAN's area is still quite small for these parameters, its latency is the second-highest of all implementations. The reason for the higher throughput is the bigger block size.

Comparing the results for the last parameter pair (64-bit blocks, 128-bit keys), PRINCE's performance really stands out. It is by far the smallest in its category and not even that far off SIMON 32/64. The latency is the lowest of all implemented ciphers, which confirms its main design requirement. The numbers for PRESENT and SIMON are similar, with PRESENT having a slightly smaller footprint and SIMON being a bit faster. However, as the area increases with the parameter size, the variations with small parameters are most interesting. The circuit is compounded by a large number of additional rounds when the size of the parameter goes up. SPECK's results don't make it an attractive alternative. The critical path is particularly long because of the adders in its design.

Looking at the different lightweight ciphers, the performance of AES is surprisingly good. It has a very large area because of the big S-boxes (8-bit to 8-bit), but its latency is competitive, given the small number of rounds and efficient permutation layer. Combined with the 128-bit blocks, this results in high throughput.

Most ASIC results are in line with the expectations from FPGA. The biggest surprise is SPECK's area being smaller than SIMON's, both for 32- and 64-bit blocks. A possible explanation for this difference is that the adders can be mapped better on ASIC than FPGA. Also note that the latency for SPECK 64/128 is very high on ASIC.

It is now possible to make some observations on the design of lightweight ciphers. Unrolling the rounds of an iterated cipher places all data operations of the round function on the critical path. Therefore, when an algorithm has more rounds, the critical path will often be longer as well (see Fig. 9). This is clear from the results for KATAN, which has a very large number of rounds. It is well known that regular arithmetic does not perform well in hardware, especially in terms of latency. SPECK's performance is a clear indication of this. Big S-boxes are also expensive, and as can be seen from the AES implementation, they have a large area requirement, especially in ASIC. Additionally, because they don't map well to the FPGA fabric, they have very long delays. The number of S-boxes used in the round function is of less importance, as they are working in parallel. Depending on the platform, using multiple-input gates could also negatively

Table 2. Size, critical path and throughput on FPGA (italics: best result in a security class, bold: best result overall)

	Cipher	Size [LUTs]	Critical path [ns]	Throughput [Gbit/s]
32/64	SIMON	**960**	*20.4*	1.46
	SPECK	1,513	40.3	0.74
32/80	KATAN	1,064	41.2	0.72
64/80	KATAN	2,550	47.3	1.26
	PRESENT	2,089	29.2	2.04
	RECTANGLE	*1,682*	*19.4*	3.08
64/128	PRESENT	2,203	32.6	1.83
	PRINCE	*1,244*	**16.4**	3.64
	RECTANGLE	1,730	19.3	3.08
	SIMON	2,688	27.3	2.18
	SPECK	3,594	50.3	1.19
128/128	AES	8,984	24.7	4.82

Table 3. Size, critical path and throughput on ASIC (italics: best result in a security class, bold: best result overall)

	Cipher	Size [GE]	Critical path [ns]	Throughput [Gbit/s]
32/64	SIMON	8,432.00	*29.6*	1.00
	SPECK	**5,893.25**	82.1	0.36
32/80	KATAN	11,939.50	61.2	0.49
64/80	KATAN	24,766.50	75.8	0.79
	PRESENT	22,063.50	39.4	1.51
	RECTANGLE	*18,160.75*	*34.87*	1.71
64/128	PRESENT	23,005.75	38.1	1.57
	PRINCE	*9,522.75*	**22.9**	2.60
	RECTANGLE	18,935.00	34.68	1.72
	SIMON	23,584.00	41.7	1.43
	SPECK	16,371.00	182.4	0.33
128/128	AES	1,26,571.00	61.6	1.93

impact the latency (e.g. a four-input XOR can be implemented in a single LUT on FPGA, while it will result in a cascade of three XORs in ASIC).

Finally, recommendations for the design of low-latency algorithms follow from these remarks. When focusing on low latency, having an unrolled design, like PRINCE, gives significantly better results. Iterated SP networks also perform well:

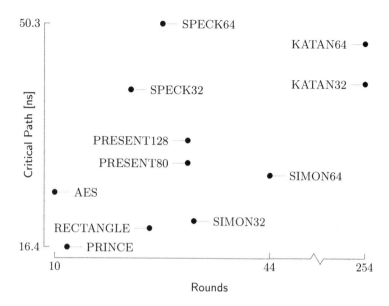

Fig. 9. Plot of the critical path on FPGA in function of the number of rounds.

the delay of small S-boxes is not very high and the permutation layer can essentially be implemented for free. The number of rounds should be as low as possible, while still maintaining an acceptable level of security. Small S-boxes are a nice component, as they have low latency as well as good area performance. Lastly, the general design rule to use boolean operations in hardware designs also applies here.

5   Conclusion

In this paper, we have given synthesis results for unrolled implementations of six families of lightweight block ciphers, along with AES for reference. It was shown that PRINCE, the only cipher specifically designed to have low latency, is the fastest of all implemented algorithms, and also has a very competitive area. For smaller block sizes, which are useful for some applications, SIMON has the smallest area and offers good throughput. However, the latency of most ciphers is too high to be useful in practice. For example, PRINCE runs at 61.039 MHz on Virtex 6, which is fast compared to the other ciphers, but is suitable only for small embedded applications. The speed in a microcontroller will be even lower once it is integrated with other components that add to the critical path. The search for new ciphers is therefore an important future research topic.

Acknowledgements. This work was supported in part by the Research Council KU Leuven: GOA TENSE (GOA/11/007). In addition, this work is supported in part by the Flemish Government through FWO G.0130.13N and FWO G.0876.14N. We would like to thank Kimmo Järvinen for his valued advice and Bohan Yang for his RECTANGLE implementation.

References

1. Ahmadian, Z., Rasoolzadeh, S., Salmasizadeh, M., Aref, M.R.: Automated Dynamic Cube Attack on Block Ciphers: Cryptanalysis of SIMON and KATAN. Cryptology ePrint Archive, Report 2015/040 (2015)
2. Alkhzaimi, H.A., Lauridsen, M.M.: Cryptanalysis of the SIMON Family of Block Ciphers. Cryptology ePrint Archive, Report 2013/543 (2013)
3. Anati, I., Gueron, S., Johnson, S., Scarlata, V.: Innovative technology for CPU based attestation and sealing. In: Proceedings of the 2nd International Workshop on Hardware and Architectural Support for Security and Privacy, p. 10 (2013)
4. Ashur, T.: Improved Linear Trails for the Block Cipher Simon. Cryptology ePrint Archive, Report 2015/285 (2015)
5. Beaulieu, R., Shors, D., Smith, J., Treatman-Clark, S., Weeks, B., Wingers, L.: The SIMON and SPECK Families of Lightweight Block Ciphers. Cryptology ePrint Archive, Report 2013/404 (2013)
6. Bernstein, D.J.: Crypto Competitions – AES: the Advanced Encryption Standard (2014). http://competitions.cr.yp.to/aes.html
7. Biryukov, A., Roy, A., Velichkov, V.: Differential Analysis of Block Ciphers SIMON and SPECK. Cryptology ePrint Archive, Report 2014/922 (2014)
8. Bogdanov, A., Knudsen, L.R., Leander, G., Paar, C., Poschmann, A., Robshaw, M., Seurin, Y., Vikkelsoe, C.: PRESENT: An ultra-lightweight block cipher. In: Paillier, P., Verbauwhede, I. (eds.) CHES 2007. LNCS, vol. 4727, pp. 450–466. Springer, Heidelberg (2007)
9. Bogdanov, A., Khovratovich, D., Rechberger, C.: Biclique Cryptanalysis of the Full AES. Cryptology ePrint Archive, Report 2011/449 (2011)
10. Bogdanov, A., Rechberger, C.: A 3-subset meet-in-the-middle attack: cryptanalysis of the lightweight block cipher KTANTAN. In: Biryukov, A., Gong, G., Stinson, D.R. (eds.) SAC 2010. LNCS, vol. 6544, pp. 229–240. Springer, Heidelberg (2011)
11. Borghoff, J., Canteaut, A., Gneysu, T., Kavun, E.B., Knežević, M., Knudsen, L.R., Leander, G., Nikov, V., Paar, C., Rechberger, C., Rombouts, P., Thomsen, S.S., Yaln, T.: PRINCE: A Low-latency Block Cipher for Pervasive Computing Applications. Cryptology ePrint Archive, Report 2012/529 (2012)
12. Canteaut, A., Fuhr, T., Gilbert, H., Naya-Plasencia, M., Reinhard, J.R.: Multiple Differential Cryptanalysis of Round-Reduced PRINCE (Full Version). Cryptology ePrint Archive, Report 2014/089 (2014)
13. Cho, J.Y.: Linear Cryptanalysis of Reduced-Round PRESENT. Cryptology ePrint Archive, Report 2009/397 (2009)
14. Daemen, J., Rijmen, V.: The Rijndael Algorithm. In: The First Advanced Encryption Standard Candidate Conference, Ventura, CA, USA, p. 45 (1998)
15. Dally, W., Towles, B.: Route Packets, Not Wires: On-Chip Interconnection Networks. In: Proceedings of the 38th Design Automation Conference (2001)
16. De Cannière, C., Dunkelman, O., Knežević, M.: KATAN and KTANTAN — A family of small and efficient hardware-oriented block ciphers. In: Clavier, C., Gaj, K. (eds.) CHES 2009. LNCS, vol. 5747, pp. 272–288. Springer, Heidelberg (2009)
17. Derbez, P., Perrin, L.: Meet-in-the-Middle Attacks and Structural Analysis of Round-Reduced PRINCE. Cryptology ePrint Archive, Report 2015/239 (2015)
18. Dinur, I.: Improved differential cryptanalysis of round-reduced speck. In: Joux, A., Youssef, A. (eds.) SAC 2014. LNCS, vol. 8781, pp. 147–164. Springer, Heidelberg (2014)

19. Giry, D., Quisquater, J.J.: Keylength – ECRYPT II Report on Key Sizes (2012). http://www.keylength.com/en/3/ (2014)
20. Hamalainen, P., Alho, T., Hannikainen, M., Hamalainen, T.: Design and Implementation of Low-Area and Low-Power AES Encryption Hardware Core. In: Proceedings of the 9th EUROMICRO Conference on Digital System Design: Architectures, Methods and Tools, pp. 577–583 (2006)
21. Isobe, T., Sasaki, Y., Chen, J.: Related-key boomerang attacks on KATAN32/48/64. In: Boyd, C., Simpson, L. (eds.) ACISP. LNCS, vol. 7959, pp. 268–285. Springer, Heidelberg (2013)
22. Jean, J., Nikolić, I., Peyrin, T., Wang, L., Wu, S.: Security analysis of PRINCE. In: Moriai, S. (ed.) FSE 2013. LNCS, vol. 8424, pp. 92–111. Springer, Heidelberg (2014)
23. Knežević, M., Nikov, V., Rombouts, P.: Low-latency encryption – Is "Lightweight = Light + Wait"? In: Prouff, E., Schaumont, P. (eds.) CHES 2012. LNCS, vol. 7428, pp. 426–446. Springer, Heidelberg (2012)
24. Menezes, A.J., Vanstone, S.A., Oorschot, P.C.V.: Handbook of Applied Cryptography, 1st edn. CRC Press Inc., Boca Raton (1996)
25. Morawiecki, P.: Practical Attacks on the Round-reduced PRINCE. Cryptology ePrint Archive, Report 2015/245 (2015)
26. National Institute of Standards and Technology: FIPS 197 (2001)
27. Parhi, K.K.: VLSI Digital Signal Processing Systems: Design and Implementation. Wiley, New York (2007)
28. Rabaey, J.M., Chandrakasan, A., Nikolic, B.: Digital Integrated Circuits: A Design Perspective, 2nd edn. Prentice-Hall, Inc., Upper Saddle River (2003)
29. Rudra, A., Dubey, P.K., Jutla, C.S., Kumar, V., Rao, J.R., Rohatgi, P.: Efficient rijndael encryption implementation with composite field arithmetic. In: Koç, Ç.K., Naccache, D., Paar, C. (eds.) CHES 2001. LNCS, vol. 2162, pp. 171–184. Springer, Heidelberg (2001)
30. Shan, J., Hu, L., Song, L., Sun, S., Ma, X.: Related-Key Differential Attack on Round Reduced RECTANGLE-80. Cryptology ePrint Archive, Report 2014/986 (2014)
31. Wang, N., Wang, X., Jia, K., Zhao, J.: Differential Attacks on Reduced SIMON Versions with Dynamic Key-guessing Techniques. Cryptology ePrint Archive, Report 2014/448 (2014)
32. Wang, Q., Liu, Z., Varc, K., Sasaki, Y., Rijmen, V., Todo, Y.: Cryptanalysis of reduced-round SIMON32 and SIMON48. In: Meier, W., Mukhopadhyay, D. (eds.) Progress in Cryptology – INDOCRYPT 2014. LNCS, pp. 143–160. Springer International Publishing, Switzerland (2014)
33. Zhang, W., Bao, Z., Lin, D., Rijmen, V., Yang, B., Verbauwhede, I.: RECTANGLE: A Bit-slice Ultra-Lightweight Block Cipher Suitable for Multiple Platforms. Cryptology ePrint Archive, Report 2014/084 (2014)
34. Zhao, G., Sun, B., Li, C., Su, J.: Truncated differential cryptanalysis of PRINCE. Secur. Commun. Netw. **8**, 2875–2887 (2015)

Improved Power Analysis on Unrolled Architecture and Its Application to PRINCE Block Cipher

Ville Yli-Mäyry[(✉)], Naofumi Homma, and Takafumi Aoki

Graduate School of Information Sciences, Tohoku University,
6-6-05, Aramaki Aza Aoba, Aoba-ku, Sendai-shi 980-8579, Japan
`ville@aoki.ecei.tohoku.ac.jp`

Abstract. This paper explores the feasibility of power analysis attacks against low-latency block ciphers implemented with unrolled architectures capable of encryption in a single clock cycle. Recently, low-latency block ciphers are attracting much attention due to the increasing requirement of real-time cryptosystems. Unrolled architectures have been expected to be somewhat resistant against side-channel attacks compared to typical loop architectures because of no memory (i.e. register) element storing intermediate results in a synchronous manner. In this paper, we present a systematic method for selecting Points-of-Interest for power analysis on unrolled architectures as well as calculating dynamic power consumption at a target function. Then, we apply the proposed method to PRINCE, which is known as one of the most efficient low-latency ciphers, and evaluate its validity with an experiment using a set of unrolled PRINCE processors implemented on an FPGA. Finally, a countermeasure against such analysis is discussed.

Keywords: Low latency cipher · Cryptographic hardware · Side-channel attacks · Unrolled architecture · Power analysis

1 Introduction

In recent years, interest in lightweight ciphers has increased greatly as the need for encryption of communication among embedded devices has grown. Many possible applications can be expected in the contexts of the Internet-of-Things (IoT) and Machine-to-Machine (M2M) communication. Lightweight ciphers have been generally designed to be efficient with respect to size and power consumption. The standardization of such ciphers has already begun with ISO/IEC29192-2, and a number of lightweight ciphers were introduced for use in environments with strictly limited resources.

A new direction in lightweight ciphers is to achieve a lower latency, that is, a lower response time to output the first encrypted/decrypted data. Possible applications that require such a lower response time include automotive authentication systems and high-speed storage. Some ciphers suitable for a low-latency

© Springer International Publishing Switzerland 2016
T. Güneysu et al. (Eds.): LightSec 2015, LNCS 9542, pp. 148–163, 2016.
DOI: 10.1007/978-3-319-29078-2_9

implementation such as Noekeon [5], mCrypton [13], and PRINCE [3] have been proposed, as explored in [10]. Among these for example, PRINCE achieves a more efficient design in delay-area (or delay-power) product in comparison with AES.

For achieving such lower latency in a block cipher, processing all rounds of the cipher in one clock cycle is an obvious choice of implementation. This kind of implementation technique is called round unrolling or unfolding, and the corresponding hardware architecture is called an unrolled or an unfolded architecture. In general, conventional block ciphers are often implemented with a "loop" architecture which usually processes one round in one or a few clock cycles and repeats the process until the last round of the cipher. This makes it possible to re-use a logic circuit for a round function and leads to a compact implementation.

On the other hand, when implementing cryptographic algorithms, the side-channel security of their physical implementation has to be also taken into consideration. In the last decade, side-channel attacks have become a serious threat to cryptographic modules. It has been shown that several types of side-channel leakage (e.g., power consumption, emitted electromagnetic radiation, and processing time) can be leveraged by an adversary to recover a secret key used in a cryptographic operation [6,11,12,15]. Most widely known side-channel attacks on cryptographic hardware have usually assumed that the target cipher is implemented with a loop architecture storing intermediate results (i.e., round outputs) into registers in a synchronous manner. This implies that hypothesis leakage models, such as Hamming weight (HW) model in DPA [12] and Hamming distance (HD) model in CPA [4], are satisfied at a specific timing during the encryption/decryption operation. Thus far, due to the popularity of loop architectures in hardware implementations, not much research has been done about the security of unrolled architectures with respect to side-channel attacks. In addition, unrolled architectures have been expected to be somewhat resistant to side-channel attacks because of no memory (i.e. register) element storing intermediate results such as in loop architectures [1]. However in the future, as the possible applications of low-latency ciphers increases, a further study on their side-channel security is highly demanded.

With the above background and motivation, we explore the feasibility of power analysis attacks against low-latency blocks ciphers implemented with unrolled architectures. In this paper, we focus on the application of a CPA-like attack without profiling to unrolled architectures. While a known-input technique has been reported for calculating dynamic power consumption in unrolled architectures [1], our challenge considered here is to find appropriate timings (i.e., Point-of-Interest (POI) samples in time domain) that make it possible to perform CPAs more efficiently under the condition that an adversary knows the inputs of obtained traces. Note here that we should search for a number of POIs to succeed in CPAs on unrolled architectures due to the asynchronous gate switching. For this purpose, we present a method for finding POI samples by exploiting the characteristics of power traces from unrolled architectures with

Welch's t-test. The conventional methods in the context of side-channel analysis have mainly exploited such statistical tests to verify the presence of leakage. For example, such a test was used for examining whether a class of plaintexts encrypted with a constant key differs significantly from the same class that has been encrypted with a randomized key in [8]. In contrast, we employ it to find the best POIs for performing side-channel attacks more efficiently, assuming that a leakage exists in observed power traces. In this paper, we then apply the proposed method to PRINCE, and evaluate its validity with an experiment using a set of PRINCE processors implemented with an unrolled architecture on an FPGA. Finally, a countermeasure against our method is discussed.

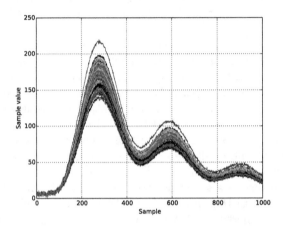

Fig. 1. Examples of power traces obtained from PRINCE processor with unrolled architecture (Color figure online).

The rest of this paper is organized as follows: Sect. 2 describes the characteristics of power traces in unrolled architectures and then presents our method to find POI samples in power traces. Usages of obtained POIs are also presented to perform power analysis attacks efficiently on unrolled architectures. Section 3 shows an application of our method to PRINCE with an unrolled architecture. Section 4 demonstrates the validity of our attack by an experiment using a set of PRINCE implementations on an FPGA. Also, a countermeasure against our attack is discussed. Section 5 concludes this paper with a summary of findings and discussion on future work.

2   Proposed Method on Unrolled Architectures

This section first describes the characteristics of power traces from unrolled architectures, and then presents the proposed method to find appropriate POIs for improving CPAs on unrolled architectures.

In unrolled architectures, since all of the round functions are executed in succession without writing intermediate values to registers, the power consumption of a single encryption/decryption operation is mainly derived from the amount of gate switching that occurs in the circuit according to the input data values. That is to say, the power consumption depends on the inside values being changed.

Figure 1 shows examples of power traces for one encryption operation in an unrolled architecture, where the difference of power traces came from the input variations. This suggests that a relationship between two successive encryption operations is critical to such dynamic power consumption. From the observation, we can find a way to characterize power consumption by knowing the relationship. Such a characterization technique was first explored and shown to be valid in [1].

Another characteristic of the power traces is that the placement and routing of logic gates have a significant effect on the timing of functions inside the circuit and indeed the output of individual functions (e.g., S-boxes) may vary greatly in the time domain due to the differences of signal path lengths. This also causes data hazards and/or glitches in the circuit, which contribute to the overall power consumption and make it harder for an adversary to formulate an accurate power model. As a result, a naive CPA, which estimates the key candidate from the maximal correlation coefficient at a single POI sample over the whole range of the observed power traces, becomes less effective because the above time differences including glitches scatter the power consumption over multiple samples. Figure 2 shows an example of such a naive CPA result on an FPGA implementation of PRINCE with an unrolled architecture (whose power traces are given as in Fig. 1), where the red and blue lines indicate the resulting correlation coefficients of the correct key guess and the wrong key guesses, respectively. Here, the correct key guess will produce highest correlation coefficients only at specific timings, but picking the maximum coefficient over the whole trace will lead to an incorrect key estimation.

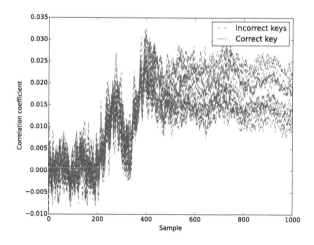

Fig. 2. Example of naive CPA results on an unrolled architecture (Color figure online).

Addressing the above difficulty, we present a method to find a set of POI samples that can be exploited in power analysis attacks. As shown in Fig. 1, the timing of a certain function in an unrolled architecture cannot be easily recognized from the power trace by a visual inspection. Our idea for finding the timing is to employ Welch's t-test [17] that examines whether a statistical difference between two sets of data exists. The difference between the sets is given as a value t, which is the confidence level of this finding. In addition, the t-test gives a probability for the null hypothesis that the two data sets belong to the same population.

The reason for using the t-test is that the power consumption of an unrolled architecture is mainly caused by gate switching activities during the encryption. If no switching occurs in a function, the corresponding power consumption is close to zero, and should differ from other power traces with switching activity. If the secret key stays constant during encryptions, an adversary can find specific input pairs where all the input bits of a target function stay constant. Such input pairs cause a slight drop in the power trace at a time indices where the target function is processed. Given a large amount of observed power traces, our method conducts a t-test with such specific traces and other traces, and finds the time indices of the targeted function from high t-values.

For selecting the specific traces above, we assume that an adversary knows a list of inputs (i.e. plaintexts) P and can measure the corresponding power trace data T. Let p_i and t_i be the ith input and the ith power trace data. Let $p_{i,j}$ be the jth part (e.g., nibble or byte) of the ith input that contributes to the input of the target function. We define T_{equal} as the set of power traces given by

$$T_{equal} = \{t_j \in T | t_j, when\, p_{i-1,j} = p_{i,j}\}. \tag{1}$$

Welch's t-test is then conducted for two data T_{equal} and $T \setminus T_{equal}$.

From the t-test results, the adversary searches for an area (i.e. time indices) indicating a sufficient confidence level. Note however that the threshold value of t should be changed flexibly depending on the condition and results. In the proposed method, we first smooth the t-test result by a low-pass filter, and search for a convex part with significant t-values. We then select a set of time indices in the convex part as the POIs for the target function. Figure 3 shows an example of a t-test result and a selected convex part, where the black and blue lines indicate the smoothed and raw t-test results, respectively. The left and right red vertical lines indicate the beginning and ending sample indices of the selected convex part, respectively. The tested power traces were obtained from a PRINCE processor described in Sect. 4. Algorithm 1 outlines the proposed method for finding POIs.

Finally, we perform a power analysis attack exploiting the obtained POIs. The usage of obtained POIs would be selected depending on the shape and distribution of t-test results. In this paper, we introduce three typical methods for calculating the correlation coefficient value used in CPA: (i) the highest value in POIs, (ii) the average value among POIs, and (iii) the weighted-average value among POIs. The first method is to calculate the correlation coefficient

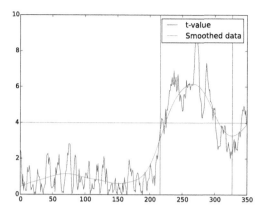

Fig. 3. Points-of-interest selected from t-test result (Color figure online).

Algorithm 1. Proposed method for choosing Points-of-Interest

Input:
plaintexts $P = \{p_0, p_1, ...p_n\}$,
power traces $T = \{t_0, t_1, ...t_n\}$,
targeted key part (e.g., nibble or byte) j,
t-value threshold for picking POIs *threshold*
Output: Points-of-Interest for the function being attacked
for $0 \leq i \leq n$ **do**
$\quad$ **if** $p_{i-1,j} == p_{i,j}$ **then**
$\quad\quad$ $T_{equal} = T_{equal} \cup t_i$

for $0 \leq k \leq max\_sample$ **do**
$\quad$ $r_k = $ t-test$(T_{equal}, T \setminus T_{equal}, k)$
$R = \{r_0, r_1, ...r_{max\_sample}\}$
$(index_{begin}, index_{end}) = $ findConvexPart(lowPassFilter(R))
$\quad$ **for** $index_{begin} \leq s \leq index_{end}$ **do**
$\quad\quad$ **if** $r_s \geq threshold$ **then**
$\quad\quad\quad$ $POIs = POIs \cup s$

return $POIs$

---

for each sample of POIs and select the highest value from the set of correlation coefficients. Note that the sample of the highest value might change with the targeted key part (e.g., S-box number). This method assumes that the critical sample point exists depending on the target function and the t-test result in the convex part is peaked. The second method is to calculate the average value of the samples at POIs and use it to calculate the correlation coefficient. This method assumes that the target function has an effect at every POI equally and the t-test result in the convex part is fairly flattened. The third method is to

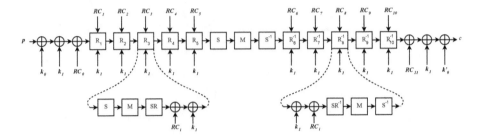

Fig. 4. PRINCE architecture

give a weight to each POI sample and use the weighted average value where the weight is proportional to the t-value to calculate the correlation coefficient. This method assumes that the target function has an effect at POIs broadly but the t-test result in the convex part is not so pronounced.

3   Application to the PRINCE Block Cipher

This section shows an application of the proposed method to the PRINCE block cipher implemented with an unrolled architecture. We first present our CPA attack on PRINCE with unrolled architecture and then apply our POI selection method to the attack.

Recent works on the security of PRINCE deal with cryptanalysis [9], and in general the protection of block ciphers from side-channel analysis [7]. To our best knowledge, in the domain of side-channel analysis, a power analysis on PRINCE has been conducted only on a loop architecture [16], but not an unrolled architecture.

3.1   PRINCE Design

PRINCE is a block cipher to be implemented with an unrolled architecture that allows for one encryption/decryption operation in a single clock cycle without any initialization phase. Figure 4 depicts the overview of the unrolled PRINCE architecture. The block size and key size of PRINCE are 64 bits and 128 bits (two 64-bit keys k_0 and k_1), respectively. Due to the reversible design, the encryption and decryption functions are performed by the same operation flow. The encryption/decryption operation consists of initial key addition, 10 round functions (R), and final key and round constant additions. Each round function consists of five sub-functions: S-Layer (S), M-Layer (M), ShiftRows (SR), AddRound-Constants and AddRoundKey. The first 5 rounds perform the five sub-functions in the above order, while the last 5 rounds perform their inverses in the reverse order. There is an intermediate function block consisting of S-Layer, M-Layer and inversed S-Layer (S^{-1}) in order of execution between the first and last 5 rounds.

3.2   Performing CPA on PRINCE with an Unrolled Architecture

What makes PRINCE different from usual CPA targets is the use of a whitening key k_0, which is added to the input before the first round function begins. The output of the first round function is determined by two 64-bit keys: the whitening key k_0 and the round key k_1. Therefore, an attack to the first round function will give an adversary an XORed key k' represented by

$$k' = k_0 \oplus k_1. \tag{2}$$

An adversary knowing only k' still cannot recover the individual key parts k_0 and k_1, and thus another attack is required for the second round function to separate k' into them. We can obtain the two keys k_0 and k_1 because the second attack gives the value of k_1. In the presented CPA, the first and second attack phases are called Phases 1 and 2, respectively.

In Phase 1, we target the S-layer function output in the first round. Since the input/output length of an S-box in S-layer is 4 bits, the whole secret key k' can be estimated from the 16 S-boxes. Let k'_j, $k_{0,j}$ and $k_{1,j}$ be the jth nibble of k', k_0, and k_1. We repeat nibble-wise attacks to obtain the whole k'. For each S-box output, we calculate the Hamming distance determined by two consecutive input data p_{i-1} and p_i, assuming that a nibble of the secret key k'_j is constant. The hypothesized power for the jth S-box M_j^1 is given as

$$M_j^1 = HD\big[Sbox(p_{i-1,j} \oplus k'_j), Sbox(p_{i,j} \oplus k'_j)\big], \tag{3}$$

where $p_{i-1,j}$ and $p_{i,j}$ correspond to the jth nibble ($0 \leq j \leq 15$) of the $i-1$th and ith input data being encrypted, respectively. The estimation of k'_j is changed from 0 to 15. The position for deriving the hypothesized power values in Phase 1 is depicted in Fig. 5.

Once k' is estimated, the adversary can use the value for Phase 2 where the whitening key k_0 is separated from k'. In Phase 2, we target the S-Layer function output in the second round. The hypothesized power for the jth S-box M_j^2 is given as

$$M_j^2 = HD\big[Sbox(Round_1(p_{i-1,j} \oplus k'_j, k_{1,j})), Sbox(Round_1(p_{i,j} \oplus k'_j, k_{1,j}))\big], \tag{4}$$

where $Round_1(p_{i-1,j} \oplus k'_j, k_{1,j})$ and $Round_1(p_{i,j} \oplus k'_j, k_{1,j})$ correspond to the jth nibble of the first round output under the condition that the estimated jth round key is $k_{1,j}$. The estimation of $k_{1,j}$ is changed from 0 to 15. The position for deriving the hypothesized power values in Phase 2 is also depicted in Fig. 5.

3.3   Applying POI Selection to PRINCE

Let $T_{equal,j}^1$ be the set of power traces where the input stays constant for the jth S-box in the first round, that is

$$T_{equal,j}^1 = \{t_j \in T | t_j, when\, p_{i-1,j} = p_{i,j}\}, \tag{5}$$

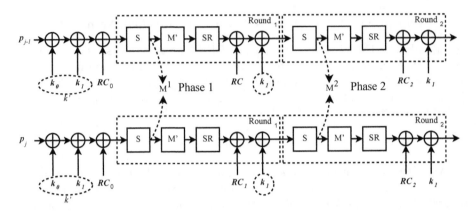

Fig. 5. Attack targets for Phases 1 and 2 in our CPA where keys recovered in the respective phases are circled.

where $p_{i-1,j}$ and $p_{i,j}$ indicate the jth nibble of the $i-1$th and ith inputs, that is, the $i-1$th and ith inputs of the jth S-box whose POIs are searched in Phase 1. We perform the t-test with $T^1_{equal,j}$ and $T \setminus T^1_{equal,j}$, and find POIs for the jth S-box in Phase 1 according to the algorithm described in Sect. 2.

For Phase 2, let $T^2_{equal,j}$ be the set of power traces where the input stays constant for the jth S-box in the second round as follows:

$$T^2_{equal,j} = \{t_j \in T | t_j, when\ Round_1(p_{i-1,j} \oplus k'_j, k_{1,j}) = Round_1(p_{i,j} \oplus k'_j, k_{1,j})\}, \quad (6)$$

where $Round_1(p_{i-1,j} \oplus k'_j, k_{1,j})$ and $Round_1(p_{j,i} \oplus k'_j, k_{1,j})$ correspond to the jth nibble of the first round output. Note here that we can evaluate the equivalence if we obtain the value of k'_j in Phase 1 (and even if we do not know the value of $k_{1,j}$). After the classification, we perform the t-test with $T^2_{equal,j}$ and $T \setminus T^2_{equal,j}$, and find POIs for the jth S-box in Phase 2 as described above. Finally, we calculate the correlation coefficient values using the timings of POIs for the proposed CPA.

4 Experiments

4.1 Setup

The validity of the proposed method is demonstrated by an experiment using a set of unrolled PRINCE processors implemented on an FPGA. In particular, we synthesized eight implementations of PRINCE with different placement and routing configurations in order to evaluate the robustness of the proposed method. To make the differences, we used three optimization flags available in Xilinx ISE (version 9.2i): optimization effort (normal, high), optimization goal (speed, area) and keep hierarchy (yes, no). The placement and routing of each setup is slightly different from each other. Table 1 shows the design names and their settings.

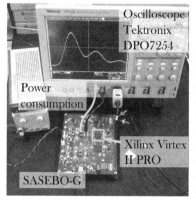

Fig. 6. Setup for experiments.

Table 1. Implementations used in experiments

Optimization flags			Design label
Effort	Goal	Keep hierarchy	
High	Area	No	high-area-no
High	Area	Yes	high-area-yes
High	Speed	No	high-speed-no
High	Speed	Yes	high-speed-yes
Normal	Area	No	normal-area-no
Normal	Area	Yes	normal-area-yes
Normal	Speed	No	normal-speed-no
Normal	Speed	Yes	normal-speed-yes

Figure 6 shows the experimental setup, where we used a SASEBO-G II board for implementing the eight variations of unrolled PRINCE processors on an FPGA (Xilinx Virtex II Pro) and acquiring the power traces from the power line by an digital oscilloscope (Tektronix DPO7254, 5Gsamples/s). Table 2 shows the experimental equipment and conditions. For each implementation, we used 250,000 power traces obtained from randomly generated plaintexts. Figure 1 shows examples of power traces measured from the design "speed-normal-yes" as described above. We also obtained similar power traces for different designs.

Table 2. Experimental environment

Digital oscilloscope	Tektronix DPO7254
Sampling Frequency	5Gsamples/s
Sampling point	Resistor (1Ω) attached to VDD
Power source	Kikusui PMC18-2A, 3.3V 2.0A
Implementation platform	Xilinx Virtex II PRO XC2VP7

4.2 Results and Discussion

Figures 7 and 8 show examples of t-test results for Phases 1 and 2 in the proposed CPA, respectively. The power traces of "speed-normal-yes" were tested for both figures. In each figure, the black and blue lines indicate the smoothed and raw t-test results, respectively. The left and right red vertical lines indicate the beginning and ending samples of the selected convex part, respectively. The results show that we can obtain a convex part for any S-box from the smoothed result. Note that a convex part (i.e., sample indices) of an S-box is different from that of another S-box for both Phases 1 and 2.

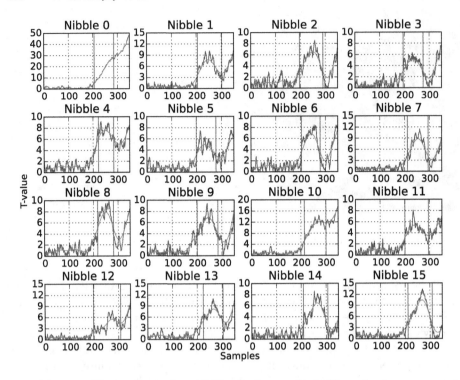

Fig. 7. Examples of POI selection results in Phase 1.

For comparison, we first show the results of the naive CPAs at a single sample point without using the proposed POI selection. Figure 9 shows the success rate of the CPA for Phase 1, where the vertical and horizontal axes indicate the number of successfully-estimated key nibbles and the number of power traces. Here, we performed the naive CPAs for all the observed sample points from index 0 to index 350. If the highest correlation coefficient value was finally obtained from the correct key guess, we took it to be successfully estimated. As a result, all the key nibbles were not estimated for all the implementations given 250,000 traces.

Figure 10 shows the success rate of the proposed CPAs with the POI selection for Phase 1, where the obtained POIs was processed by the usage (i) described in Sect. 2, that is, the maximal coefficient was simply selected from all the coefficients given at POI sample indices. Figure 11 shows the corresponding success rate with the usage (ii), where the averaged POI samples was used to calculate correlation coefficient for the proposed CPA. Figure 12 shows the corresponding success rate with the usage (iii), where the weighted-average values were used to calculate correlation coefficient for the proposed CPA and each weight was simply given by the normalized t-value in POIs. As a result, we confirmed that the efficiency of the proposed CPA was significantly improved for all the usages of the obtained POIs in comparison with the naive CPA without our POI selection

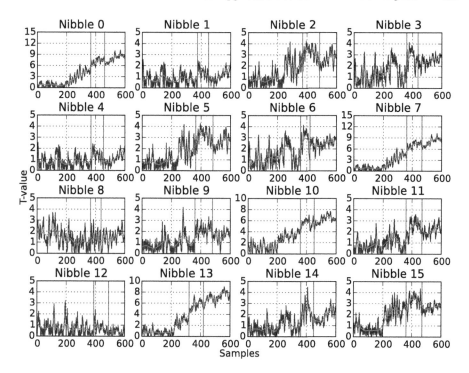

Fig. 8. Examples of POI selection results in Phase 2.

shown in Fig. 9. These results suggest that our selection method successfully find good POIs for various implementations in a robust manner.

On the other hand, the results also suggest that each usage of POIs is not a conclusive solution to maximize the efficiency of the proposed CPA. The usage of (i) works best on S-boxes where the output switching is concentrated heavily on one sample, but does not take into consideration cases where the target function output is affected by glitches and its power consumption is scattered onto multiple samples. The usage of (ii) would be suitable for the above cases. But an adversary using POIs greedily (including those with relatively-low t-values) will have a reduced signal-to-noise ratio if a concentrated output switching is observed. In the above sense, the usage of (iii) compromising between (i) and (ii) seems to be the best among the three usages because samples with higher confidence levels by the t-test, that is, with higher probability of performing the target function, are weighted more highly in calculating the correlation. However, it still does not leave the other two methods in the dust in this experiment. Considering the above properties of the three usages, the optimal strategy might be to switch them depending on the shape and distribution of the convex part selected by the t-tests. A more adaptive weighting (or sophisticated thresholding in POI selection) is being conducted for future works.

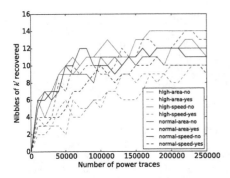

Fig. 9. Success rate of naive CPAs without POI selection for Phase 1 (Color figure online).

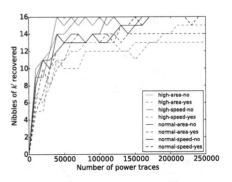

Fig. 10. Success rate of proposed CPAs with POI usage (i) for Phase 1 (Color figure online).

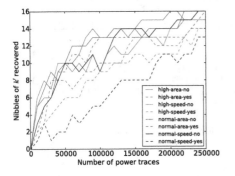

Fig. 11. Success rate of proposed CPAs with POI usage (ii) for Phase 1 (Color figure online).

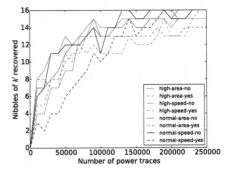

Fig. 12. Success rate of proposed CPAs with POI usage (iii) for Phase 1 (Color figure online).

Table 3 shows the summarized results of the naive and proposed CPAs for Phase 1. We have successfully estimated the correct key nibbles with a higher success rate for Phase 1 in comparison with the naive CPA. Though there were some nibbles that could not be estimated with 250,000 traces even by the proposed CPAs, the results showed our POI selection method improved the efficiency of CPAs.

One note in Phase 2 is that the probability for finding specific input pairs that an S-box input does not change is dramatically reduced since the second round S-box inputs depend on 16 input bits. In such cases, an adversary requires to observe a substantial set of power traces for the t-test. In our experiments, we found only 20–30 power traces from 250,000 randomly-generated inputs (e.g., power traces). Obviously if the probability of finding suitable data from randomly generated ones is low, the total number of required power traces for the CPA will increase significantly. Therefore, the efficiency of the proposed CPA would be improved if specific inputs suitable for the t-tests were chosen. In addition,

Table 3. Number of key nibbles recovered with 250000 traces.

	Phase 1			
Design label	w/o POIs	(i)	(ii)	(iii)
high-area-no	13	16	16	16
high-area-yes	10	12	16	16
high-speed-no	14	16	15	15
high-speed-yes	10	15	14	16
normal-area-no	11	16	16	16
normal-area-yes	13	14	13	15
normal-speed-no	11	16	16	16
normal-speed-yes	9	16	13	16

the accuracy of POI samples' position would be increased by a larger number of such chosen inputs. Such improvement based on a chosen-input scenario is being left for the future study. Due to this, the recovered key bits in the attack's second phase are considerably lower than that of the first phase and full recovery of the key bits was not possible with the used 250,000 traces.

4.3   Countermeasure

A simple countermeasure against CPAs, such as the proposed method, was presented in [1], where random values were introduced to the data inputs between encrypted inputs. This countermeasure removes the relationship between two inputs, and therefore makes it harder for an adversary to know how much gate switches occur in some certain parts of the circuit. On the other hand, such a countermeasure is unattractive in the context of low-latency applications because it essentially doubles the cipher's latency by one additional clock cycle which is required to drive random values into the circuit. When considering countermeasures, it is worth noting that every round function can be implemented independently of other rounds in unrolled architectures, and the area-wise cost of protecting only targeted S-boxes with tamper-resistant implementation (e.g., a threshold implementation [14]) is relatively low compared to the implementation without such a countermeasure. In the case of PRINCE, only the first and second round S-boxes need to be protected by the threshold implementation whereas the rest of the rounds' S-boxes can implemented as-is. With regard to the threshold implementation of PRINCE, we note that according to S-box classification done in [2], a 5-share threshold implementation exists for the "default" S-box given in PRINCE [3].

5   Summary

In this paper, we explored the feasibility of power analysis attacks against low-latency block ciphers designed based on unrolled architectures which are expected be inherently more resistant to such attacks. In particular, we presented a method for selecting POIs by a statistical test under the condition that the adversary knows input data. We also presented a two-phase CPA attack on PRINCE and applied the proposed POI selection method for the attack.

The validity of the proposed CPA including the POI selection method was demonstrated through an experiment using eight variations of unrolled PRINCE implementations on an FPGA. The results showed that our method can improve the efficiency of the proposed CPAs in comparison with the naive CPAs without such POI selection. On the other hand, a more efficient usage of obtained POIs still remains for future work. One possible strategy would be an adaptive weighted-averaging depending on the shape and distribution of the convex part which is given by the t-test. A further improvement of the proposed attack in the case of chosen-input scenarios would be valuable for future study.

Also, this paper briefly discussed a countermeasure against the proposed CPAs. A partial threshold implementation would be a possible solution. However, a study into an efficient countermeasure focusing on the minimum overhead in latency would be an interesting topic in the field of lightweight cryptosystems.

Acknowledgements. This work has been supported by JSPS KAKENHI Grant No. 25250006. We are grateful for their support.

References

1. Bhasin, S., Guilley, S., Sauvage, L., Danger, J.-L.: Unrolling cryptographic circuits: a simple countermeasure against side-channel attacks. In: Pieprzyk, J. (ed.) CT-RSA 2010. LNCS, vol. 5985, pp. 195–207. Springer, Heidelberg (2010)
2. Bilgin, B., Nikova, S., Nikov, V., Rijmen, V., Stütz, G.: Threshold implementations of all 3×3 and 4×4 S-boxes. In: Prouff, E., Schaumont, P. (eds.) CHES 2012. LNCS, vol. 7428, pp. 76–91. Springer, Heidelberg (2012)
3. Borghoff, J., et al.: PRINCE a low-latency block cipher for pervasive computing applications. In: Wang, X., Sako, K. (eds.) ASIACRYPT 2012. Lecture Notes in Computer Science, vol. 7658, pp. 208–225. Springer, Heidelberg (2012)
4. Brier, E., Clavier, C., Olivier, F.: Correlation power analysis with a leakage model. In: Joye, M., Quisquater, J.-J. (eds.) CHES 2004. LNCS, vol. 3156, pp. 16–29. Springer, Heidelberg (2004)
5. Daemen, J., Peeters, M., Rijmen, V., Assehe, G.V.: Nessie Proposal: Noekeon (2000). http://gro.noekeon.org/
6. Gandolfi, K., Mourtel, C., Olivier, F.: Electromagnetic analysis: concrete results. In: Koç, Ç.K., Naccache, D., Paar, C. (eds.) CHES 2001. LNCS, vol. 2162, pp. 251–261. Springer, Heidelberg (2001)
7. Gérard, B., Grosso, V., Naya-Plasencia, M., Standaert, F.-X.: Block ciphers that are easier to mask: how far can we go? In: Bertoni, G., Coron, J.-S. (eds.) CHES 2013. LNCS, vol. 8086, pp. 383–399. Springer, Heidelberg (2013)
8. Goodwill, G., Jun, B., Jaffe, J., Rohatgi, P: A testing methodology for side channel resistance validation. In: NIST non-invasive attack testing workshop (2011). http://csrc.nist.gov/news_events/non-invasive-attack-testing-workshop/papers/08_Goodwill.pdf

9. Jean, J., Nikolić, I., Peyrin, T., Wang, L., Wu, S.: Security analysis of PRINCE. In: Moriai, S. (ed.) FSE 2013. LNCS, vol. 8424, pp. 92–111. Springer, Heidelberg (2014)

10. Knežević, M., Nikov, V., Rombouts, P.: Low-latency encryption – Is "Lightweight = Light + Wait". In: Prouff, E., Schaumont, P. (eds.) CHES 2012. LNCS, vol. 7428, pp. 426–446. Springer, Heidelberg (2012)

11. Kocher, P.C.: Timing attacks on implementations of diffie-hellman, RSA, DSS, and other systems. In: Koblitz, N. (ed.) CRYPTO 1996. LNCS, vol. 1109, pp. 104–113. Springer, Heidelberg (1996)

12. Kocher, P.C., Jaffe, J., Jun, B.: Differential power analysis. In: Wiener, M. (ed.) CRYPTO 1999. LNCS, vol. 1666, pp. 388–397. Springer, Heidelberg (1999)

13. Lim, C.H., Korkishko, T.: mCrypton – A lightweight block cipher for security of low-cost RFID tags and sensors. In: Song, J.-S., Kwon, T., Yung, M. (eds.) WISA 2005. LNCS, vol. 3786, pp. 243–258. Springer, Heidelberg (2006)

14. Nikova, S., Rechberger, C., Rijmen, V.: Threshold implementations against side-channel attacks and glitches. In: Ning, P., Qing, S., Li, N. (eds.) ICICS 2006. LNCS, vol. 4307, pp. 529–545. Springer, Heidelberg (2006)

15. Quisquater, J.-J., Samyde, D.: ElectroMagnetic Analysis (EMA): measures and counter-measures for smart cards. In: Attali, I., Jensen, T. (eds.) E-smart 2001. LNCS, vol. 2140, pp. 200–210. Springer, Heidelberg (2001)

16. Selvam, R., Shanmugam, D., Annadurai, S.: Side Channel Attacks: VulnerabilityAnalysis of PRINCE and RECTANGLE using DPA. IACR ePrint Archive, paper2014/644 (2014)

17. Welch, B.L.: The generalization of 'Student's' problem when several different population variances are involved. Biometrika **34**(1–2), 2835 (1947)

Author Index

Printed in the United States
By Bookmasters

Printed in the United States
by Baker & Taylor Publisher Services